Miscellanies, Volume 1...

Harriet Martineau

MISCELLANIES.

BY

HARRIET MARTINEAU.

IN TWO VOLUMES.

VOLUME I.

BOSTON:

HILLIARD, GRAY AND COMPANY.

M DCCC XXXVI.

CAMBRIDGE PRESS:
METCALF, TORRY, AND BALLOU.

PREFACE.

THESE two volumes contain the greater part of my contributions to periodicals during the years 1829, 30, 31, and 32. They are miscellaneous in their character, and were written without the slightest reference to each other. Each one presents the thought with which my mind was engrossed at the time; and, in each case, the thought fashioned for itself the form in which it should appear. Hence the diversity of styles of composition in these pieces, and their proportionate inequality of merit. Hence, also, the classification which is exhibited in the table of contents; a classification intended only for convenience of reference.

On looking over these pieces, after an interval of four years, during which they were wholly forgotten, it is evident to me that one presiding idea must have been in my mind during the composition of the whole; dawning over the first, and brightening up to the last. One piece bears the name of The Progress of Worship. This name might, with equal propriety, be given to the tale called Solitude and Society; to the parable of the Hermit who went out to his matins; to the verses headed The Three Ages of the Soul; and to the 2d No. of the Sabbath Musings: and I am finally tempted to give this title to the whole book. Its application, however, might not appear so clear to others as to myself; and I shall therefore confine myself to indicating it by a second classification in this Preface.

The Religious Sentiment, in its early periods, may be weak or strong, steady or wavering ; but its operation is, in each case, imperfect. Not having gone through the process of tribulation, experience, and hope, it cannot have so much of love in it as to make it, what it may afterwards become, the perpetual feast of the spirit. It has so much of fear as to induce it to bind itself strictly to forms ; and it alternates with other sentiments, instead of intermingling with them all. God is then the object of intermitting regards. Religion is then a yoke ; easy and light in comparison with slavery to Chance and Passion ; but still a yoke. This is the state of the child who hides his face in his pillow while relating to his mother the transgressions and self-conquests of the day. This is the state of the youth whose heart leaps up at the golden sunrise, but who lets the gorgeous moments pass away because he dares not indulge himself with them till he has gone through his form of prayer ; on rising from which, he finds the glow departed alike from his spirit and from the sky. This is the state of the man who excludes his worldly interests from his mind on Sundays, and finds trains of sweet thoughts arising, and ancient kindly emotions stirring within him, as the choir sings rest to tormenting cares, and the voice of the preacher tells how the dead rest from their labors. He wonders why he did not think of these things during his week-day troubles ; and resolves, for his own sake, to think oftener of God. This is the state of the aged when the experience of life has taught them nothing more than that here there is no abiding place ; that they must soon go to some strange region, where they suppose they shall be taken care of. Their highest hope concerning this new place probably is, that there they shall not have to be afraid any more. Such, whether in the child or the sexagenarian, is the early stage of the religious sentiment; a condition of fear, forms, and intermitting regards.

Of the following pieces, none were written under the idea of the religious sentiment at this stage. The materials are too few, and have too little life in them to afford any inducement to brood over them. That such is the beginning of worship is barely matter of inference from what follows.

From occasionally remembering God, the worshipper proceeds to search for him, particularly by self-inquisition. Now he takes upon him his burden of self-consciousness, and is carefully, and often painfully, employed in settling points of belief and of conduct, fixing methods of observance, watching for manifestations (that is, virtues and vices) in others, and treating these manifestations with anxious approbation or reprobation, as ultimate facts. He probably draws out in his own mind some such table of virtues as Dr. Franklin ruled and lettered down upon paper, and is surprised to find that as often as he makes progress in the one on which he is most intent, improvement in others seems to follow of course. This state is far superior to the former; for, though the love of manifestations is far below that of principles, it is far above that of forms.

Many of the following pieces were written under the idea of this condition of the religious sentiment. Some encourage self-inquisition; as the Essays on the reciprocal Operation of Feelings and Habits; on the Uses of the Retrospective and Prospective Powers; and the 1st, 3d, and 5th Nos. of the Sabbath Musings.*

---

* It can scarcely be necessary for me to explain that I am speaking throughout of my idea of the progress of the religious sentiment;

a *

The reviews of Crombie's Natural Theology, and of the
Essays on the Pursuit of Truth, &c. come under this head;
and also the Essays on the Art of Thinking; these all attempt
to settle points, and prescribe methods, first for intellectual,
and then for moral purposes. Next comes the Letter to
the Deaf. This is of later date than any other such close
prescription of methods; but it was designed to meet a
peculiar case, on which, from want of sympathy and recorded
experience, principles had not been brought to bear with
sufficient distinctness and steadiness.

With the above may be classed the fragments called the
Survivor; the Ode to Religious Liberty; the Address to the
Avowed Arians of the Synod of Ulster; and Consolation.
Also, the parables Faith and Hope, the Hermit beside the
Rock, and the Spirits of the Night.

The worshipper next proceeds to a higher labor. He finds
that preachers who treat of virtues and vices in their dis-
courses do little to help him in his alliance with the one, and
his warfare with the other. The contemplation of beautiful
or ugly abstractions may have a good general effect in exalting and refining the moral taste, but it is no safeguard under
the actual pressure of temptation. He finds that they are
manifestations; and that they must be fitful, if that of which
they are manifestations be fluctuating. Weary of self-refer-
ence, and finding himself afloat again and again, after all his

---

and not of my progress. Little could be learned of this last from my
writings, because some which appear to bear an autobiographical
character are only ideal and sympathetic. Of these, the 5th No. of
the Sabbath Musings is one. Others are strictly experiences. It
will not be expected of me that I should indicate them.

labor in fastening himself to points and methods, he arrives at the conviction that there is nothing immutable but God; and in his anxiety to lay hold on this immutability for his own repose, he takes a survey of what is around him, and a retrospection of what is behind him, in order to discover, by a study of Providence, the principles which constitute the language by which God speaks to man. Principles being infallible as God himself, the faith of the worshipper grows with each new word of the oracle which falls upon his ear. Providence being benignant, the love of the worshipper kindles as often as the light of God's countenance reaches him from behind some dark cloud of circumstance. His burden of consciousness is loosened. The voice of conscience becomes more clear and sweet as the din of selfish fears and questionings subsides. The religious sentiment is now exalted almost into a condition of repose.

Under the idea of such a process of spiritual induction as this, the next class of pieces seem to have been composed : — the amplification of Lessing's Hundred Thoughts, the Reviews of the Religion of Socrates, and of Nature and Providence to Communities : and the parables of the Wandering Child, Heli and Antar, and Young Life.

The highest condition of the religious sentiment is when it has attained repose; when the worshipper not only sees God every where, but sees nothing which is not full of God. In the serenity of this assured faith it is that men endure, at the call of duty, as a matter of course, the most protracted and the fiercest woes of life and of death. In this consciousness, — no longer of self, — but of God, it is that philosophers and philanthropists go forth through Nature and Society, to sound the processes of the one, and test the institutions of the other. The induction which they have gone through has furnished them with the instrument by which they can interpret the mysteries of God, and prove the ways of men. Though they sit in the serene sunshine of Providence, they are not to be idle. To them is appointed labor, — irksome labor, in the guardianship of their race. By them alone can fraud and fallacy be exposed without passion ; abuse rebuked without malice ; and the whole work of proof, detection, and rectification be intrepidly carried on in a lowly and peaceable spirit. In a word, the highest process of worship is going on when the worshippers are the most conscious of God, unconscious of self, and mindful of their race ; when they are the fulfillers of the first and great commandment, and of the second, which is like unto it.

Under the idea of such a state of duty and privilege, were others of these pieces composed. Some attempt to apply proof to institutions ; as the Essay on the Hanwell Lunatic Asylum ; the reviews of Romanism and Episcopacy, of Jacotot's System of Education, of West India Slavery, and of Witchcraft in Salem. Others are intended to explode errors, advocate rights, and indicate duty ; as the reviews of Scott's Demonology and Witchcraft, of Doddridge's Life and Correspondence, and of Godwin's Thoughts on Man ; the Essays on the Characteristics and Achievements of the Genius of Scott, on the Duty of Studying Political Economy, on Moral Independence, and on Theology, Politics, and Literature ; * the 4th and 6th Nos. of the Sabbath Musings ; the Tale called The Early Sowing ; the Reform Song, and the first Hymn.

---

* Written for the first Number of a new Series of a periodical.

I am far from imagining that there is any thing new or
peculiar in this idea of the progress of worship: but, though
it may be found traced out in every page of the Gospel, and
wrought out in the lives of the noblest of heathens before,
and the wisest of Christians since its date, it can hardly be
said to be sufficiently familiar to us as long as we see religion
treated as a concern apart from all other concerns; waited
for, as for a morning and evening breeze, instead of being
unconsciously breathed, as the element by which we live. It
cannot be said to be sufficiently familiar to us as long as any
intend to be men of business in the prime of life, and Christians some time or other. It cannot be said to be sufficiently
familiar to us while any of us are supine under the abuses of
society, or terrified at the march of events, or paralyzed by
human opinion, or falling short in any way in those duties in
which religious sentiment is designed to be a sufficient stimulus and support. Indifference in such duties is a sufficient
proof that our religion has not engaged our human affections;
that our worship, if we worship, has not advanced beyond
the second stage of its progress.

My belief that the presiding idea under which my work
was composed is a true one, by no means implies that I
believe my work to be a good one. The revision of the
pieces has been far from gratifying to me. But they are
true representations of what I felt and thought when they
were written; and I believe it right to offer as many as
may be here found, lest others should present them in a
mode which would impair their truth by destroying their
connexion. I should not have issued them at present in
England; but it gives me much pleasure to prepare for my

American friends, at the suggestion of some beloved ones among them, a book in which they may read with the eyes of their consciousness, invisible records of the gratitude and love of a stranger, whom they have gladdened by their hospitality, and honored with their friendship.

Boston, January 1, 1836.

CONTENTS.

PHILOSOPHICAL ESSAYS.

PHILOSOPHICAL ESSAYS.

CHARACTERISTICS OF THE GENIUS OF SCOTT.

THE advent of genius is the most striking, and will, in time, be perceived to be the most important species of circumstance which can befall society. When, as in the case of Scott, it manifests itself, not only in a highly popular form, but in a peculiarly healthy state, it becomes equally interesting to analyze it as an object of psychological research, and a duty to inquire into the process of education by which it has been brought to sound maturity. Such an inquiry may serve as an instrument wherewith to measure the achievements of genius in this particular instance of its manifestation, and also as an indication how most wisely to cherish any future revelation of the same kind with which the world may be blessed. This is a social service enjoined upon survivors by departing genius; a service which may not be refused, though emotions of grief must be largely mingled with the awe and hope which arise out of the contemplation of the past and future influences of the high presence which has become hidden. We, therefore, proceed, first, to inquire into the discipline of the genius of Scott, and the characteristics of its maturity; and, next, to attempt an estimate of the services that genius has rendered to society.

1

Walter Scott was happy in his parentage and condition in life. His father had good sense, benevolence, and sincerity; his mother added to these virtues vigorous and well-cultivated talents. The experience of pain which appears to be essential to the deepening and strengthening of genius, was not, in his case, derived from hardships which infuse bitterness with strength, and corrupt while they expand. There was neither the domestic oppression under which Byron grew restive, nor the over-indulgence which prepares its victim for finding the world an oppressor. Scott was, it appears, surrounded with a kindly moral atmosphere from his birth. There was no thwarting of his early tastes; his young sayings were laid up in his mother's heart; his brothers were his friends; and we have his own word for the tenderness with which he was regarded in his second home — his grandfather's farm at Sandyknow : —

> " For I was wayward, bold, and wild,
>   A self-willed imp, a grandame's child;
>   But half a plague, and half a jest,
>   Was still endured, beloved, carest."

Neither was his experience of pain derived from poverty, from a baffling of desires, from a deprivation of means to an earnestly-desired end, from the irksomeness of his occupations, or a sense of the unfitness of his outward condition to his inward aspirations. He was spared all that sordid kind of suffering which irritates while it excites, and even while communicating power, abstracts its noblest attribute, — its calmness.

Of this class of evils, from which genius has extensively suffered, Walter Scott knew nothing; and, happily for him, it did not therefore follow that he was raised above that experience of real life, which is the most nourishing aliment of intellectual power. It is a rare thing, and happier than it is

rare, to lay hold of reality under a better impulse than that
of hardship, and with sufficient power to make it serve its
true end. The lordling knows nothing of reality. What he
is told he believes, be it what it may. What he is command-
ed he does, or leaves undone, according to a will which is
not the more genuine for being perverse; — a will which
springs out of convention, and is swayed by artificial impulses. His very ailments are scarcely teachers of reality, for
they are not only artificially beguiled, but are made the
building materials of a spurious experience. The fever of a
lordly infant leaves its victim less wise than the fever of a
cottage child, which is to the latter an evil felt in its full
force, but uncompounded with other evils. On recovery, the
cottage child knows best what sickness is; and, yet, bodily
affections are the least susceptible of admixture of any:
they afford to the lordling the best means of gaining genuine
experience. All else is with him passive reception or conventional action, though he may travel in his own country and
abroad, and learn to play trap-ball at Eton. As for those
who have to do only with what is real, the hewers of wood
and drawers of water, they are too generally unprepared to
make use of reality. Their power, as far as it goes, is superior to the lordling's; but it is a scanty and unfruitful power.
They are for ever laying a foundation on which nothing is
seen to arise. This is better than building pagodas of cards
on a slippery surface like the lordling; but it is not the final
purpose for which the human intellect was made constructive.
It is not enough for the little cotton-spinner, or ploughboy, to
know what the lordling only believes, — of the qualities of
twist, and the offices of machinery, and the economy of the
nests of larks and field-mice. They should be led beyond
cotton-spinning and field labors by such knowledge; but it
as seldom happens that they are so as that the lordling exchanges his belief for knowledge; which is the same thing

as saying, that genius is as rare in the one class as in the
other ; being, in the one, overlaid with convention ; in the
other, benumbed by want. , The most efficacious experience
of reality must be looked for in the class above the lowest,
and in individuals of higher classes still, fewer and fewer in
proportion to the elevation of rank, till the fatal boundary of
pure convention be reached, within which genius cannot live
except in the breast of one here and there, who is stout-
hearted enough to break bounds, and play truant in the regions of reality.   The individuals who may thus come out
from the higher ranks (where all efficacy is supposed to
reside in teaching, instead of enabling to learn) may generally be observed to bear some mark of Providence, which
they themselves may endure with humiliation, which their
companions regard with ignorant compassion ; but in which
the far-sighted recognise, not only a passport to the select
school of experience, but a patent of future intellectual no-
bility.   What this mark may be, signifies little.   The important point is, that there should be pain, — inevitable pain, —
not of man's infliction, — natural pain, admitting of natural
solace, so that it may produce its effects pure from the irritation of social injury, and be bearable for a continuance in
silence.   Whether the infliction be orphanhood, leading to
self-reliance ; whether it be the blindness which has exalted
the passion of many bards, or the deafness which deepened
the genius of Beethoven, or the lameness which agonized the
sensibilities of Byron, or mere delicacy of health (which has
often, after invigorating genius, been itself invigorated by
genius in its turn) ; whether the infliction be any of these
or of the many which remain, matters little ; its efficacy
depends on the degree in which it is felt ; that is, on the
degree of the knowledge of reality which it confers.

To pain thus inflicted, to a knowledge of reality thus conferred, was Scott, in a great measure, indebted for the pro-

digious overbalance of happiness which afterwards enriched himself, and the world through him. He suffered in childhood and youth from ill health and privation. His ill health caused his removal into the country, where, from circumstances of situation, &c. those tastes were formed which predominated in him through life, while the passion with which they were cherished must have been deepened by the one affliction which he had to bear alone, — his lameness. Few have any idea of the all-powerful influence which the sense of personal infirmity exerts over the mind of a child. If it were known, its apparent disproportionateness to other influences would, to the careless observer, appear absurd; to the thoughtful, it would afford new lights respecting the conduct of educational discipline; it would also pierce the heart of many a parent who now believes that he knows all, and who feels so tender a regret for what he knows, that even the sufferer wonders at its extent. But this is a species of suffering which can never obtain sufficient sympathy, because the sufferer himself is not aware till he has made comparison of this with other pains, how light all others are in comparison. Be the infirmity what it may, as long as it separates, as long as it causes compassion, as long as it exposes to the little selfishness of companions, to the observation of strangers, to inequality of terms at home, it is a deep-seated and perpetual wo; one which is, in childhood, never spoken of, though perpetually brooded over; one which is much and universally underrated, because it is commonly well borne; and, again, well borne, because underrated, and, therefore, unsympathized with.

That this was the case with Walter Scott, is certain. His lameness in childhood was, no doubt, thought much less of by every one, even his mother, than by himself. Not an hour of any day, while with his young companions, could this pain of infirmity have been unfelt. In all sports, in all domestic plans, in all schoolboy frolics, he either was, or be-

lieved himself to be, on unequal terms with his playmates;
and though he happily escaped the jealousy which arises too
often from a much less cause, he suffered enough to drive
him to a solace, whose pure and natural pleasures might best
counterbalance his peculiar and natural pain. We have
notices of these things from himself; a touching recurrence
in one of his lightest pieces, to the days when the little lame
boy lagged behind with the nurse-maid, while his brothers
were running wild; when he was painfully lifted over the
stiles which others were eager to climb. More at large we
have tidings of the opposite pleasures, in which he found the
best repose from his mortifications. His worship of Smalholm
Tower, amidst the green hills; his quest of wallflowers and
honeysuckles, and of the blossoms of traditionary verse which
adorn the retreats where he sought his pleasures. The immediate enjoyment arising from the study of nature, is probably as much less in childhood than in mature years, as the
pain arising from personal infirmity is greater — the pleasure
being enhanced and the pain alleviated, by the variety and
complexity of associations with which each becomes mingled;
and Walter Scott, therefore, gained in pleasure with every
year of his youth. But yet there was a sufficient balance of
enjoyment, even in these early days, to render his genius of
that benignant character which proves its rearing to have
been kindly. He not only gained power by vicissitude,
(which is the most rapid method of knowing realities,) but
pleasure fast following upon pain, the pain was robbed of its
irritation, and the pleasure was enhanced by a sense of freedom, the welcome opposite of the constraint which any species of infirmity imposes in society. Scott's childhood was,
in short, spent in *feeling*, the best possible preparation for
after *thinking*. His limbs were stretched on the turf, his
hands grasped the rough crags, and wallflower scents reached
him from crumbling ruins, and streams ran sparkling before

his eyes ; and these realities mingled with the no less vivid ones which he had just brought with him from society.

Nor were these the only vicissitudes he knew. His tastes thus formed, suited little with his school pursuits ; and hence arose wholesome and strengthening exercises of fear and love. It seems strange, contemplating Walter Scott in his after life, as firm as mild, to think that he could either experience or cause fear ; but there is no doubt whatever that this formed part of the discipline of his genius. He was a naughty schoolboy, as far as learning lessons went. He tells us of disgraces and punishments for being idle himself and keeping others idle, — and of the applause of his school-fellows for his tale-telling being a sort of recompense for what he thus underwent. Since he felt this applause a recompense, the evil of punishment was feared and felt. Since he continued to incur punishment, his love of nature and romance was yet stronger than his fear. This alternation went on for years, for he never gained credit as a learner of languages, and finished in possession of " little Latin and less Greek." For a long continuance then, there was disgrace in school, and honor in the playground ; fear in school, and a passion of love among the green hills ; slavery between four walls, and rapturous liberty when rambling with a romancing companion amidst the wildest scenery that lay within reach. A glorious discipline this for a sensibility which could sustain and grow under it !

Half the work was now done. Through the exercise of the sensibility the faculties were strengthened. There was yet little knowledge, but there was power, — power which would soon have preyed upon itself, if objects had not, by a new set of circumstances, been presented for it to employ itself upon. An illness confined him long to his bed, in a state which admitted of no other amusements than chess and reading. He read ravenously, and, as he himself says, idly ;

that is, he devoured all the poems and novels which a large
circulating library afforded, till he was satiated, and then
took to memoirs, travels, and history. He continued this
practice of desultory reading, when afterwards removed once
more into the country on account of the state of his health;
and thus was he initiated into the second of the three great
departments of knowledge, which it was necessary to traverse
in preparation for the work of his later years. He had now
made acquaintance with nature in her aspects, though not in
her constitution, and with man as he is displayed in books.
History showed him man in his social capacity; tales of real
and fictitious adventure showed him man in contest with natural difficulties, and passing through the diversified scenery
of various climates and nations; memoirs showed him man
going through the experience of human existence; but all
this was at second-hand. The third great study which remained was, man as he appears in actual life. It remained to
verify what man seems in books by what he is before the eyes.
And for this also opportunity was afforded by another change
of circumstance. Walter Scott recovered his health, or
rather became, for the first time, vigorous in body, and able
to enter the world on the same terms with others. He studied law in college as well as under his father, and mixed in
society far more than ever before; and though looked upon
rather as an abstracted young man, very fond of reading,
than as a particularly sociable personage, he was actually at
this time, and for some years afterwards, making acquaintance with human nature under a great variety of forms,
whether in the courts, or in his own rank of society, or wandering, as was still his wont, among the vales of Tweeddale,
gathering legends from the shepherds, or domesticating himself by the farmer's fireside. During this stage of his preparation, it was an important circumstance that he became
enrolled in a cavalry regiment, formed under the apprehension

of an invasion from France. Here he was far from being considered "an abstracted young man;" being highly popular, from his good humor and his extraordinary powers of entertainment, which probably were exercised ·in a somewhat different way from the goblin romancing, which made him a favorite among his school-fellows. He now probably communicated the results of his observation of actual life, while he no doubt improved them at the same time.

During the next few years he continued to enlarge his knowledge in all these three departments, by travelling, by the study of German literature, and by the performance of the active duties imposed upon him by his office of Sheriff of Selkirkshire; an office which, no less than his travels, brought him into communication with human nature under a variety of modifications. The study of German literature alone, — (we say nothing of the language, as, by Sir Walter's own confession, he only used it as a means of scrambling into the literature) — this new acquisition alone might serve, to a mind so prepared as his, as a sufficient stimulus to the work he afterwards achieved; and to it we cannot but attribute much of that richness of moral conception, much of the transparent depth of his philosophy of character, which is, to merely English readers, the most astonishing of his excellencies.

Here, then, we have gained some faint insight into the process by which an organization (probably of great original excellence) was made the most of, and rendered the constituent of a genius as kindly as it was powerful; that is to say, as healthy as it was rare. Such an organization may not be rare. We cannot tell; so little do we know of its mysteries, and so complicated is the machinery of education and of society, by which it may be ruined or impaired. As probable as that there might be a Milton or a Hampden in Gray's presence, when he pondered his elegy, is it that there may be many Scotts in our regal halls, in our factories, in our grammar or dame schools ; one weakened in the hot-bed of aristocracy, another withered by want and toil, a third choked with what is called learning, a fourth turned into a slave under the rod. It seems that some light is thrown upon the matter of education by such a case as the one before us. Here is a discipline diametrically opposite to received notions of what is fitting.   Here is a boy, — not so unlike other boys in the outset as to make this case an exception to all rules, — here is a boy lying about in the fields when he should have been at his Latin grammar ; romancing when he should have been playing cricket ; reading novels when he should have been entering college ; hunting ballads when he should have been poring over parchments ; spearing salmon instead of embellishing a peroration ; and, finally, giving up law for legends, when he should have been rising at the bar. Yet this personage came out of this wild kind of discipline, graced with the rarest combination of qualifications for enjoying existence, achieving fame, and blessing society ; with manners which were admitted by a king to ornament a court, although his accomplishments were to be referred solely to intellectual culture, and in no degree impaired the honesty of his speech and action ; deeply learned, though neither the languages nor the philosophy of the schools made part of his acquisitions ; robust as a ploughman, able to walk like a pedlar, and to ride like a knight-errant, and to hunt like a squire ; business-like as a bailiff ; industrious as a handicraftsman ; discreet and frank to perfection at the same time ; gentle as a woman ; intrepid as the bravest hero of his own immortal works. Here is an extraordinary phenomenon, to result from an education which would give most people the expectation of a directly contrary issue. Here is enough to put us on inquiring, not whether learning, and even school-discipline, be good things, but whether the knowledge usually thought most

essential, the school discipline which is commonly esteemed
indispensable, be in fact either the one or the other; whether
the study of nature, in her apparent forms, may not be found
a much more powerful stimulus to thought than it is at present allowed to be, let the study be pursued among the hills of
Tweeddale, or in the Laboratory, Botanic Garden, or Observ-
atory: whether again, the discipline of pain and pleasure,
appointed by Providence, may not effect more by being less
interfered with than it is under our present educational
methods, which leave scarcely any experience pure from artificial admixture. Many parents will say that they do not
wish their children to become poets and romance writers,
and will plead that Walter Scott was but little of a lawyer
after all. But it should be remembered, that the generation
and direction of power are very different things. It was the
discipline of natural vicissitude which generated power in
Walter Scott; its direction was owing to local and individual
circumstances. The example might be followed exactly in
the first particular, and only analogically in the other. This
might be done without any apprehension; for no one will
deny the practicability that there was for turning Sir Walter's
genius in some other direction, if it had been thought desirable. There was such a practical character about all his
undertakings, such good sense pervading his conversation and
views of life, that there can be no doubt of his power being
of that highest kind, which is as flexible as it is strong;
which can change its aims as readily as it can pursue them
perseveringly. The question is, how to obtain this power,
much more than how to direct it. The movements of society
must not, it seems, be trusted to originate it; but the pressure of society may probably be trusted to direct it.

While few inquiries can be more interesting than that of
how the genius of Scott grew up, few contemplations can be
more pleasurable, more animating, than that of the same

genius in its matured state.   It is difficult to decide where to
begin in reviewing the qualities which serve as tests of its
healthfulness; but perhaps the most striking, not from its
predominance, (where none can be said to predominate,) but
from its importance, is its *purity*.

This purity is not solely to be ascribed to the purity of the
aliment on which the genius was nourished.   All the aliment
presented to genius is pure in itself, whether it be the tranquil beauty of blue skies and verdant hills, or the mournful
beauty which sanctifies the relics of things passed away, or
the idealized beauty of works of art, or the suggestive beauty
of passing circumstances, or that moving pageant, in which
many see no beauty, that display of society, in which crime,
littleness, and wo, are mixed up with whatever is more honorable to humanity.   All these things are pure, in as far as
their action upon genius is concerned, as stimulants of sensibility, and provocatives to thought; and there can be little
doubt that Scott would, if placed, without Byron's training,
in Byron's position, amidst the licentious intrigues of fashionable life, have painted that life in all its hideous truth, with
perfect purity of spirit.   There is no more reasonable doubt
of this than that Byron would have carried his stormy passions with him into the stillest nooks of Tweeddale, and
wakened the echoes of Smalholm Tower with his bitter
mockery of certain of his race.   It is not the material on
which genius employs itself that can ever be impure; since
genius has nothing conventional in its constitution, and the
purity or impurity which is thought to reside in objects, is
wholly conventional.   All depends upon how the material is
received; whether as the food of appetite, or of the affections, chastened by philosophy.   It is not true genius which
defiles its own aliment for its own pleasure; and where
depravity exists in combination with genius, it is by a forced
connexion, and the depravity goes to feed the appetites,

while the genius finds its nourishment elsewhere. Such a combination exhibits the two-headed monster of the moral world, one of whose countenances may be regarding the starry heavens, while the other is gloating over the garbage of impurity beneath it. The employment of the one has nothing whatever to do with the contemplation of the other. The genius of an artist is no more answerable for his gluttony or drunkenness, than his gluttony and drunkenness for his genius. Where genius is somewhat less unfortunate in its connexion, where it is linked with the licentiousness of caste and custom, rather than with that of brutality, it is supposed to be nourished by this licentiousness, and Don Juan is appealed to as a proof; but it is not the licentiousness, but the knowledge of human passions, gained by its means, (a knowledge which might be much better gained by a thousand higher means,) by which the genius is enriched. Genius accepts the knowledge, and rejects the poison amidst which it is conveyed. The more the experience savors of impurity, the less is there for genius to appropriate; the more there is of philosophic investigation, (and this was at the bottom of much of Byron's pursuit of experience,) the more is genius profited, and the less base are the excesses with which it is mixed up. Where, with this philosophical investigation, is united that chastened affection for humanity which makes the observer far-sighted, and connects him with his race by generous sympathies instead of selfish instincts, no impurity can attend any knowledge whatever of the doings of the race: no more than pollution could dim the brightness of an angelic presence passing through a Turkish harem, or kindle unholy fires in the eyes of the Lady while watching the rabble-rout of Comus. The genius of Scott was not only innocent as the imagination of a child — all genius is so in itself — it was also pure; that is, it did not bring into combination with itself any thing which could deteriorate its

2

power, or defile its lustre.   His purity of thought and feeling
was not of the still and cold, but of the active and genial
character.   It was not like the mountain snow, which is all
whiteness under common circumstances, but which, if by
chance melted, may be found to have held many dark specks
congealed within it ; but rather like the running stream,
which catches light, warmth, and coloring from all substances
through which it passes, and sweeps away, or buries, all with
which it has no affinity.   No one can dispute Walter Scott's
knowledge of life, and his insight into the mysteries of society.   He could have told, more than most men, of the intrigues of courts, the licentiousness of nobles, the secret
revels of divers classes of men, and the excesses which
follow close on both the gratification and the disappointment
of all the stronger passions.   No one had a warmer sympathy with the stirrings in men's bosoms, or could make larger
allowance for frailty, or feel more genially the pleasures
of conviviality and other social excitement ; yet no man was
ever more remarkable for combining perfect purity of conception with truth and freedom of delineation.   He was himself temperate in his habits as genial in his temperament ;
and his works are like himself.   The Templar, Varney, Mike
Lambourne, Christian, Dalgarno, find each their place in his
pictures of life — they are not made the text of a sermon,
but rather allowed to speak for themselves in a not very
sermon-like style ; and the issue is, that they leave on the
mind of the reader not a single impression which can defile,
but instead, a conviction that, as respects the mind of the
author, they came and went, leaving no spot or stain behind.
   Closely allied with the purity of Scott's genius, was its
modesty — a modesty as astonishing to his distant admirers
as it ever was amusing to his near friends.   It is scarcely
possible to imagine how, with his quick sense of the good and
the beautiful, he should have remained so innocent of all

suspicion of how much there was of both in his own works.
If the ingenuousness of his mind had been less remarkable
than it was, there would have been a pretty general suspicion
that he was not above the common affectation of pretending
to dispute the decision of the public; but the entire simplicity
of his speech and conduct places his ingenuousness beyond
question.   It is certain that he alone failed to perceive or to
bear in mind the power and richness of his own conceptions
and delineations; while it is no less certain that, if he had
met with the most insignificant of his characters in any other
novel, or had (like Dr. Priestley) stumbled upon a forgotten
odd volume of his own, without the titlepage, and had not
known whither to refer it, he would have fallen into an enthusiasm of admiration upon it, as, to the great amusement of
his friends, he was wont to do about productions of much
inferior merit.   Credulous as he was where merit was to be
ascribed, here only he declined taking every body's word.
Deferential as he was to the voice of society, here only he
evaded its decision.   Sometimes he seemed scarcely aware
what was comprehended in the words of its laudatory de-
crees : sometimes he ascribed his success to novelty, sometimes to .fashion ; now to one temporary influence, now to
another — to any thing rather than his own merit.   This
modesty so verges upon excess as to cause some passing feelings of regret, that it was impossible to inspire him with a
due sense of what he had done, with that virtuous complacency which is the fair reward of such toils as his ; till we
remember that he could not but have had his private raptures
over the beauties of his own creation ; his thrillings of pleasure in converse with the divine Die Vernon, and of lofty
emotion when winding up his most solemn scenes ; and his
paroxysms of mirth after calling up a Friar Tuck, or a Trip-
tolemus Yellowley ; till, reminded by the world that all these
bore the closest connexion with himself, they, with the pride

and pleasure they had afforded, were swallowed up and forgotten in his modesty.   That they should be thus forgotten
or lightly esteemed, still seems unfair, however the fact may
be accounted for ; and it is a positive relief to meet with a
notice here and there, in Sir Walter's notes and prefaces,
which indicate that he did derive some gratification from his
success, that he did consent to taste a little of the delicious
brimming cup which his brethren of the craft are usually all
too ready to drain before it is half full.   "I have seldom,"
he says, " felt more satisfaction than when, returning from a
pleasure voyage, I found Waverley in the zenith of popularity, and public curiosity in full cry after the name of the
author.   The knowledge that I had the public approbation
was like having the property of a hidden treasure, not less
gratifying to the owner than if all the world knew that it was
his own."   We thank him for having let us know this.   It is
one of the most precious passages in his writings, though, if
occurring in those of almost any other of the *genus irritabile*,
it is probably one to which we should have given little attention.   The delicacy of his modesty appears in the following
passage, which, coming from a man who had stood as severe
a trial of his humility as was ever afforded by the sudden
acquisition of unbounded fame, bears a very high value, and
ought to be taken to heart by many who are more frail,
though less tempted than himself.   Our readers have all
probably seen it before ; but a second, or even a twentieth,
reading can do them no harm.

" I may perhaps be thought guilty of affectation, should I
allege, as one reason of my silence, [as to the authorship of
the novels,] a secret dislike to enter on personal discussions
concerning my own literary labors.   It is in every case a
dangerous intercourse for an author to be dwelling continually
among those who make his writings a frequent and familiar
subject of conversation, but who must necessarily be partial

judges of works composed in their own society. The habits of self-importance which are thus acquired by authors are highly injurious to a well-regulated mind; for the cup of flattery, if it does not, like that of Circe, reduce men to the level of beasts, is sure, if eagerly drained, to bring the best and the ablest down to that of fools. The risk was in some degree prevented by the mask which I wore; and my own stores of self-conceit were left to their natural course, without being enhanced by the partiality of friends, or adulation of flatterers."

It may, however, be observed, that this degree of discretion is desirable, perhaps practicable, only where the authorship relates to light literature; and that it would be an injustice to works of a grave and scientific character, to deprive them of whatever advantage the author may gain by the discussion of his subject during its progress. In these cases, however, the discussion should be of the topics, not of the authorship; of the work, not of the writer. Simplicity is the true rule, as in all other cases, so in this: the simplicity which was exemplified in the Author of Waverley, and which is equally far removed from the jealous unsocial secrecy of Newton respecting his scientific researches, and the prattling vanity of those weak-minded literati and philosophers who do all that in them lies to bring contempt on their calling.

In fairness, it should be added, that the genius of Sir Walter owed some of its modesty to his Toryism, which prescribed other objects of ambition than literary fame. To his aristocratic taste it was more agreeable to be ranked among the landed proprietors than among the authors of his country. He was better pleased to be looked upon as the local dispenser of justice than as the enchanter of Europe. He wrote a score of matchless romances for the sake of improving a patch of bad land; and while apparently insensible to flattery on the score of his works, and unable to account for

2 *

even reasonable praise, he exhibited a gratified complacency in his title of " the Shirra," and in his rank as a country gentleman of Roxburghshire. So much for the variety in men's estimates of good !

This, his modesty, guarded by his Toryism, partly accounts for the extraordinary union of *frankness* and *discretion* in his character. It could only be by lightly valuing his achievements, by thinking little of himself and his doings, that a man of his sincerity could have been such a secret-keeper. It was not by measures of precaution as regarded his own conduct ; it was not by plot and underplot, that the public was misled as to the authorship of the novels. It was by the coolness of his manner, and the simplicity of his speech and demeanour, that inquirers were baffled ; and this coolness could scarcely have been preserved by one so ardent and simple, if he had thought his achievements as marvellous as they appeared to others, or if they had been the objects of his principal interest. In what light he regarded them may be gathered from a passage in which he offers us his views of the duties of those who are entering on a literary life.

" Upon the whole, as I had no pretension to the genius of the distinguished persons who had fallen into such errors, [vanity and irascibility,] I concluded there could be no occasion for imitating them in such mistakes, or what I considered as such. With this view, it was my first resolution to keep as far as was in my power abreast of society ; continuing to maintain my place in general company, without yielding to the very natural temptation of narrowing myself to what is called literary society. By doing so, I imagined I should escape the besetting sin of listening to language which, from one motive or another, ascribes a very undue degree of consequence to literary pursuits, as if they were indeed the business rather than the amusement of life."

Whatever may be conjectured as to how much Sir Walter included under the term " literary pursuits," and as to how differently he might have estimated them if he had beheld another in his own position, the above passage vindicates the truth, that " out of the abundance of the heart the mouth speaketh." The abundance of his heart did not consist of that of which he did not speak — of himself and his fame. He spoke of politics, of other men's literature, of antiquities, of planting and farming, of law and justice, of fishing and shooting ; " of man, of nature, of society ; " and of these things his heart was full. He did not speak or encourage others to speak of his labors of the desk, and of their rewards ; and of these things his heart was not full.

It seems rather strange that he should have spoken thus lightly of literature, when he himself applied its forces to some of the gravest purposes in which they can be employed, — in the delineation of the working of the darker passions. If the inquiry had been brought home to him, he would scarcely have persisted that there was mere amusement to himself in the conception, or to his readers in the contemplation of such characters as his Dirk Hatteraick, Front-de-Bœuf, the Templar, Tony Forster, Varney, and Leicester, and Rashleigh Osbaldistone, and many more, whose dark thoughts and deeds it would be as wrong as it is impossible to allow to pass before us as a mere spectacle, and be forgotten. There is too solemn a character belonging to the sufferings of Amy Robsart, and of the Master of Ravenswood, to permit their having no permanent effect on philosophy and morals, and too much depth in the genius which delineated them to justify the speaking lightly of such of its efforts as those in question. If the office of casting new lights into philosophy, and adding new exemplifications and sanctions to morals, be not the " business " of literary genius, we know not what is. It is the " business," the first business of every man to deduce these very lessons from actual life; and we can conceive of no more important occupation than his who does the same thing for many, while doing it for himself; presenting the necessary materials, and their issues, unravelled from the complications, and separated from the admixtures which may impair their effect in real life, but no less palpably real than if they had passed under actual observation. This is the task, the real " business" of moral philosophers of all ranks and times; of Socrates, Zeno, and Epicurus, in the temple and the garden; of the Fathers of the Church in their twilight cells of learning; of the philosophers and bards of the middle ages; and, in the present, of Scott in his study, no less than of the divine in his pulpit. How much more conscious Scott really was than he seemed, of the importance of his office as an exhibitor of humanity, can probably never now be known; but that that office did, in fact, constitute the real business of his life, is as certain as it will be evident, when not one stone of Abbotsford shall be left upon another, when the last tree of his planting shall have tottered to its fall, and the last relic of the man shall have been lost, except that which is enshrined in his works.

It may be said, that he had little to do with the darker passions, and proved that there are but few villains among the host of characters; but these dark passions cast their shade far and wide, and one villain modifies the fortunes of many innocent persons. Rashleigh is at the bottom of all that happens in Rob Roy, and ambition gives its entire coloring to the romance of Kenilworth. These dark passions cause the predominant impression left by moral pictures; as a thunder cloud characterizes the summer landscape, though the streams of sun-light may far outnumber the flashes of the lightning. That dark passions are introduced, and have excited an interest, is a sufficient basis for the argument, that their exhibition constituted an important part of the business of his life, who conceived and portrayed their workings.

The world, at least that part of it which knows what it is talking about, has ceased to be astonished at the union of *mirth* and *pathos* in the effusions of genius. That mirth is often found without pathos, and pathos without mirth, is no argument against their coëxistence ; as there have been some in every age to prove, beginning (at the nearest) from Solomon, when writing the Proverbs and Ecclesiastes, and finishing with Sir Walter Scott. Indeed, as an acute discrimination of analogies is the basis equally of poetry and wit, and as the same discrimination, applied to the workings of human emotion, is the chief requisite to pathos, the wonder is rather, that Milton should have been able to keep ludicrous combinations of ideas always out of sight, than that Shakspeare should have been profuse in them ; that the Man of Feeling should never have been moved to mirth, than that Uncle Toby should have brushed away his tears with a laugh. The power produced by this union has seldom been more fully shown than in the Abbot Boniface of Scott. While the Abbot of the Monastery, he is little better than contemptible. The man moves no sympathy, and is regarded as a fine satirical sketch, as a representation of an obsolete class, and in nowise interesting as an individual. How miraculously he comes out as the old gardener, grown innocent in his tastes, and crossed in his sole desire, — their harmless indulgence ! The comic aspect of his official character is preserved, while we are made to feel a respectful compassion for the individual ; and his last words sink deep into the heart, and return for ever upon the memory and the ear.

" The Ex-Abbot resumed his spade. ' I could be sorry for these men,' he said ; ' ay, and for that poor Queen ; but what avail earthly sorrows to a man of fourscore? and it is a rare dropping morning for the early colewort.' "

The most remarkable circumstance attending Scott's opposite powers of moving is, not their coëxistence, but their keeping one another in check, as they ever did, except in the one (repented ?) instance in which he allowed his wit to run riot — in his sketches of the Covenanters in Old Mortality. None probably deny, that fanaticism is a most tempting subject for wit to divert itself upon, and that there may be little exaggeration in the reports given of Mause Headrigg's conversation and achievements ; but there are also few to defend a needless outrage upon the religious prejudices of a nation, at the risk of disturbing something better than prejudices. Sir Walter did not excuse himself for this single indiscretion, or probably intend to do so, by his subsequent exposition of the absurdity of men of the present day clinging to the letter of the faith and practice of their forefathers. In all other instances his mirth was as discreet and innocent as his pathos was deep and true. Each enhanced, while it controlled the other ; and their union afforded an infallible test of the power of the genius whose healthy development it characterized.

In no respect has the character of genius been more importantly vindicated by Sir Walter than in his habitual *cheerfulness.* There may be, and ought to be, an end for ever to the notion, that melancholy is an attribute of genius ; for Sir Walter was as little given to melancholy as any whistling ploughboy within the realm of Scotland. If it be true, that genius dives deep into the recesses where pain shrouds itself from the light, it is also true, that genius opens up new and everspringing sources of joy ; while the common and wearing troubles of life are thrown off by its elasticity, and its own light sheds beauty on all that surrounds it. That many geniuses have been moody men, is not owing to their genius, but to habit of body or mind, which their genius was not powerful enough to evercome. If the mind be its own place, the highest mind must hold the happiest place ; the wider its ken, the more numerous the objects of good within the circle ; the more various its powers, the more harmonious the creation of which those powers take cognizance. Thus was it with Sir Walter Scott; his internal cheerfulness breathing music through the fiercest storms that gathered at his spell, and forming the basis of all the varied melodies which he drew from the chords of the human heart. It is never lost — not in the darkest scenes where his personages are raging, suffering, sinking under violence and wo: there is even here a principle of vigor in the humanity displayed, — a tacit promise, that there are better things beyond, which, without any obtrusion of the author's individuality, supports the reader's spirits upon the buoyancy of the writer's. We will not flatter even the dead. We will not say that this cheerfulness appears to us to spring so much from a lofty faith in humanity as from other causes, equally pure, but with which it is a pity that the faith we speak of should not coëxist. Walter Scott had a perpetual spring of joy within him from his love of nature, from his secret sense of power, from his wise regulation of his tastes and desires, and from the kindliness of disposition which endeared him to every one, and every one to him ; but there are no traces of that long clear foresight of the issues of social struggles, no evidences that he caught the distant echoes of that harmony into which all the jarrings of social interests must subside ; no aspirations after a better social state than the present ; no sympathy beaming through its tears, for the sacrifices of patriotism, and the patient waiting of the oppressed for redress. No one showed more respect for opinion as the basis of practice, or more sympathy for individual sorrows : no one could put a more benevolent construction on what passed before his eyes, or was more disposed to make the best of whatever is ; but his perpetual, fond recurrence to the past, his indisposition to change ; in a word, his Toryism prevented his recognising the ultimate purposes of society, and reposing amidst that faith in man which is, next to trust in God, (of which indeed it forms a

part,) the best resting place of the spirit amidst the tumults
and vicissitudes of life. It was from a deficiency of support
of this kind that his spirit once quailed : that once, that will
never cease to be mourned, when multitudes, far his inferi-
ors in all besides, were enabled to rejoice while he suffered,
trembled, supplicated, all the more keenly, ·all the more
urgently, from the might of the heart within him. The fear
of change perplexed him, and he warned and petitioned
against it ineffectually, and to his own great injury ; when, if
he could but have seen that change was inevitable, and might
be directed to the most magnificent achievements, he might
have been one of the adored leaders of a heroic nation, instead of being made a spectacle to the people while offering
his affecting farewell — "*Moriturus vos salutat.*" He had
vigor to support his own misfortunes, and to set about repair-
ing them with unflinching heroism. But he had not faith in
man collectively as he had in individual man, and could not
resist the sadness with which political change inspired him,
and which, more than any private sorrows, was thought to
accelerate his decline. From the hopefulness which springs
out of faith in man's progression, he was cut off. It was a
great misfortune. Far be it from us to taunt his memory
with it, or to ascribe it to any thing but the outward circumstances of his training. If the world lost something by it,
he lost more, and moreover suffered by infliction as well as
deprivation : and all this makes the depth and continuity of
his cheerfulness the more remarkable. This cheerfulness,
this tendency to put a kindly construction on all which has
been and is, accounts for his popularity notwithstanding his
Toryism, and is, in its turn, partly accounted for by his
industry, — another test of the healthiness of his genius.

On this industry little can be said. Its achievements are
before every one's eyes, and are, we suppose, nearly as unaccountable to most people as to ourselves. We give up the

attempt to settle how he did all, and when he did it. We
have his own word for his works (except during an interval
of two years) being all written by his own hand; and if we
had not had this unquestionable word, we should have dis-
sented from Göthe's supposition, that he sketched and touched
up, and left it to inferior hands to compose the bulk of his
works. There is such a character of unity amidst all the
diversity; the dullest scenes are so evidently enjoyed by the
author, however little they may be so by the reader; there is
such gusto, such an absence of all sense of drudgery throughout, that we could (as we said at the time) have staked our
character for penetration upon the fact, before the disclosure
was made, that every chapter in this library of novels was
written by the same hand. How it was done is another
matter. How he wrote for years together, sixteen pages
of print per diem, on an average, while discharging his official duties in town, or before beginning his daily occupations
and pleasures of hospitality in the country, — sixteen pages
of historical, as well as fictitious, narrative, including all the
research which either required, is to us matter of pure astonishment. We must be content with it as a fact; and taking
it thus, we can understand how so perpetual a flow of fresh
ideas, so animating a consciousness of power, so ever-present
an evidence of achievement must have fed the springs of his
cheerfulness, and have given that character of luxury to his
intellectual refreshments which bodily toil gives to the meal
and the couch of the laborer. There is a delight appertain-
ing to earned pleasures which is common to all classes in the
intellectual and social world; and herein was Sir Walter
least of all aristocratic. His example of this truth is so
valuable, his sanction so impressive, that we must be excused
the triteness of our morality. If there be any in whose eyes
Industry has not hitherto been majestic, they may now perhaps be led to appreciate her dignity. All others will dwell

thankfully on every new testimony to her congeniality with genius.

It is not easy to see how it can ever be tolerable to genius to be idle. To conceive achievements, and not attempt them; to discriminate beauty, and not reach after it; to discern that action is necessary to further contemplation, and not to act; — these things seem, if not contradictory, unnatural; and the impulses arising from them are quite sufficient, without any help from the ambition of which Sir Walter had a very small share, to account for any degree of exertion that physical and mental energy can sustain. They are enough to render the spirit willing; and where the spirit is willing, the might is strong; and this willingness and might together constitute industry; an indispensable grace of the lofty, (whatever some who are great in their own eyes may think,) as well as the most ennobling virtue of the humble. Genius implies toil, both as its cause and its consequence; and the example of Walter Scott (unnecessary as a proof, though welcome as a sanction to some) will open the eyes of many as to a new truth. And herein we recognise another of his mighty services as a vindicator of genius.

The *practical character* of his conduct and conversation was another of his valuable characteristics, — implied in his industry, indeed, but remarkable apart from that. Good sense is as remarkable a feature of his most imaginative writings as illustration and humor were of his homeliest conversation. He had a considerable degree of worldly sagacity; not only of that which, being worked out in the study, makes a good show upon paper, but of that shrewdness which is ready for use in all the rapid turns of life, and sudden occasions of daily business. This is evident, not only in his portrait, and in his exposition of the system of Scotch banking, but in his most delicate delineations of his fairest heroines; in his records of the conversation of the glorious Die

Vernon, in the *tête-à-têtes* of Minna and Brenda, and conspicuously in the interview between Rebecca and Rowena. It is the practical character, *i. e.* the reality which pervades his loftiest scenes, that gives to them their permanent charm : in the same manner as the writer himself was respected as a man of superior rationality, and beloved as an endearing companion, instead of being regarded as a wayward dreamer, merely tolerated on account of supposed genius.

Here we must stop for the present. In pursuing this inquiry into the education and characteristics of his genius, we seem to have done little towards expressing the emotions which his name awakens, exalted as it is amidst the coronach of a nation. We shall hereafter attempt some estimate of his achievements, and of his services to his race — services of whose extent he was himself nearly as unconscious as his contemporaries are proud.

ACHIEVEMENTS OF THE GENIUS OF SCOTT.

Having already tendered our homage to the memory of Scott in his capacity of vindicator of the character of Genius, we proceed to discuss his other claims to the veneration and gratitude of society.

In doing this, we shall not enter into any elaborate criticism of his compositions as works of art. This has been done a hundred times before, and will be done a hundred times again, to the great benefit of literature and the fine arts, and to the exalted entertainment of both those who lead and those who follow in the discrimination of the manifold beauties and graces with which Scott has adorned the realms of taste. We apply ourselves to the contemplation of the

works of Scott, in their effects as influences, rather than to
an analysis of their constitution as specimens of art. If we
include in our inquiry the services which he rendered to
society negatively as well as positively, unconsciously as well
as designedly, it may appear that the gratitude of one age
and one empire is but a sample of the reward which his
achievements deserve and will obtain.

There is little reason to question that Scott has done more
for the morals of society, taking the expression in its largest
sense, than all the divines, and other express moral teachers,
of a century past. When we consider that all moral sciences are best taught by exemplification, and that these exemplifications produce tenfold effect when exhibited unprofes-
sionally, it appears that dramatists and novelists of a high
order have usually the advantage, as moralists, over those
whose office it is to present morals in an abstract form. The
latter are needed to systematize the science, and to prevent
its being lost sight of as the highest of the sciences ; but the
advantage of practical influence rests with the former. When
we, moreover, consider the extent of Scott's practical influence, and multiply this extent by its force, there will be little
need of argument to prove that the whole living phalanx of
clergy, orthodox and dissenting, of moral philosophers, of all
moral teachers, except statesmen and authors of a high order,
must yield the sceptre of moral sway to Scott. If they are
wise, they will immediately acknowledge this, estimate his
achievements, adopt, to a certain extent, his methods, and
step forward to the vantage ground he has gained for them.
If they be disposed to question the fact of the superiority of
his influence, let them measure it for an instant against their
own. Let them look to our universities, and declare whether
they have, within a century, done much for the advancement
of morals at home, or to bring morals into respect abroad.
Let them look to the weight of the established clergy, and

say how much they actually modify the thoughts and guide
the conduct of the nation; taking into the account, as a balance against the good they do, the suspicion there exists
against them in their character of a craft, and the disrepute
which attaches itself to what they teach, through an admixture of abuses. Let them look to the dissenting clergy, —
far more influential as they are than the established, — and
say, whether they operate as extensively and benignantly
upon the human heart, as he who makes life itself the language in which he sets forth the aims and ends of life; who
not only uses a picture-alphabet, that the untutored and the
truant may be allured to learn, but imparts thereto a hiero-
glyphic character, from which the most versed in human life
may evolve continually a deeper and yet deeper lore. Let
our moral philosophers (usefully employed though they be in
arranging and digesting the science, and enlightened in mod-
ifying, from time to time, the manifestations of its eternal
principles,) — let our moral philosophers declare whether
they expect their digests and expositions to be eagerly listened
to by the hundred thousand families, collected, after their
daily avocations, under the spell of the northern enchanter;
whether they would look for thumbed copies of their writings
in workshops and counting-houses, in the saloons of palaces,
and under many a pillow in boarding-schools. Our universities may purify morals, and extend their influence as far as
they can; their importance in this case runs a chance of
being overlooked: for Scott is the president of a college
where nations may be numbered for individuals. Our clergy
may be and do all that an established clergy can be and do;
yet they will not effect so much as the mighty lay preacher
who has gone out on the highways of the world, with cheerfulness in his mien and benignity on his brow; unconscious,
perhaps, of the dignity of his office, but as much more powerful in comparison with a stalled priesthood, as the trouba-

dour of old, — firing hearts wherever he went with the love
of glory, — than the vowed monk.   Our dissenting preachers
may obtain a hold on the hearts of their people, and employ
it to good purpose ; but they cannot send their voices east
and west to wake up the echoes of the world.   Let all these
classes unite in a missionary scheme, and encompass the
globe, and still Scott will teach morals more effectually than
them all.   They will not find audiences at every turn who
will take to heart all they say, and bear it in mind for ever ;
and if they attempt it now, they will find that Scott has been
before them every where.   He has preached truth, simplicity,
benevolence, and retribution, in the spicy bowers of Ceylon,
and in the verandahs of Indian bungalowes, and in the per-
fumed dwellings of Persia, and among groups of settlers at
the Cape, and amidst the pine woods and savannahs of the
western world, and in the vineyards of the Peninsula, and
among the ruins of Rome, and the recesses of the Alps, and
the hamlets of France, and the cities of Germany, and the
palaces of Russian despots, and the homes of Polish patriots.
And all this in addition to what has been done in his native
kingdom, where he has exalted the tastes, ameliorated the
tempers, enriched the associations, and exercised the intellects of millions.   This is already done in the short space of
eighteen years ; a mere span in comparison with the time
that it is to be hoped our language and literature will last.
We may assume the influence of Scott, as we have described
it, to be just beginning its course of a thousand years ; and
now, what class of moral teachers, (except politicians, who
are not too ready to regard themselves in this light,) will
venture to bring their influence into comparison with that of
this great lay preacher ?

If they do so, it will be on the ground, not of disputing the
extent of his influence, but its moral effect; which, therefore, we proceed to investigate ; beginning with his lesser,
and going on to consider his greater achievements.

His grateful countrymen, of all ranks, acknowledge that he has benefited Scotland, as much morally as in respect of her worldly prosperity. Not only has he carried civilization into the retreats of the mountains, and made the harmonious voices of society float over those lakes where the human war-cry once alternated with the scream of the eagle; not only has he introduced decency and comfort among the wilder classes of his countrymen, a full half century before they could have been anticipated, and led many thousands more into communion with nature, who would not, but for him, have dreamed of such an intercourse; not only has he quickened industry, and created wealth, and cherished intelligence within the borders of his native land; he has also exercised a direct moral influence over the minds of those on whom Scotland's welfare largely depends; softening their prejudices, widening their social views, animating their love of country while drawing them into closer sympathy with men of other countries. It may be said, — it is said, — that his country is not sensible of his having done all this; that she cannot be sensible of it, since she suffered his latter days to be overclouded by sorrows which she could have removed, and his mighty heart and brain to be crushed by a weight of care and toil of which she could have relieved him. The fact is undeniable; and it is on record for ever, with a thousand similar facts, from which it is to be hoped that men will in time have philosophy enough to draw an inference, and establish a conclusion in morals to which Walter Scott has failed to lead them, even by the mute eloquence of his own sufferings. They may in time perceive that the benefactor of a nation should be the cherished of a nation, before he has become insensible of their affection; and that it is a small thing to make splendid the narrow home of him who was allowed to perish unsheltered in the storm. It is not enough to abstain from the insult which aggravated the sufferings of Lear;—to be innocent of inflicting his woes. It is not enough for the subjects of this intellectual king to have honored him equally when his train was shortened, and to have uncovered their heads as he passed, in respectful compassion for his reverses; they ought to have felt that in having been made their king, he had become their charge; and that whencesoever adversity arose, it was their duty to avert it from his honored head. It is folly to talk of the evil of a precedent in such a case. The line of intellectual sovereigns is not so long as to make the maintenance of their prerogative a burdensome imposition; and we ask no loyalty to pretenders. As for the present case, bitterly as we feel the crudeness of the world's morality of gratitude, we are as far as was the illustrious departed from imputing blame to individuals,—to any thing but the system under which he suffered. He was too humble—too little conscious of his own services to apply to himself the emotions with which the lot of other social benefactors was regarded by him, and with which his own is too late regarded by us—the emotions of grief and shame that society has not yet learned to prize the advent of genius; that the celestial guest is still permitted to tread, solitary and unsheltered, the rugged highways of the world, however eagerly its deeds of power and beneficence may have been accepted. That the countrymen of Scott feel truly grateful to their benefactor, we doubt not. We implore them to strengthen this gratitude from a sanction into a principle of conduct; that, if it should please Heaven again to bless them with such a guest, they may duly cherish him while yet in the body, delay his departure to the latest moment, and be disturbed by no jarring mockeries of shame and remorse while chanting their requiem at his tomb.

To do his next work of beneficence, this great moralist stepped beyond the Border, and over continents and seas. He implanted or nourished pure tastes, not only in a thousand homes, but among the homeless in every land. How many indolent have been roused to thought and feeling, how many licentious have been charmed into the temporary love of purity, how many vacant minds have become occupied with objects of interest and affection, it would be impossible to estimate, unless we could converse with every Briton, from the Factory Terrace at Canton round the world to the shores of the Pacific, and with every foreigner on the Continent of Europe whose countenance lights up at the name of Scott. If one representative only of every class which has been thus benefited were to repair to his grave, the mourning train would be of a length that kings might envy. There would be the lisping child, weeping that there should be no more tales of the Sherwood Foresters and the Disinherited Knight; there would be the school-boy, with his heart full of the heroic deeds of Cœur de Lion in Palestine; and the girl, glowing with the loyalty of Flora, and saddening over the griefs of Rebecca; and the artisan who foregoes his pipe and pot for the adventures of Jeanie Deans; and the clerk and apprentice, who refresh their better part from the toils of the counting-house amidst the wild scenery of Scotland; and soldier and sailor relieved of the tedium of barracks and cabin by the interest of more stirring scenes presented to the mind's eye; and rambling youth chained to the fireside by the links of a pleasant fiction; and sober manhood made to grow young again; and sickness beguiled, and age cheered, and domestic jars forgotten, and domestic sympathies enhanced;—all who have thus had pure tastes gratified by the creations of his genius, should join the pilgrim train, which will be passing in spirit by his grave for centuries to come. Of these, how many have turned from the voice of the preacher, have cast aside "good books," have no ear for music, no taste for drawing, no knowledge of any domestic accomplishment which might keep them out of harm's way, but have found that they have a heart and mind

which Scott could touch and awaken!   How many have thus
to thank him, not only for the solace of their leisure, but for
the ennobling of their toils !

Another great service rendered is one which could be administered only by means of fiction — a service respecting
which it matters not to decide whether it was afforded designedly or unconsciously. We mean the introduction of the conception of nature, as existing and following out its own growth
in an atmosphere of convention; a conception of very great
importance to the many who, excluded from the regions of
convention, are apt to lose their manhood in its contemplation.
There is little use in assuring people of the middling ranks,
that kings eat beef and mutton, and queens ride on horseback ;
they believe, but they do not realize.   And this is the case,
not only with the child who pictures a monarch with the
crown on his head, on a throne, or with the maid-servant who
gazes with awe on the Lord Mayor's coach; but, to a much
greater degree than is commonly supposed, with the father of
the child, the master of the maid, — with him whose interests
have to do with kings and courts, and who ought, therefore,
to know what is passing there.   It would be impossible to
calculate how much patriotism has lain dormant, through the
ignorance of the plain citizen, of what is felt and thought in
the higher regions of society, to which his voice of complaint
or suggestion ought to reach, if he had but the courage to lift
it up.   The ignorance may be called voluntary: it may be
truly said that every one ought to know that human hearts
answer to one another as a reflection in water, whether this
reflection be of a glow-worm on the brink, or of the loftiest
resplendent star.   This is true; but it is not a truth easy in
the use; and its use is all-important.   The divine preaches
it, as his duty, to humble courtly pride, and to remind the
lowly of their manhood: but the divine himself realizes the
doctrine better while reading Kenilworth, or the Abbot, than

while writing his sermon; and his hearers use this same sermon as a text, of which Nigel and Peveril are the exposition.
Is this a slight service to have rendered?— to have, perhaps
unconsciously, taught human equality, while professing to exhibit human inequality?—to have displayed, in its full proportion, the distance which separates man from man, and to
have shown that the very same interests are being transacted
at one and the other end of the line? Walter Scott was exactly the man to render this great service; and how well he
rendered it, he was little aware. A man, born of the people,
and therefore knowing man, and at the same time a Tory
antiquarian, and therefore knowing courts, he was the fit person to show the one to the other. At once a benevolent in-
terpreter of the heart, and a worshipper of royalty, he might
be trusted for doing honor to both parties; though not, we
must allow, equal honor. We cannot award him the praise
of perfect impartiality in his interpretations. We cannot but
see a leaning towards regal weaknesses, and a toleration of
courtly vices. We cannot but observe, that the same licentiousness which would have been rendered disgusting under
equal temptation in humble life, is made large allowance for
when diverting itself within palace walls. Retribution is allowed to befall; but the vices which this whip is permitted to
scourge are still pleasant vices, instead of vulgar ones. This
is not to be wondered at; and perhaps the purity of the writer's own imagination may save us from lamenting it; for he
viewed these things, though partially, yet too philosophically,
to allow of any shadow of an imputation of countenancing, or
alluring to vice, with whatever wit he may have depicted the
intrigues of Buckingham, or whatever veil of tenderness he
may have cast over the crimes of the unfortunate Mary. His
desire was to view these things in the spirit of charity; and
he was less aware than his readers of a humble rank, that he
threw the gloss of romance over his courtly scenes of every

character, and that, if he had drawn the vices of the lower
classes, it would have been without any such advantage.
Meanwhile, we owe him much for having laid open to us the
affections of sovereigns, — the passions of courtiers, — the
emotions of the hearts, — the guidance of the conduct, — the
cares and amusements, — the business and the jests of courts.
He has taught many of us how royalty may be reached and
wrought upon; and has therein done more for the state than
perhaps any novelist ever contemplated. That he did not
complete his work by giving to courts accurate representations
of the people, seems a pity; but it could not be helped, since
there is much in the people of which Walter Scott knew
nothing. If this fact is not yet recognised in courts, it soon
will be; and to Walter Scott again it may be owing (as we
shall hereafter show) that the true condition and character of
the people will become better known in aristocratic regions
than they are at present.

The fictions of Scott have done more towards exposing
priestcraft and fanaticism than any influence of our own time,
short of actual observation; and this actual observation of
what is before their eyes is not made by many who see the
whole matter plainly enough in the characters and doings of
Boniface, Eustace, and the monks in Ivanhoe, — of Balfour,
Warden, and Bridgenorth. It is, we allow, no new thing to
meet with exposures of spiritual domination; but the question
is, not of the newness, but of the extent of the service. These
things are condemned in the abstract by books on morals;
they are disclaimed from the pulpit, and every Christian
church demonstrates its odiousness by the example of every
other; but these exposures do not effect half so much good as
exemplification from the hand of a philosophical observer, and
disinterested peace-maker. Men may go on for centuries
bandying reproaches of priestcraft and superstition on the one
hand, and irreligion on the other; — men may go on long point-

ing out to those who will not see, the examples of all which may be seen at every turn,—of priestcraft nourishing superstition, and superstition inducing irreligion; and less will be done by recrimination towards finding a remedy, than by the illustrations of a master-hand, choosing a bygone age for the chronology, orders long overthrown for the instruments, and institutions that have passed away for the subjects of his satire. Many who take fire at any imputation against their own church, have become aware of its besetting sins by pictures of a former church, and will easily learn to make the application where it may be serviceable. Many who look too little to the spirit through the forms of religion, are duly disgusted with the foibles of the puritans; and, perceiving how much the vices of the cavaliers were owing to the opposite vices of the contrary party, acquire a wholesome horror of spiritual pride and asceticism in the abstract, and become clear-sighted to the existence of both, in quarters where they had not before been recognised. Sir Walter says, in one of his prefaces, " I am, I own, no great believer in the moral utility to be derived from fictitious compositions;" but, in saying this, he either meant that sermons are not commonly found to produce so good an effect when introduced into a novel as when offered from the pulpit, or he was thinking at the moment of his own fictitious compositions, which, he was singularly apt to imagine, could have little influence to any good purpose. If he had looked at his own writings as those of any other man, he would have thought, as others think, that his vivid pictures of the effects of a false religion are as powerful recommendations of that which is true, to those who will not read divinity, (and they are many,) as works of divinity to those who will not read Scott's novels, (and they are few.) When to such a picture as that of his Louis XI. is added such a commentary as is found in the preface, we have a fine exposition

4

of an important point of morals, and a satire upon every species of profession which rests in forms.

"The cruelties, the perjuries, the suspicions of this prince, were rendered more detestable, rather than amended, by the gross and debasing superstition which he constantly practised. The devotion to the heavenly saints, of which he made such a parade, was upon the miserable principle of some petty deputy in office, who endeavours to hide or atone for the malversations of which he is conscious, by liberal gifts to those whose duty it is to observe his conduct, and endeavours to support a system of fraud, by an attempt to corrupt the incorruptible. In no other light can we regard his creating the Virgin Mary a countess, and colonel of his Guards, or the cunning that admitted to one or two peculiar forms of oath the force of a binding obligation, which he denied to all others; strictly preserving the secret, which mode of swearing he really accounted obligatory, as one of the most valuable of state mysteries. It was not the least singular circumstance of this course of superstition, that bodily health and terrestrial felicity seemed to be his only objects. Making any mention of his sins when his bodily health was in question, was strictly prohibited; and when, at his command, a priest recited a prayer to St. Eutropius, in which he recommended the king's welfare, both in body and soul, Louis caused the two last words to be omitted, saying, it was not prudent to importune the blessed saint by too many requests at once. Perhaps he thought, by being silent on his crimes, he might suffer them to pass out of the recollection of the celestial patrons whose aid he invoked for the body."

It may be said, that all this may be found in history. True; but how many have been impressed with this and all other instances, from the rise of popery to the decline of puritanism, in comparison with the numbers who have received, and will receive, a much stronger impression to the same effect from Scott's novels?

Another important moral service, which belongs almost exclusively to fiction, is that of satirizing eccentricities and follies, commonly thought too insignificant to be preached against, and gravely written about; but which exert an important influence on the happiness of human life. The oddities of women he has left almost untouched; but we have a brave assemblage of men who are safe from pulpit censure; (unless another Henry Warden should rise up to preach against the sixteen follies of a Roland Græme under sixteen heads;) but who may be profited by seeing their own picture, or whose picture may prevent others becoming like them. Is it not wholesome to have a Malagrowther before us on whom to exhaust our impatience, instead of venting it on the real Malagrowthers of society? Shall we not have fewer and less extravagant Saddletrees, and Shaftons, and Halcroes, and Yellowleys, for these novels? and will not such bores be regarded with more good humor? Will not some excellent Jonathan Oldbuck now and then think of the Antiquary, and check his hobby? — and many a book-worm take a lesson from Dominie Sampson? Whether such a direct effect be or be not produced, such exhibitions are as effectual as comedy ought to be on the stage, and mirthful raillery in real life, in enforcing some of the obligations, and improving the amenities of society. The rich variety of Scott's assemblage of oddities, and the exquisite mirth and good-humor with which they are shown off, are among the most remarkable particulars of his achievements. There is not only a strong cast of individuality (as there ought to be) about all his best characters; but his best characters are none of them representatives of a class. As soon as he attempted to make his personages such representatives, he failed. His ostensible heroes, his statesmen and leaders, his magistrates, his adventurers, his womankind, whether mistresses or maids, leave little impression of individuality ; while his sovereigns, real heroes, and oddities are inimitable.   The reasons of this failure of success may be found under our next head.   The result is, that Walter Scott is not only one of the most amiable, but one of the most effective satirists that ever helped to sweep the path of life clear of the strewn follies under which many a thorn is hidden.

In ascending the scale of social services, for which gratitude is due to the illustrious departed, we next arrive at one which is so great that we cannot but mourn that it was not yet greater.   There can be no need to enlarge upon the beauty and excellence of the spirit of kindliness which breathes through the whole of Scott's compositions ; a spirit which not only shames the Malagrowthers of society, just spoken of, but charms the restless to repose, exhilarates the melancholy, rouses the apathetic, and establishes a good understanding among all who contemplate one another in these books.   It is as impossible for any one to remain cynical, or moody, or desponding, over these books, as for an infant to look dismally in the face of a smiling nurse.   As face answers to face, so does heart to heart ; and as Walter Scott's overflowed with love and cheerfulness, the hearts of his readers catch its brimmings.   If any are shut against him, they are not of his readers ; and we envy them not.   They may find elsewhere all imaginable proofs and illustrations of the goodliness of a kindly spirit ; but why not add to these as perfect an exemplification as ever was offered ?   It may be very well to take one abroad in the grey dawn, and tell him that the hills have a capacity of appearing green, the waters golden, and the clouds rose-colored, and that larks sometimes sing soaring in the air, instead of crouching in a grassy nest ; but why not let him remain to witness the effusion of light from behind the mountain, the burst of harmony from field and copse ? Why not let him feel, as well as know, what a morning of sunshine is? Why not let him view its effects from every accessible point, and pour out his joy in snatches of song responsive to those which he hears around him, as well as his thankfulness in a matin hymn ? If it be true, as no readers of Scott will deny, that it exhilarates the spirits, and animates the affections, to follow the leadings of this great Enchanter, it is certain that he has achieved a great moral work of incitement and amelioration. The test of his merits here is, that his works are for the innocent and kindly-hearted to enjoy ; and if any others enjoy them, it is by becoming innocent and kindly for the time, in like manner as it is for the waking flocks and choirs to welcome the sunrise : if the fox and the owl choose to remain abroad, the one must abstain from its prey, and the other hush its hootings.

The kindliness of spirit being of so bright a quality, makes us lament all the more, as we have said, that it had not the other excellence of being universally diffused. We know how unreasonable it is to expect every thing from one man, and are far from saying or believing that Walter Scott looked otherwise than benignantly on all classes and all individuals that came under his observation. What we lament is, that there were extensive classes of men, and they the most important to society, that were secluded from the light of his embellishing genius. His sunshine gilded whatever it fell upon, but it did not fall from a sufficient height to illuminate the nooks and valleys which he found and left curtained in mists. What is there of humble life in his narratives ? What did he know of those who live and move in that region? Nothing. There is not a *character* from humble life in all his library of volumes ; nor had he any conception that character is to be found there. By humble life we do not mean Edie Ochiltree's lot of privileged mendicity, nor Dirk Hatteraick's smuggling adventures, nor the Saxon slavery of

4 *

Gurth, nor the feudal adherence of Dougal, and Caleb Bald-
erstone, and Adam Woodcock, nor the privileged depend-
ance of Caxon and Fairservice.   None of these had any thing
to do with humble life : each and all formed a part of the
aristocratic system in which Walter Scott's affections were
bound up.   Jeanie Deans herself, besides being no original
conception of Sir Walter's, derives none of her character or
interest from her station in life, any farther than as it was the
occasion of the peculiarity of her pilgrimage.   We never
think of Jeanie as poor, or low in station.   Her simplicity is
that which might pertain to a secluded young woman of any
rank ; and it is difficult to bear in mind — it is like an extra-
neous circumstance, that her sister was at service, the only
attempt made throughout at realizing the social position of
the parties.   We do not mention this as any drawback upon
the performance, but merely as saving the only apparent exception to our remarks, that Sir Walter rendered no service
to humble life in the way of delineating its society.   Faithful butlers and barbers, tricky lady's maids, eccentric falcon-
ers and gamekeepers, are not those among whom we should
look for the strength of character, the sternness of passion,
the practical heroism, the inexhaustible patience, the unassu-
ming self-denial, the unconscious beneficence — in a word,
the *true-heartedness* which is to be found in its perfection in
humble life.   Of all this Walter Scott knew nothing.   While
discriminating, with the nicest acumen, the shades of character, the modifications of passion, among those whom he
did understand, he was wholly unaware that he bounded
himself within a small circle, beyond which lay a larger, and
a larger ; that which he represented being found in each, in
a more distinct outline, in more vivid coloring, and in striking and various combinations, with other characteristics of
humanity which had never presented themselves to him.   He
knew not that the strength of soul, which he represents as

growing up in his heroes amidst the struggles of the crusade, is of the same kind with that which is nourished in our neighbours of the next alley, by conflicts of a less romantic, but not less heroic cast. He knew not that the passion of ambition, which he has made to contend with love so fearfully in Leicester's bosom, is the same passion, similarly softened and aggravated, with that which consumes the high-spirited working man, chosen by his associates to represent and guide their interests, while his heart is torn by opposite appeals to his domestic affections. He knew not that, however reckless the vice of some of his courtly personages, greater recklessness is to be found in the presence of poverty; that the same poverty exposes love to further trials than he has described, and exercises it into greater refinement; and puts loyalty more severely to the test, and inspires a nobler intrepidity, and nourishes a deeper hatred, and a wilder superstition, and a more inveterate avarice, and a more disinterested generosity, and a more imperturbable fortitude, than even he has set before us. In short, he knew not that all passions, and all natural movements of society, that he has found in the higher, exist in the humbler ranks; and all magnified and deepened in proportion as reality prevails over convention, as there is less mixture of the adventitious with the true. The effect of this partial knowledge is not only the obliteration to himself and to his readers, as far as connected with him, of more than half the facts and interests of humanity, but that his benevolence was stinted in its play. We find no philanthropists among his characters; because he had not the means of forming the conception of philanthropy in its largest sense. He loved men, all men whom he knew; but that love was not based on knowledge as extensive as his observation was penetrating; and it did not therefore deserve the high title of philanthropy. We have no sins of commission to charge him with, no breaches of charity, not a thought or expression which is tinged with bitterness against man, collectively or individually; but we charge him with omission of which he was unconscious, and which he would, perhaps, scarcely have wished to repair, as it must have been done at the expense of his Toryism, to which the omission and unconsciousness were owing. How should a man be a philanthropist who knows not what freedom is?—not the mere freedom from foreign domination, but the exemption from misrule at home, the liberty of watching over and renovating institutions, that the progression of man and of states may proceed together. Of this kind of freedom Sir Walter had no conception, and neither, therefore, are there any patriots in his *dramatis personæ*. There are abundance of soldiers to light up beacons and fly to arms at the first notice of invasion; many to drink the healths and fight the battles of their chiefs, to testify their fidelity to their persons, and peril life and liberty in their cause; plenty to vindicate the honor of England abroad, and to exult in her glory at home. But this is not patriotism, any more than kindliness is philanthropy. We have no long-sighted views respecting the permanent improvement of society,—no extensive regards to the interests of an entire nation; and, therefore, no simple self-sacrifice, no steadfastness of devotion to country and people. The noble class of virtues, which go to make up patriotism, are not even touched upon by Scott. The sufferings of his heroes are represented to arise from wounded pride, and from the laceration of personal, or domestic, or feudal feelings and prepossessions; and in no single instance from sympathy with the race, or any large body of them. The courage of his heroes is, in like manner, compounded of instincts and of conventional stimuli; and in no one case derived from principle of philanthropy, or of patriotism, which is one direction of philanthropy. Their fortitude, howsoever steadfast, when

arising from self-devotion at all, arises only from that unrea-
soning acquiescence in established forms, which is as inferior to the self-sacrifice of philanthropy, as the implicit
obedience of a child is inferior to the concurrence of the
reasoning man.   None of Scott's personages act and suffer
as members and servants of society.   Each is for his own ;
whether it be his family, his chief, his king, or his country,
in a warlike sense.   The weal or woe of many, or of all,
is the only consideration which does not occur to them —
the only motive to enterprise and endurance which is not
so much as alluded to.   There is no talk of freedom, as
respects any thing but brute force, — no suspicion that one
class is in a state of privilege, and another in a state of sub-
jugation, and that these things ought not to be.   Gurth,
indeed, is relieved from Saxon bondage, and Adam Woodcock is as imperious and meddling as he pleases, and the
ladies' maids have abundant liberty to play pranks ; but this
sort of freedom has nothing to do with the right of manhood,
and with what ought to be, and will be, the right of woman-
hood — it is the privilege of slavery, won by encroachment,
and preserved by favor.   Gurth got rid of his collar, but in
our days he would be called a slave : and Adam Woodcock
and Mistress Lilias lived by the breath of their lady's nos-
trils, in the same manner as the courtiers of Cœur de Lion
gained an unusual length of tether from their lord's knightly
courtesy, and those of the second Charles from his careless
clemency.   There is no freedom in all this.   *Slave* is written on the knightly crest of the master, and on the liveried
garb of the servitor, as plainly as even on the branded
shoulder of the negro.   But it must be so, it is urged, when
times and scenes of slavery are chosen as the groundwork
of the fiction.   We answer, Nay; the spirit of freedom may
breathe through the delineation of slavery.   However far
back we may revert to the usages of the feudal system, there

may be,—there must be, if they exist in the mind of the
author,— aspirations after a state of society more worthy of
humanity.   In displaying all the pomp of chivalry, the heart
ought to mourn the woes of inequality it inflicted, while the
imagination revels in its splendors.   But this could not be
the case with Scott, who knew about as much of the real
condition and character of the humble classes of each age
as the Japanese; perhaps less, as he was a reader of Basil
Hall.   Beyond that which seemed to him the outermost
circle, that of the domestics of the great, all was a blank;
save a few vague outlines of beggar-women with seven small
children, and other such groups that have by some chance
found their way into works of fiction.   His benignity, therefore, alloyed by no bitterness of disposition in himself, was
so far restricted by the imperfection of his knowledge of
life, as to prevent his conveying the conception of philanthropy in its largest sense.   His services to freedom are of
a negative, rather than a positive character; rendered by
showing how things work in a state of slavery, rather than
how they should work in a condition of rational freedom;
and it follows, that his incitements to benevolence are also
tendered unconsciously.   Through an exhibition of the
softening and brightening influence of benignity shed over
the early movements of society, he indicates what must be
the meridian splendor of philanthropy, penetrating every
where, irradiating where it penetrates, and fertilizing, as
well as embellishing whatever it shines upon.

Much has Walter Scott also done, and done it also unconsciously, for woman.   Neither Mary Wollstonecraft, nor
Thompson of Cork, nor any other advocate of the rights of
woman, has pleaded so eloquently to the thoughtful,—and
the thoughtful alone will entertain the subject, — as Walter
Scott, by his exhibition of what women are, and by two or
three indications of what they might be.   He has been found

fault with for the poverty of character of the women of his
tales; a species of blame against which we have always pro-
tested. If he had made as long a list of oddities among his
women as his men, he would have exposed himself to the
reproach of quitting nature, and deserting classes for extravagant individualities; since there is much less scope for
eccentricity among women, in the present state of society,
than among men. But, it is alleged, he has made few of
his female characters representatives of a class. True; for
the plain reason, that there are scarcely any classes to represent. We thank him for the forcible exhibition of this
truth: we thank him for the very term *womankind;* and can
well bear its insulting use in the mouth of the scoffer, for
the sake of the process it may set to work in the mind of the
meditative and the just. There is no saying what the common use of the term *canaille* may in time be proved to have
effected for the lower orders of men; or in what degree the
process of female emancipation may be hastened by the
slang use of the term *womankind,* by despots and by fools.
It may lead some watchful intellects — some feeling hearts —
to ponder the reasons of the fact, that the word *mankind*
calls up associations of grandeur and variety, — that of
womankind, ideas of littleness and sameness; — that the one
brings after it conceptions of lofty destiny, heroic action,
grave counsel, a busy office in society, a dignified repose
from its cares, a steadfast pursuit of wisdom, an intrepid
achievement of good; — while the other originates the very
opposite conceptions, — vegetation instead of life, folly instead of counsel, frivolity instead of action, restlessness in
the place of industry, apathy in that of repose, listless accomplishment of small aims, a passive reception of what
others may please to impart; or, at the very best, a halting,
intermitting pursuit of dimly-discerned objects. To some it
may be suggested to inquire, Why this contrast should

exist?—why one-half of the rational creation should be so
very much less rational?—and, as a consequence, so much
less good, and so much less happy than the other? If
they are for a moment led by custom to doubt whether,
because they are less rational, they are less happy and less
good, the slightest recurrence to Scott's novels is enough to
satisfy them, that the common notion of the sufficiency of
present female objects to female progression and happiness
is unfounded. They will perhaps look abroad from Scott
into all other works of fiction—into all faithful pictures of
life—and see what women are; and they will finally perceive, that the fewer women there are found to plead the
cause of their sex, the larger mixture of folly there is in
their pleadings; the more extensive their own unconsciousness of their wrongs, the stronger is their case. The best
argument for Negro Emancipation lies in the vices and subservience of slaves: the best argument for female emancipation lies in the folly and contentedness of women under the
present system,—an argument to which Walter Scott has
done the fullest justice; for a set of more passionless, frivolous, uninteresting beings was never assembled at morning
auction, or evening tea-table, than he has presented us with
in his novels. The few exceptions are made so by the strong
workings of instinct, or of superstition, (the offspring of
strong instinct and weak reason combined;) save in the two
or three instances where the female mind had been exposed
to manly discipline. Scott's female characters are easily
arranged under these divisions:—Three-fourths are *womankind* merely: pretty, insignificant ladies, with their pert
waiting maids. A few are viragoes, in whom instinct is
strong, whose souls are to migrate hereafter into the she-
eagle or bear,—Helen M'Gregor, Ulrica, Magdalen Græme,
and the Highland Mother. A few are superstitious,—
Elspeth, Alice, Norna, Mother Nicneven. A few exhibit

the same tendencies, modified by some one passion; as Lady Ashton, Lady Derby, and Lady Douglas. Mary and Elizabeth are womankind modified by royalty. There only remain Flora M'Ivor, Die Vernon, Rebecca, and Jeanie Deans. For these four, and their glorious significance, womankind are as much obliged to Walter Scott as for the insignificance of all the rest; not because they are what women might be, and therefore ought to be; but because they afford indications of this, and that these indications are owing to their having escaped from the management of man, and been trained by the discipline of circumstance. If common methods yield no such women as these; if such women occasionally come forth from the school of experi-ence, what an argument is this against the common meth-ods, — what a plea in favor of a change of system! Woman cannot be too grateful to him who has furnished it. Hence-forth, when men fire at the name of Flora M'Ivor, let women say, " There will be more Floras when women feel that they have political power and duties." When men worship the image of Die Vernon, let them be reminded, that there will be other Die Vernons when women are impelled to self-reliance. When Jeanie is spoken of with tender esteem, let it be suggested, that strength of motive makes heroism of action; and that as long as motive is confined and weak-ened, the very activity which should accomplish high aims must degenerate into puerile restlessness. When Rebecca is sighed for, as a lofty presence that has passed away, it should be asked, how she should possibly remain or re-appear in a society which alike denies the discipline by which her high powers and sensibilities might be matured, and the objects on which they might be worthily employed? As a woman, no less than as a Jewess, she is the representative of the wrongs of a degraded and despised class: there is no abiding-place for her among foes to her caste; she wanders

5

unemployed (as regards her peculiar capabilities) through
the world; and when she dies, there has been, not only a
deep injury inflicted, but a waste made of the resources of
human greatness and happiness. Yes, women may choose
Rebecca as the representative of their capabilities: first,
despised, then wondered at, and involuntarily admired;
tempted, made use of, then persecuted, and finally banished
— not by a formal decree, but by being refused honorable
occupation, and a safe abiding place. Let women not only
take her for their model, but make her speak for them to
society, till they have obtained the educational discipline
which beseems them; the rights, political and social, which
are their due; and that equal regard with the other sex in
the eye of man, which it requires the faith of Rebecca to
assure them they have in the eye of Heaven. Meantime,
while still suffering under injustice, let them lay to heart, for
strength and consolation, the beautiful commentary which
Walter Scott has given on the lot of the representative of
their wrongs. If duly treasured, it may prove by its effects,
that our author has contributed, in more ways than one, to
female emancipation; by supplying a principle of renovation to the enslaved, as well as by exposing their condition;
by pointing out the ends for which freedom and power are
desirable, as well as the disastrous effects of withholding
them. He says, —

"The character of the fair Jewess found so much favor
in the eyes of some fair readers, that the writer was cen-
sured, because, when arranging the fates of the characters
of the drama, he had not assigned the hand of Wilfred to
Rebecca, rather than the less interesting Rowena. But,
not to mention that the prejudices of the age rendered such
an union almost impossible, the author may, in passing,
observe, that he thinks a character of a highly virtuous and
lofty stamp, is degraded rather than exalted by an attempt

to reward virtue with temporal prosperity. Such is not the recompense which Providence has deemed worthy of suffering merit; and it is a dangerous and fatal doctrine to teach young persons, the most common readers of romance, that rectitude of conduct and of principle are either naturally allied with, or adequately rewarded by, the gratification of our passions, or attainment of our wishes. In a word, if a virtuous and self-denied character is dismissed with temporal wealth, greatness, rank, or the indulgence of such a rashly formed or ill-assorted passion as that of Rebecca for Ivanhoe, the reader will be apt to say, Verily, virtue had its reward. But a glance on the great picture of life will show, that the duties of self-denial, and the sacrifice of passion to principle, are seldom thus remunerated; and that the internal consciousness of their high-minded discharge of duty, produces on their own reflections a more adequate recompense, in the form of that peace which the world cannot give or take away."

These, then, are the moral services, — many and great, — which Scott has rendered, — positively and negatively, — consciously and unconsciously, to society. He has softened national prejudices; he has encouraged innocent tastes in every region of the world; he has imparted to certain influential classes the conviction that human nature works alike in all; he has exposed priestcraft and fanaticism; he has effectively satirized eccentricities, unamiableness, and follies; he has irresistibly recommended benignity in the survey of life, and indicated the glory of a higher kind of benevolence; and finally, he has advocated the rights of woman with a force all the greater for his being unaware of the import and tendency of what he was saying. The one other achievement which we attribute to him, is also not the less magnificent for being overlooked by himself.

By achieving so much within narrow bounds, he has taught
how more may be achieved in a wider space. He has
taught us the power of fiction as an agent of morals and
philosophy; "and it shall go hard with us but we will better
the instruction." Every agent of these master spirits is
wanted in an age like this; and he who has placed a new
one at their service, is a benefactor of society. Scott might
have written, as he declared he wrote, for the passing of his
time, the improvement of his fortunes, and the amusement
of his readers: he might have believed, as he declared he
believed, that little moral utility arises out of works of fiction: we are not bound to estimate his works as lightly as
he did, or to agree in his opinions of their influences. We
rather learn from him how much may be impressed by exemplification which would be rejected in the form of reasoning,
and how there may be more extensive *embodiments* of truth
in fiction than the world was before thoroughly aware of.
It matters not that the truth he exemplified was taken up at
random, like that of all his predecessors in the walks of
fiction. Others may systematize, having learned from him
how extensively they may embody. There is a boundless
field open before them; no less than the whole region of
moral science, politics, political economy, social rights and
duties. All these, and more, are as fit for the process of
exemplification as the varieties of life and character illustrated by Scott. And not only has he left the great mass of
material unwrought, but, with all his richness of variety, has
made but scanty use of the best instruments of illustration.
The grandest manifestations of passion remain to be displayed; the finest elements of the poetry of human emotion
are yet uncombined; the most various dramatic exhibition
of events and characters is yet unwrought, for there has yet
been no recorder of the poor; at least, none but those who
write as mere observers; who describe, but do not dramatize

humble life. The widest interests being thus still untouched, the richest materials unemployed, what may not prove the ultimate obligations of society to him who did so much, and pointed the way towards doing infinitely more; and whose vast achievements are, above all, valuable as indications of what remains to be achieved? That this, his strongest claim to gratitude, has not yet been fully recognised, is evident from the fact, that though he has had many imitators, there have been yet none to take suggestion from him; to employ his method of procedure upon new doctrine and other materials. There have been many found to construct fiction within his range of morals, character, incident, and scenery; but none to carry the process out of his range. We have yet to wait for the philosophical romance, for the novels which shall relate to other classes than the aristocracy; we have yet to look for this legitimate offspring of the productions of Scott, though wearied with the intrusions of their spurious brethren.

The progression of the age requires something better than this imitation; — requires that the above-mentioned suggestion should be used. If an author of equal genius with Scott were to arise to-morrow, he would not meet with an equal reception; not only because novelty is worn off, but because the serious temper of the times requires a new direction of the genius of the age. Under the pressure of difficulty, in the prospect of extensive change, armed with expectation, or filled with determination as the general mind now is, it has not leisure or disposition to receive even its amusements unmixed with what is solid and has a bearing upon its engrossing interests. There may still be the thoughtless and indolent, to whom mere fiction is necessary as a pastime; but these are not they who can guarantee an author's influence, or secure his popularity. The bulk of the reading public, whether or not on the scent of utility,

cannot be interested without a larger share of philosophy,
or a graver purpose in fiction, than formerly; and the writer
who would effect most for himself and others in this department must take his heroes and heroines from a different
class than any which has yet been adequately represented.
This difference of character implies, under the hands of a
good artist, a difference of scenery and incident; for the
incidents of a fiction are worth nothing, unless they arise out
of the characters; and the scenery, both natural and moral,
has no charm unless it be harmonious with both.   Instead
of tales of knightly love and glory, of chivalrous loyalty, of
the ambition of ancient courts, and the bygone superstitions
of a half-savage state, we must have, in a new novelist, the
graver themes — not the less picturesque, perhaps, for their
reality — which the present condition of society, suggests.
We have had enough of ambitious intrigues; why not now
take the magnificent subject, the birth of political principle,
whose advent has been heralded so long?   What can afford
finer moral scenery than the transition state in which society
now is!   Where are nobler heroes to be found than those
who sustain society in the struggle; and what catastrophe
so grand as the downfall of bad institutions, and the issues
of a process of renovation?   Heroism may now be found,
not cased in helm and cuirass, but strengthening itself in
the cabinet of the statesman, guiding the movements of the
unarmed multitude, and patiently bearing up against hardship, in the hope of its peaceful removal.   Love may now
be truly represented as sanctified by generosity and self-
denial in many of the sad majority of cases where its course
runs not smooth.   All the virtues which have graced fictitious delineations, are still at the service of the novelist;
but their exercise and discipline should be represented as
different from what they were.   The same passions still
sway human hearts; but they must be shown to be intensi-

fied or repressed by the new impulses which a new state of things affords. Fiction must not be allowed to expire with Scott, or to retain only that languid existence which is manifest merely in imitations of his works : we must hope, — not, alas! for powers and copiousness like his, — but for an enlightened application of his means of achievement to new aims : the higher quality of which may in some measure compensate for the inferiority of power and richness which it is only reasonable to anticipate.

It appears, then, from the inquiry we have pursued, that the services for which society has to be eternally grateful to Walter Scott are of three distinct kinds. He has vindicated the character of genius by the healthiness of his own. He has achieved marvels in the province of art, and stupendous benefits in that of morals. He has indicated, by his own achievements, the way to larger and higher achievements. — What a lot for a man, — to be thus a threefold benefactor to his race! to unite in himself the functions of moralist, constructor, and discoverer! What a possession for society to have had! and to retain for purposes of amelioration, incitement, and guidance! He can never be lost to us, whatever rival or kindred spirit may be destined to arise, or whether he is to be the last of his class. If the latter supposition should prove true, — which, however, appears to us impossible, — he will stand a fadeless apparition on the structure of his own achievements, distanced, but not impaired by time : if the former, his spirit will migrate into his successors, and communicate once more with us through them. In either case, we shall have him with us still.

But, it will be said, the services here attributed to Scott were, for the most part, rendered unconsciously. True; and why should not the common methods of Providence have place here as in all other instances? Scott did voluntarily all that he could; and that he was destined to do yet more

involuntarily, is so much the greater honor, instead of dero-
gating from his merit.   That some of this extra service .was
of a nature which he might have declined if offered a choice,
is only an additional proof that the designs of men are over-
ruled, and their weakness not only compensated for by divine
direction, but made its instruments.   Great things are done
by spontaneous human action : yet greater things are done
by every man without his concurrence or suspicion; all
which tends, not to degrade the character of human effort,
but to exemplify the purposes of Providence.   Scott is no
new instance of this, nor deserves less honor in proportion to
his spontaneous efforts than the sages of Greece, or the histo-
rians of Rome, and the benefactors of every age, who have
been destined to effect more as illustrators than even as
teachers and recorders.   He was happy and humbly compla-
cent in his creative office ; it is so much pure blessing that
we can regard him with additional and higher complacency
as a vindicator of genius, and an unconscious prophet of its
future achievements.

NORWICH, 1832.

ESSAYS ON THE ART OF THINKING.

I.

So much has been written and said on the importance of habits of accurate thought, that scholars and wise men have had enough of the subject. But it is not for them that we write. It is possible that we may be aware of errors of judgment to which they are liable, and into which we apprehend they frequently fall. We may occasionally take notice of the perverted ingenuity of the acute theorist, or smile at the difficulties which the skeptic labors to accumulate, or wonder at the strange interpretations which the biblical critic puts upon motives and actions, or sigh over the partial delusions to which the moral philosopher is himself subject. But our wonder and regret we keep to ourselves, and are far from the thought of offering any observations worthy to occupy intellects of a rank so much higher than our own. They have Bacon, Newton, Locke, and a host of advisers besides. We take up the pen in the service of those who have never studied nor are likely to study under these masters in the art of thinking. Of all the multitudes who have never been taught to think, or who have learned the art but imperfectly, there may be some who, laboring under a fellow-feeling of infirmity with ourselves, may turn to these pages with a hope of assistance and consolation. To such we address ourselves; and, taught by our own difficulties to appreciate theirs, we assure them that we feel deep compassion for that painful consciousness of deficient observation, perverted judgment, unchastened imagination, indolent attention, treacherous memory, and all intellectual faults and deficiencies whatever, which is a daily subject of regret and shame to a reflecting mind. We invite them to accompany us in a brief inquiry into some of the causes of these evils, and the best modes of cure for ourselves, and of prevention for those over whose intellectual discipline we may have any control.

Every one allows that habits of accurate thought are of
great importance ; but the philosophical observer alone is
aware of how much. Whether he looks back upon the history of the world, or watches the events which pass before
his eyes, or anticipates the results of causes now in operation,
and speculates on the future condition of the human race, he
is more and more impressed with the importance of employing the intellectual powers on legitimate objects, and directing them diligently to attainable ends. If all men could see
with his eyes, and follow the convictions of his understanding,
there would be an end at once to half the evils that afflict
humanity. Let no one accuse us of exaggeration ; but if surprised at our statement, let him pause and consider the
illimitable influence which the intellectual and moral powers
have on one another ; let him reflect on the tendency of difference of opinion to excite bad passions, and the reciprocal
influence of bad passions in perverting the judgment and
clouding the understanding. If he objects that we disregard
the large class of natural evils, we reply, that natural and
moral evil produce and reproduce each other perpetually.
Moreover, natural evils might be neutralized or destroyed to
an extent which we can yet scarcely conceive, if men's minds
were directed to an efficacious inquiry into their origin and
results. If natural philosophers had always known what they
were about, if they had determined what end they meant to
attain, and had early discovered the right road to their object, there is no saying how far our race might by this time
have triumphed over the ills that flesh is heir to. If all the
time, thought, and labor, which have been spent on the study
of alchymy, had been devoted to chemical science worthy
the name, who can say how far the kindred sciences would
have advanced, or what splendid results would have appeared
by this time? If there had been no empiricism in medical
practice, if physicians had known how to study, and their

patients what to expect from them, and how far to believe them, who can say how often the plague might have been staid, how many dreadful diseases might have been extirpated, how many victims to quackery and credulity might have been spared? If legislators had, some ages ago, hit upon the right mode of ascertaining the proper objects and best modes of civil government, and if the nations had urged them on, and supported them in the inquiry, and exercised a due check on the power they conferred, they might have been saved the inflictions of famine, fire, and sword, and all the countless evils which follow in the train of war. If, again, our objector insists that all this is mere speculation, we request him to listen to a very few facts, which may show what a host of evils has arisen from infirmities of the understanding, and for one century after another spread its desolating march over the most civilized portion of mankind. Among so great a variety of instances as history lays before us, it is difficult to say what facts are the most striking; and we will, therefore, confine ourselves to those which approach the nearest, and detail a few of the mistakes of civilized, enlightened, and Christian Europe. Passing over the destructive wars among savage nations, arising from trivial causes, but perpetuated from generation to generation — passing over the cases of the innumerable victims to superstition in India, to etiquette in China, to bigotry among the Mahometans, and to brute force uncontrolled by intellectual power in all regions of the globe, let us see what was done in neighbouring countries, in times not very far distant from our own.

The Emperor Constantine labored for a long series of years, with the best intentions, to establish a perfect uniformity of faith in the Christian world. For want of understanding the plain truth that the minds of men are differently constituted, and can never be assimilated by human authority, he encouraged heart-burnings and dissensions more hostile to the spirit of

religion than the despised institutions of barbarous states.
To what condition his own mind was brought by mistaken
zeal, we learn from his rescript against the Novatians and
other heretics, wherein he terms them enemies of truth, ad-
versaries of life, abettors of the most abominable wickedness,
which a whole day would not suffice to describe. He de-
clares it impossible to bear their most destructive tenets any
longer, and orders the destruction of their places of assembly,
and the banishment of the heretics, whose offence it was to
differ from the emperor as to whether a person who sinned
after baptism should be forgiven by the church as well as by
God.

The fulfilment of this edict, as of many which were passed
by persecuting emperors, occasioned much bloodshed, and
violences at which humanity shudders. On the questions
whether the body of Christ was corruptible, whether he was
capable of feeling hunger and thirst after his resurrection,
whether Christ was created out of nothing or out of something,
whether the union between the Son of God and the Son of
Man was an union of *nature* or of *person*, or only of *will and
affection*, and whether Mary was the mother of one, or both,
or neither; whether the Holy Ghost was silent respecting himself to the Apostles for the sake of giving them a lesson not to
commend themselves, or for some other reason,—the minds
of men were agitated for centuries, the true spirit of Christianity was lost, lives were sacrificed without number, the laws
of society violated, and the bond of human sympathies broken.
Bishops made war upon one another, or ranged themselves
under the banners of princes; their followers imitated their
example, and perpetrated the most dreadful cruelties. In the
eighth century, midnight murders, by the hands of the clergy,
were frequent: heretics were torn limb from limb in the streets
and churches, and, to use the words of the historian, " Des
yeux et des langues arrachées sont les évènemens les plus

ordinaires de ces siècles malheureux." These fiend-like passions were roused by disputes about words, the more violent because they were without ideas. The horrid effects of these passions were not confined to one period or country, but drew a veil of thick darkness over the minds of countless multitudes through successive generations.

The belief of the infallibility of the Pope, arising from an erroneous interpretation of *one* sentence of Scripture, occasioned the most terrible series of calamities under which the Christian world has groaned. An absurd credulity respecting the efficacy of pilgrimages led to the sacrifice of millions of lives in the Crusades. Perverted notions of the character of the Deity, and of the obligations of his creatures, occasioned the institutions of Monachism, which, though overruled to beneficial purposes by Divine Wisdom, will ever be a monument of the folly of the human race, and an example of the pitiable weakness of human reason. In former times, the number of beings thus cut off from the duties and pleasures most congenial to their nature, was greater than many persons have now an idea of. In Egypt alone, in the fourth century, there were 70,000 monks. If we thus cast a cursory glance over the state of Europe during the dark ages, taking into our view the disasters of wars abroad, of dissensions at home, of frequent and dreadful persecutions, — if the perils of the human soul under the influence of superstition be considered, the general belief in the efficacy of indulgences, the license which thousands allowed themselves on pretence of zeal for religion, and under promise of atonement in gold, — if we feel compassion for the innocent hearts which have been either hardened or broken under monastic penalties, or for the immortal faculties which have been wasted on unworthy objects, or debased by crime, — if we mark the progress which our race has made since divine truth has part unveiled her awful face, we shall be confirmed

6

in our conviction that the right pursuit of truth would cancel half the evils which afflict humanity.

The errors we have mentioned arose in the department of religion alone. What were men doing in philosophy in the mean while? Disputes about names and forms and essences were involving society in the evils of bloodshed. The *seraphic doctor* was wasting powers, which even now are a marvel to the learned, in treatises on the nature of angels. Some of the Christian fathers were anathematized for hinting the existence of Antipodes. Galileo was consigned to the dungeons of the Inquisition at Rome, and obliged to do penance by repeating the seven penitential psalms once a week for three years, for asserting that the earth moved on its own axis; while the *perspicuous*, the *most resolute*, the *marvellous*, the *angelical*, the *irrefragable* doctors in philosophy were arguing with more heat than light whether 2×3 makes 5 or 7, whether nonentities have qualities, and whether angels can go from end to end without passing through the middle.

It is easy to despise these follies, and every one can laugh at them: but are we at all times, and on all subjects, wiser? Is there any one of us who can declare himself free from a perversion as absurd on every point on which he ought to exercise his reason? To judge from the absurdities which are daily uttered in conversation, and which are so common as to pass often unnoticed, the noble faculty of Reason has as yet received but a very partial cultivation, and is placed in an undue subservience to her lively sister, Imagination, or is set up as a laughing-stock to her mocking rival, Folly. Go into what society you will, especially where there is a numerical majority of the fair sex, and you will hear much said which, to perfected reason, (if there were such a thing,) would appear as absurd as the magic jargon of the dark ages, or the senseless assertions of ancient academies on unfathomable subjects. If we go among the poor of a manufacturing district, we are not surprised to find one person venerating the left-leg stocking above the right, or a woman dying of the small-pox, with a slice of fat bacon round her throat, or a man bruised by machinery lamenting that he did not take warning when he heard his shoes dancing on the stairs by their own motion: but we are too little aware how absurdities, as real, though not as glaring, pass current in the intercourse of persons comparatively enlightened. We do not allude to superstitions which are prevalent in particular districts, and which, being early instilled by our grandmothers, are apt to remain when we have become ashamed of them. It is true, we have heard very sensible young ladies excuse themselves from being married on a Friday; not that they really suppose one day worse than another, but sad examples are extant, and if any thing should happen, it would be disagreeable that the world should say, and so forth. Such superstitions we leave to find their own way out of the world. It is enough that their believers are half-ashamed of them. It is our purpose to point out the errors of which we are not ashamed, of which we are not generally aware.

Who is not apt, on occasion, to assign a multitude of reasons when one will do? This is a sure sign of weakness in argument. Who, in the possession of power, political or domestic, is not driven to rivet an assertion or a command on the last link of his chain of reasoning? What gentleman, unless he have gone through a course of logic, does not sometimes quit his hold of a knotty point, and heap incontrovertible assertions on a subject which no one is inclined to dispute? What youthful lady, growing warm in a discussion on a matter of taste, does not fly from argument to rapture, and touch on a hundred unconnected subjects, leaving her opponent (if he be a rational person) totally unable to follow her zigzag course, and looking as foolish as a mathematician in pursuit of a butterfly? These inconsistencies

may be thought only amusing, or, at most, provoking: but
they are more. A habit of inaccuracy in trifles (supposing
such discussions to be trifling) soon extends to more important things, and he who utters carelessly the ideas that come
uppermost, will in time have nothing better to communicate;
and being content idly to watch the foam which dances on
the waves, will become unable to dive for the treasures of
the deep. The faculty which is bestowed to be his guide
and guard amidst the mutable and conflicting influences
which are to mould him to immortality, is not incorruptible,
and will assuredly prove treacherous, if a careful watch is
not kept over her fidelity. Involuntary error is a calamity.
Negligence of truth is more — it is a crime: and every indulgence in indolence and carelessness of thought is crimi-
nal, when we know that such indulgence tends to limit our
capacity for the reception of divine truth, and to deteriorate
the noblest gift that God has conferred on man. When we
shuffle away from an argument which we have not courage
to face, when we skim over a subject which we are too idle
to examine, when we banish reflections which it is our duty
to entertain, we are doing worse than omitting a present
duty — we are incapacitating ourselves for the charge of
future responsibilities. We do not mean that every subject
on which our reason can be employed should be thoroughly
examined whenever it presents itself. Life would thus be
spent in reasoning, and the moral faculties be sacrificed to
the intellectual. What we mean is, that *when* we reason, it
should be so as to form our minds to a habit of judging cor-
rectly; that we should argue accurately or not at all; and
that where we are called on to decide instead of to reason,
we should, on no account, allow ourselves to impose on our
own minds or those of others, by insufficient or fallacious
arguments, whatever may be their number.

We are also to consider the welfare of others, and remember what we owe to their improvement and their peace. If their minds are inferior to our own, we incur a heavy responsibility by helping to pervert and blind their reason. If they are our equals in mind and station, we run the risk of originating disputes. If superior in mind, and beneath us in other respects, we inflict an injury by urging reasons which are perceived to be false, but which must not be questioned. A command, however unreasonable, is welcome in comparison. A lady wishing to be undisturbed, desires a sensible, conscientious servant to say that she is not at home if any one calls. The servant, left to himself, would say that his mistress is particularly engaged: but the lady, aware of what may be passing in the mind of the domestic, condescends to give various reasons why there is no harm in the practice her conscience all the while condemns, why every body does it, and is right to do it, how it is no lie, because every body understands the hidden meaning of the phrase, and so on. The servant would reply if he dared, "Why, then, all this talk? If every body understands that you are engaged at home, why not say so?" But he must hold his tongue, or argue with his mistress, and be silenced. We pity his feelings.

The case is worse in families where the parents have more taste for power than for right reason. Their children are intelligent and conscientious. They are strongly recommended to do something which they do not altogether approve, but they think it will occasion less harm to comply than to resist, or even object. It is easy to obey a simple command, or observe a plain recommendation; but the parent, conscious of a disagreement of opinion, adduces abundance of reasons which are no reasons at all. If the young folks are silent, or can turn the conversation, it is well; but we could not much blame them if they were urged to reply, or wonder if argument led to resistance, or at least took away all the grace of compliance. Such cases we have seen, and were forcibly reminded of the king of the beasts with his four strong reasons for appropriating the four quarters of the prey. If such parents, if parents in general, were aware of the unquiet thoughts thus stirred up, they would be equally careful to cherish right reason in themselves and their children ; or if unable to do this, they would be wise to rule by authority and affection alone, and attempt no more to use reason as a bond of union. Alas ! how much uneasiness arises in families from disputes originating in mistake, and carried on in misunderstanding ! If among those who are thus divided, or who fret under the yoke which they have no wish to cast off, every individual were enabled to perceive where the exact difference lies — if each were able to make his words correspond with his ideas, and to govern his ideas by right reason, all would find that they had been perplexed in a mist which made a mole-hill appear like a mountain, exalted dwarfish difficulties into gigantic, and displayed imaginary obstacles while it concealed real perils. This chilling influence withdrawn, they would rejoice once more in the sunshine of peace, and hail the brightened flow of genial sympathies.

It would give us much satisfaction to assist any who have suffered from such perplexities and delusions, either in the individual pursuit of truth, or in the more melancholy case to which we have just adverted. We shall hereafter proceed to describe some of the phantoms by which we have been deluded or terrified, which for ages enslaved the noble faculty of reason, and sat like an incubus upon the nations, till the great enchanter arose who put it in the power of the weakest to keep them aloof, and of the most timid to chase them away.

NORWICH, 1829.

ESSAYS ON THE ART OF THINKING.

II.

THE same errors which retarded for centuries the progress of science, and rendered abortive the most exalted efforts of cultivated intellect, beset our daily exertions of thought, and are the cause of our disappointment when trifling results follow arduous labor. One of the principal of these errors is the wrong choice of subjects of thought. There are various ways of making a wrong choice. We may speculate, like a host of philosophers of old, on subjects which are not only in part beyond the reach of human intellect, but on which there is no possibility of gaining any knowledge,—where there is no foundation for speculation, and where the imagination forms the only basis for subsequent reasoning. It is far from being desirable that our range of thought should be always confined to such subjects as we can fully comprehend. If this were established as a rule, we should be excluded from the contemplation of the grandest objects on which our faculties can be employed, — the nature and attributes of the Deity, and the course of his providence. It is of the greatest importance to our intellectual as well as moral strength, that our minds should be enlarged more and more by a perpetual recurrence to these awful subjects of meditation; because, however vast, however incomprehensible as a whole, a firm and broad foundation exists for the operations of the reasoning power, and a clear light is cast on one portion of the path which, issuing from impenetrable darkness beneath, is lost in unapproachable radiance on high. The nature of God is necessarily incomprehensible by us, his attributes infinite, the course of his providence an object of faith rather than of knowledge; yet will true philosophy find her noblest and most frequent employment in the contemplation of these things; because, though vast, they are real, and the conceptions they originate, though faint, are clear, and though limited, are true. Our ideas of power, of wisdom, of holiness and love, are, or ought to be, as distinct as any we can form; and in contemplating the perfections of God, we are not obliged to form new conceptions which can be applied to this subject alone, but the same ideas of natural and moral perfection which we daily entertain are here applied, though elevated and enlarged to the utmost of our power. Such exercise of the mind, in which the imagination and the reason animate and improve each other, is in the highest degree beneficial to both. But if we proceed so far, or deviate so widely, that they can no longer accompany each other, it is time to stop and inquire whether we are not wasting our powers in wild reverie or fruitless speculation. To meditate occasionally on eternity, infinity &c., till we have convinced ourselves that all attempts to comprehend them are vain, is morally useful, as it humbles the pride of reason, and marks the limit of our faculties; but he would be little better than mad who should imagine that he had passed this limit, who should continue to speculate when reason was left far behind, and proceed to build theories on such speculations. Yet this has been done, and by philosophers who were regarded as the lights of the age in which they lived, and who would have been so, had they been wise in their choice of subjects of thought. Of the essences of beings, though much has been written, nothing is known. Of the essences of beings which (for want of knowing better) we call *spiritual*, nothing can be ascertained; yet the illustrious Thomas Aquinas wasted his precious days and his marvellous powers in treating of the nature of angels. It is a matter of astonishment to those who have read his works and admired the strength and acuteness of his reasoning, that he should have founded his arguments on no firmer basis than the dreams of his imagination, and have employed himself in labors as fruitless and nearly as absurd as those of the philosopher who endeavoured to extract sunbeams from cucumbers.

Yet while we wonder and smile at the mistakes of these philosophers, we may find something analogous to them in ourselves. Our meditations are often on subjects on which no knowledge can be attained, from which no intellectual or moral strength can be derived. How many hours of our lives are spent in speculating upon the future! To lay plans for our future employments, to form resolutions for our future conduct, to anticipate the recurrence of temptation, to hope for the renewal of virtuous pleasures, — to meditate on these things is worthy of a rational being; but to imagine ourselves the heroes of adventures which may never take place, and to ponder events which we have no ground for anticipating, is an excess which may be pardonable in a young imagination, but is a subject of shame and regret to a well-disciplined mind. We are aware that there are some who defend this waste of thought on the plea that the mind is thus prepared for whatever may happen, and secured from surprise by any remarkable concurrence of circumstances: but, in our opinion, the best preparation for the future is the present development and improvement of all the faculties. Our present pursuits should be always such as may fully employ our various powers, leaving no room for the rambling excursions of the imagination, and no opportunity for the perversion of reason. How many of us lose our time, and sometimes our tempers, in discussions of subjects where discussion is unavailing! We have listened to a long and warm argument as to the place of abode of the virtuous after death: —not whether it will be on this globe or elsewhere, (on which something may be said,) but, if elsewhere, whether in one of the planets, or in a region wholly unknown. We have detected ourselves in the midst of a speculation on the nature of the new senses

with which our glorified bodies may be endowed, and have
listened, first with surprise and then with regret, to a protracted argument on the transmigration of the soul.   It is
said, and with truth, that such discussions tend to enliven
the imagination, and sharpen the faculties generally.
If occasionally indulged in with this view, they may be
harmless or useful.   But our objection to such speculations
is in full force when they are pursued as subjects of philosophical inquiry.   We wish to point out that when bent on
the acquisition of *knowledge*, it is foolish to lay hold of subjects on which no knowledge can be obtained.   It should be
a rule with us, before we enter on a new inquiry, to ascertain whether the knowledge we seek is within our reach;
or we shall be in a similar condition with him who builds
a tower without counting the cost, or goes out to war without having computed his forces.

We make a wrong choice when we pursue an object which
our ignorance unfits us to attain.   It is not certain that the
interpretation of all the prophecies in the Revelation is still
beyond the reach of human faculties; and learned men,
who sit down calmly to study the mysterious book, with no
other purpose than to discover the truth, deserve our respect
and gratitude.   But we have heard that women who understand no language but their own, and are but superficially
acquainted with history, have spent their hours in attempts
to explain the prophecies, and have left behind them, as a
monument of perverted ingenuity, volumes of unfounded
speculation on subjects before which the most enlightened
intellects are compelled to bow.   Many a strange interpretation have we heard advanced with confidence by unlearned
persons on difficult passages of the Old Testament, where
the profoundest Hebrew scholars ventured to offer nothing
more than a conjecture.   Many an argument and many an
assertion have we listened to from those who had never

studied the philosophy of the human mind, on the subject of liberty and necessity. Whether or not we allow that certainty is to be attained on this point, it can only be by those who have prepared themselves for a comparison of the general course of Providence with the operations of the human mind, by the careful study of both. Painful but salutary is the rebuke conveyed to us in the midst of the warmth of such discussions, by the smile on the face of one who has experienced difficulties that we dream not of; and who is perhaps kind enough to show us that we had better adjourn the debate for an indefinite time. On such occasions is the rule brought home to us, to ascertain whether the object we aim at is within the reach, not only of our faculties, but of our knowledge.

The consequence of our wrong choice of subjects of thought is so great a degree of uncertainty in our aim, that our efforts must unavoidably fail of their object, though something valuable may be achieved by the way. Our advance cannot always be progressive, or our labors effective, if our purpose be ill-defined or wholly obscure. This is too evident to need illustration.

The cause of these mistakes is that which the world has for ages had reason to lament — ignorance of the true principle of philosophizing. We are apt to set out wrong. Either explicitly or unconsciously, we form a theory, and (as we all like our own theories) we make all circumstances bend to it, and all our observations go to support it. Thus, the old philosophers had each one theory or more: some came pretty near the truth; others wandered, in a most eccentric orbit, far from the source of light. How was it to be decided who was in the right? By the observation of facts, as all agreed. They searched the heavens and the earth for facts, and all gleaned a plenteous store, and apparently with nearly equal success. At all events, illustrations,

which each contended to be facts, abounded. Where was
the next appeal to be made? No one knew; so the philosophical world was divided among jarring factions, till Bacon
published the right method of discovering truth, which has
caused philosophy to advance with rapid strides, and a new
light to dawn on the world of science. This principle is so
simple that it seems extraordinary that it should not sooner
have been adopted; and yet so vast in its operation, that attempts to estimate its effects are vain. This method is to bring
together an accumulation of facts previous to the formation of
a theory; and having carefully observed their bearing upon
a particular point, to deduce from them a principle which
may be applied to the explanation of new facts. Had Newton lived before Bacon, he might have formed an erroneous
theory of optics, and have been confirmed in it by a partial
observation of facts; but he drank deeply of the spirit of
the new philosophy, and by it regulated his inquiries. He
brought together a vast collection of facts in relation to light
and colors, viewed them in all possible situations, tried a
great variety of experiments upon them, carefully preserving
his mind from fanciful theories, and at length founded, on
actual experience, his system of optics, by which light, one
of the most subtile of all things, is reduced to certain laws,
as truly as the most gross and solid bodies. In like manner
were his other inquiries conducted, and their magnificent
results obtained. In like manner must science continue to
advance, and the mysteries of nature be unravelled. In
like manner must we all, if our object be truth, conduct
every inquiry. And if tempted to smile at thus comparing
great things with small, the researches of a Newton with the
feeble efforts of intellects puny as ours, let us remember that
if an object be worth pursuing at all, it is worth pursuing in
the best way. We may work away in our closets, and, after
all our labor, only discover what thousands have known

before us ; but the pleasure of useful exertion, and the privilege of substantial knowledge will be our own,—a power of accurate thought, a capacity of increasing wisdom, which are of high importance to rational and immortal beings. A child intent on the management of his little garden plot, or of his cage of birds — a young inquirer beginning his study of the human mind—the mother anxious to form plans of education for her child — and the philosopher whose objects of research are removed beyond the reach of the naked eye and the excursions of unassisted imagination, are alike liable to mistake and failure, if they form theories on any other basis than a careful examination of facts. To habituate the mind to follow the inductive method in all researches, is the first general rule which the lovers of truth should ever keep in view.

It is the tendency of our minds to become too firmly attached to a theory deduced by ourselves, especially when well-founded. We should be on our guard, therefore, to apply it to that class of objects alone to which it relates. To stretch one theory to the explanation of every class of facts is as fruitful a source of error as to apply half a dozen theories to the explanation of so many similar appearances. To this error those are most liable whose range of inquiry is contracted, who love truth, but have little leisure or opportunity for study. These, having once laid hold of a solid truth, are unwilling to part with it ; are liable to overrate its value ; and, when they meet with new difficulties, are tempted to recur to a favorite solution, rather than be at the trouble of finding a new one. But because it sometimes happens that the same key will open more doors than one, it does not follow that it is suited to every lock ; and it is wiser to seek patiently for the right instrument, than to end the difficulty by force or straining. How simple are the principles on which the philosophy of nature is founded, and how few

7

the agents by which it is conducted, is a disclosure reserved
for a day when science shall have attained a greater maturity; at present it is clear that we shall fall into error if we
devise a separate solution for each particular fact, or if we
apply a principle, however well ascertained, to the explanation of all appearances between which we can fancy a resemblance.   In the education of a family of children, there
ought to be some general rules, the enforcement of which
must be salutary to each; but as no two minds are alike in
all points, it would be as absurd to regulate all in a precisely
similar manner, as to have a totally different system for each.
Some weaknesses, faults, and follies, are common to all young
minds, while there is an infinite variety in their capacities
and dispositions; and he is the truly wise parent who knows
how to enforce general rules with steadiness, while he ap-
plies particular methods with discernment.   Such discrimination should be our aim in our interpretation of the common
events of life, in our judgment of human character, in the
lessons we draw from circumstances, and in our study of
books and of the world of nature.   We must be careful not
to conclude that because actions resemble each other, the
motives must in all cases be alike, that events which have
been once connected are for ever inseparable, that one department of research, however good, will make us universally
wise, or that one method of discipline, however salutary,
will secure ourselves or others from the insinuations of all
moral evil.   While our observation of facts is very limited,
a small portion of philosophical knowledge may be sufficient
to account for them; but if we seek to extend our range, we
must be careful that our minds are so disciplined as to receive new ideas without prejudice, that they are strengthened for the formation of new conceptions, prepared to apply
well-known truths in their proper places, and to leave them
behind when we enter on unexplored and extended regions.

Ideas are impressed on all minds in the order of time; but the modes in which they are afterwards disposed are various. Upon the mode of classification depends much of the clearness and strength of the intellect. A well-trained intellect will, with ease, retain valuable impressions, and dismiss those that are unimportant; while a young or weak mind will retain both indiscriminately, and a perverted one will let slip all that should be retained, and grasp only what is trifling and useless. How large a portion of useful knowledge we daily forego, how awfully we weaken our minds by the retention of ideas which can minister to no good, we cannot at present estimate; but we may form some faint idea by drawing a contrast between the mind of Milton and that of a fashionable fop, between such a man as Hartley and a scoffing, dissolute infidel. The habit of classifying our impressions as they are received, and arranging our ideas in such an order as that we may know where to find them, and when to produce them, must be formed by early attention and considerable labor; but the acquisition is worth any degree of exertion. The habit once formed, the benefit is secured for ever; the mind converts all things to wholesome aliment, and the process of assimilation goes on with ease, and without intermission. A mind totally destitute of a power of classification, is of rare occurrence, except among the most ignorant of our race; but the exercise of the power is deficient in most, and perfect, perhaps, in none. The weakest minds arrange all their impressions in the order of time, the most philosophical in that of cause and effect.

We have all smiled at the nurse in Romeo and Juliet, with her long story to prove Juliet's age, the absurd detail of unconnected circumstances, related merely because they happened near the same time; but we may all be conscious of something of the same folly in ourselves, and may observe that we can scarcely relate the shortest story, the most simple incident, without introducing some detail which is not to the purpose. In forming a judgment from events which pass before our eyes, how unapt are we at selecting the available circumstances, and passing over those which only encumber the inquiry! In reading on any particular subject, this difficulty is in some measure obviated by the skill of the writer, if he be a good one; but no care can supersede our own; and though much knowledge may be gained, it will not be accompanied by an appropriate share of wisdom, unless we train our own thoughts to a methodical arrangement of facts, as well as to clear insight into them. One person reads Waverley with great interest; but retains only a confused assemblage of agreeable ideas, in which it is difficult to say what class predominates. He remembers that there are beautiful descriptions of scenery, and fine delineations of character; that the story is engrossing, and the situations splendid; but he mingles all these together in his report of the book, and intersperses his account with notices of where he was when he read it, what neighbour called and interrupted him in an interesting scene, how he was persuaded to leave it and go out to dinner, what company he met, and so on, in strange disorder. A more accurate thinker would give a widely different report. He would bring together in his conversation, as previously in his mind, various examples of the same excellence : of these excellences he would speak separately, and class them in what he believed to be their due degrees, so as to give the hearer a distinct conception of the extent of the design, and the scope of the story; he would speak of the book alone, while it was the theme of conversation; and especially, as totally irrelevant to the subject, he would omit all mention of himself. Can there be a question which of these two has read the book with the greatest profit and enjoyment?

If it be objected that it is harsh to require the mind to be always philosophizing, always bent on the acquisition of knowledge, we reply that such is not our intent. A state of unrelaxing effort is as hurtful to the mind as to the body. But we maintain that a habit of accurate thought once formed, the workings of the intellect will always be true. New ideas will, without effort, be arranged, and valuable acquisitions will be made, while the thinker leaves his mind to itself, and is conscious of no exertion. We believe that no relaxation is more salutary than the repose which is enjoyed in a country walk, when the mind, wholly passive, is left open to the influences of nature. But while the mind of a philosopher is as susceptible of pleasure in the fields and woods as that of a sportive child, while he surrenders himself up to enjoyment, there is no question but that the impressions received by each will be widely different in nature and value. A child's ideas will be jumbled together, and the greater part of them will be unconnected and transitory; those of the philosopher will have found each its appropriate place; and when he repairs to his closet, he will find that he has gained, not only vigor and refreshment, but further confirmation of some valuable fact, or illustration of some well-grounded theory. An orderly mind is a temple where truth condescends to appear, and delights to be worshipped; and those who dare to pile upon her altars all that comes within their reach, who deck her shrine with weeds as well as flowers, must expect to see their garlands fade unnoticed, and their sacrifices rejected as unacceptable, if not impious.

7*

ESSAYS ON THE ART OF THINKING.

III.

WE have stated that, in the most philosophic minds, ideas are classed in the order of Cause and Effect. In this manner alone can the true relations of things be ascertained : by this method alone can our experience be made useful to us, or our present circumstances become conducive to our future good. Though we have no knowledge of the nature of the connexion between causes and effects, and can only reason from the fact that certain antecedents have invariable consequents, it is plain that without a distinct apprehension of this truth, there can be no real knowledge. This distinct apprehension, in the mind of the most ignorant of mankind, will produce rational conduct, in so far as its influence extends : while its obscurity may subject the profound philosopher to error at which he will hereafter stand astonished. The child who, having been stung, fears a wasp, is inspired by a more rational terror than the many wise men who in former days dreaded that the downfall of a kingdom would be the consequence of an eclipse of the sun. In the present infancy of our faculties and of our knowledge, we are subject to error in every speculation, and to hindrance in every pursuit, by our imperfect perception of the important relation of which we speak : but by steadily adhering to established truth, and by enlightened efforts to extend the inquiry, we may obtain substantial knowledge and enlarge our capacity for an increasing store.

A chemist wishes to ascertain the cause of a particular phenomenon. If he be unenlightened, he will mix his materials together at random, and thus fail entirely, or succeed only by a fortunate accident. If he be rendered somewhat wiser by an exercise of observation, he will discover that the

appearance arose after the combination of a certain set of
ingredients: he will combine these substances anew, and
place them in the same circumstances as when he first observed them; and will thus obtain the desired result. If he
be wise, however, he is not yet satisfied; but continues his
experiments till he has discovered whether all, and which, of
the ingredients he uses are necessary to the production of the
phenomenon under observation. He takes away first one
and then another substance, and simplifies the process by
degrees, till he can affirm, with certainty, that such and such
a cause will produce such and such an effect: and this fact
will then become a foundation for further inquiries. A similar process should be attempted by the followers of truth in
every form; and those who have no time and opportunity for
study by books and philosophical experiment, should observe
the same rule in their daily course of life; or they. will be
necessarily subject to disappointment in their schemes, and
failure in their exertions. The father who expects his boy to
be a prodigy because he sends him to the same school which
has produced a prodigy, deserves to be disappointed. So
does the mother who pampers the appetite of her children
with delicacies, and expects them to be healthy, because she
knows a family of children who happen to have thriven in
spite of such indulgence, and not in consequence of it. To
similar disappointments shall we be liable while we overlook
or mistake the relation between causes and effects, whether
the risk we incur be trifling or important: whether we assure
ourselves that the sky will be clear at a certain hour to-day,
because it was yesterday, or expect that the current of our
highest affections will continue in bright and full flow, while
we neglect to purify and replenish the springs.

The only manner in which our past experience can be
made useful to us is by showing what effects will be produced
by certain causes: and if no care be taken to observe and

record such experience, life is, so far, spent in vain. No
one but an idiot can pass through life wholly untaught by
such observation; but in proportion to our attention to experience will be our wisdom. The weak mind receives impressions as they arise, and perhaps retains them in all their
vividness, but in a series which renders them useless or even
hurtful. The young mind which has been oppressed by a
first calamity, and has found relief from that oppression in
the soothings of friendship and in praises, kindly meant but
injudicious, as well as in higher consolations, is ill-prepared
for another infliction, if he ascribes his recovered peace in
an equal degree to human sympathy and to religious hopes,
and thus places his dependence where it would be well for
him that it should fail. In the pursuit of science, the most
fruitful source of error is the liability to mistake temporary
and accidental for permanent connexion. We smile at the
simplicity of a savage who believes an eclipse to be the consequence of the discharge of a musket, because the events
occur in immediate succession; and if we suppose him capable of following a chain of reasoning on this false assumption,
his conclusions will be necessarily absurd; but not more so,
perhaps, than our own, if we fall into a similar error at the
commencement, or in the course, of a philosophical inquiry.
Not more absurd, perhaps, than the reasoning of persons who
affirm that actions may be independent of motives, and yet
profess invariably to estimate the value of actions by the purity of motives. Not more absurd, perhaps, than the empirics
(by profession or by taste) who expect the cure of all disor-
ders from the operation of one medicine. Not more absurd,
perhaps, than the opinions of those who ascribe the increase
of crime to the diffusion of education, and foretell a further
augmentation of the evil from the continued advancement of
knowledge. We knew a lady (of unquestionable benevolence) who on being applied to for her annual contribution to

a school, declined subscribing again, "for," said she, "I have had three very bad servants lately, and they could all read and write." There are many who, like her, can never be persuaded that mental illumination is no more the cause of moral darkness than the flash of a musket of an eclipse of the sun, or than the erection of Tenterden steeple of the formation of Goodwin sands.

Our anticipation of the future will be no less faulty than our recollection of the past, or observation of the present, if we fall into the error in question. If we believe that the same causes will produce various effects, we shall be liable to expose ourselves to temptations under which we have formerly fallen, and we shall commit acts of imprudence in the vain hope that the consequences will not again be disastrous. We shall, with the impetuosity of our earlier years, rush into dangers of which experience has already warned us; and, with the folly of childhood, expect grand results from trifling operations, and magnificent effects from inadequate causes. The most harmless form which this error assumes is the confidence with which the schemer continues to multiply his expectations in proportion to their failure, and is ever looking for gratifications which never arrive. As happiness consists in the full employment of our faculties in some pursuit, such a man as this may enjoy a considerable portion, provided he takes care to involve none but himself in his disappointments: but his happiness can bear no proportion, cæteris paribus, to that of a man who pursues well-defined objects by adequate means, and who guards himself against all failures but those which proceed from influences beyond his control. If they both live to old age, the one will have obtained ample stores of knowledge, will have so enlarged his capacities of improvement as to be prepared to enter on the state which must next be revealed; and, unruffled by disappointment, unmoved by anxiety, will calmly and cheerfully await the opportunity of

exercising his powers on the objects of the unseen world.
The other, unstable in all his ways, confused in all his
thoughts, will be tossed about by hopes and fears, vague and
groundless; his experience will be worth little more than that
of the new-born infant: and there is but too much reason to
fear that when he exchanges this life for another, he will not,
only have almost every thing to learn, but much to unlearn.
This may be thought an exaggerated picture. We put it as
an extreme case: but it should be remembered that the operation of causes, though often obscure, is as invariable in the
moral as in the physical world, and that he who neglects the
observation of them in the one, is little likely to know much of
their connexion in the other.

In our observation of the relation of cause and effect, too
much care cannot be exercised, lest our views should be too
confined, lest in our conviction of their invariable sequence,
we should overlook the thousand circumstances which may
intervene to modify the results for which we confidently look.
If we watch the operation of one cause when many are at
work, the result will be different from what we expect. If
we expect that a certain agent will produce a certain effect
upon various bodies because it does upon one, if we believe
that a scheme which has been invariably successful, will
always be so, under every change of circumstances, we de-
ceive ourselves, and presumptuously imagine that we know
more than it is in our power to know, and can judge more
accurately than our limited capacity allows. A medicine
which cures a head-ache to-day, may aggravate it to-morrow;
not because the effects of the medicine are opposite, other
influences remaining the same; but because we have fewer
ailments to-day than we shall have to-morrow, and our state
of body being different, the effects of the medicine will not
be the same. In like manner, a reproof which will bring a
child to tears at one time, will produce no emotion at anoth-

er ; and laborious exertion which has hitherto met with its appropriate reward, may hereafter be frustrated, through no fault of our own, and without inferring any breach of the law of cause and effect. Such experience should teach us to be moderate in our expectations, and though firm, yet modest in our convictions : as, unless we knew all the causes that are at work, we cannot reckon with positive certainty on any event; and in the pursuit of truth are as liable to error and uncertainty, as in the practical labors in which we are daily impressed with our short-sightedness and weakness. While we rejoice that we have sufficient assurance to encourage and reward the labor of our heads and hands, we must beware lest we depend on this assurance too far, and become liable to new disappointments, and the victims of error the more humbling as it is allied to presumption. In some departments of science, the operation of causes is less obscure than in others, and results may therefore be predicted with greater certainty. An astronomer foretels an eclipse, and it happens on the very day and hour specified, perhaps, a hundred years before. But the wisest parent, watching with the most unremitting attention over the education of his child, cannot pretend to judge what his intellectual, and still less his moral character will be, ten years hence. Such differences in the various departments of study should be carefully marked by the lover of truth; or he will be apt to determine the ratio at which his intellectual progress shall proceed, or to fly to the other extreme, and place little reliance on the calculations of astronomers, and question the demonstrations of the mathematician.

We must not leave unnoticed one most abundant source of error to which all are liable, but more especially inexperienced and shallow thinkers; we mean the liability to attend to words rather than the ideas of which they are the symbol. It is so impossible to press into our limits what

ought to be said on this subject, that we feel some hesitation
in adverting to it at all. But the slightest warnings are
better than none; and when we mention that it is by taking advantage of this infirmity that sceptics and infidels
have acquired every advantage of which they can boast,
there can be no further question of the importance of care
lest we be thus seduced from the path of truth. Language
is far from being a perfect mode of communication. We
have more ideas than words, and the same word must often,
therefore, express more ideas than one; and a proposition
which may be perfectly true when a word bears one sense,
may be false if the meaning be changed. Artful reasoners
take advantage of this imperfection of language to mislead
the unwary; and careless reasoners are themselves led astray
by it. The greater part of Hume's arguments which have
done the most mischief are easily refuted by clear thinkers,
who are accustomed to begin an inquiry by fixing the meaning of the various terms employed, and adhering steadily to
it through every step of the argument.

We well remember the dismay and perplexity with which
we first read Hume's Dialogues; being unable to discover
where he was wrong, though perfectly convinced that there
was artifice somewhere; the chain of argument seemed for
the most part complete, though errors were apparent here
and there. When at length the deception was discovered, it
was still difficult to detect it in every false step of the argument: to find at once the exact place where the meaning of
a word was changed, or to discover how many significations
it was made to bear. Such pains, however, are well bestowed; the result cannot but be satisfactory in all such inquiries.
Among the many excellent works which have for their object
the exposure of this species of deception, and the offer of assistance to the weak and inexperienced thinker, we cannot
but mention Cogan's Ethical Questions, as one which has

done and will continue to do good service in the cause of truth, by exposing the fallacies of her opponents.

Careless reasoners who, without dishonest intentions, make use of ambiguous terms, are unable to arrive at truth themselves, and do much to obstruct the progress of others. They make out a verbal truth, and are satisfied; while they fearlessly build one proposition upon another, till they come to some monstrous conclusion, and are confounded. If they have patience to go back, step by step, till they find where the error lies, it is well : they have then only to lament their lost time and labor, and have gained a valuable lesson. If they give up the point in despair, they are in a worse condition than when they set out. If they prefer believing and acting upon the false conclusions to which they have arrived, their situation is awful. Happily, it does not always happen that

> " False conclusions of the reasoning power,
> Make the eye blind, and close the passages
> By which the ear converses with the heart ; "

and the mind may be guarded by favorable influences from the baneful effects of error and unbelief, and may preserve a practical faith when the speculative is shaken or overthrown. But such instances are rare ; and the risk of moral as well as intellectual perversion is so fearful, that no precautions can safely be neglected which may preserve us from the sophistry of infidelity and the snares of perverted reason.

Where neither artifice nor carelessness exists, there is room for much misunderstanding from the inadequacy of language. It is probable that no two persons affix precisely the same idea to any one term ; as our ideas are compounded originally from our sensations, and there is no reason to believe that any two persons receive and retain impressions in precisely the same manner. At any rate, as we can communicate our ideas by no method more exact than language, we

8

cannot ascertain how nearly similar the perceptions of others are to our own. This imperfection it is beyond our power to remedy; and we only mention it as a thing to be borne in mind when we are baffled in the pursuit of truth, and as a hint to exercise candor when we see others perplexed by difficulties which we do not perceive. This consideration should also prove an inducement to us to exercise the utmost care in our use of the instrument which, though imperfect, is the best we can command for the communication of our ideas. We should early accustom ourselves to a scrupulous accuracy in our modes of expression, at least on subjects intended to employ the reasoning faculty. This may be done without pedantry, without formality; as is proved by the instances which we may all have had the advantage of noticing, of persons who, without premeditation, pour out stores of valuable thought in a flow of appropriate language, and without affectation speak on the commonest subjects with an energy and delicacy which incline us to hope that the imperfections of language may at length vanish away.

If the utmost attention to the meaning of words cannot always secure us from error, what must be the plight of those who think little about the meaning at all, but are influenced by sound rather than sense! How many such are there! How many rational theologians are called fanatics or methodists because they use language which, though scriptural, is out of favor, because it has been abused to the purposes of fanaticism! How many bad arguments are heard and dismissed as valid, because expressed in imposing language! How much utter nonsense is cried up as fine poetry, because dressed in words which awaken pleasant associations as they pass over the ear! How many sonnets are read with delight and committed to memory by young lovers of poetry which contain absolutely nothing except in the last line! This is so frequently the case with English sonnets, that we believe many readers join in the practice which we have long adopted of never venturing on a sonnet without glancing at the closing rhyme. We are ready to acknowledge that the sense is by no means the only thing to be regarded in poetry : all that we mean is, that it ought not to be dispensed with. We are very fond of the measured diction and studied harmony of our classical poets : but the beautiful versification of Pope would find no favor in our eyes, if it were not for the depth of meaning condensed in his flowing lines. Wordsworth expresses our ideas exactly in one of his prefaces, where he places in immediate contrast the passage from the Proverbs, "Go to the ant, thou sluggard," with its pompous paraphrase by Johnson. The effect is ludicrous ; yet who knows but that some have admired the paraphrase more than the original ?

From the weakness of regarding sound rather than sense it arises, that some minds are invariably influenced by the last speaker, or even writer. We have heard some persons lament this in themselves as a deplorable weakness, and others treat it as a jest. When the point in dispute is a controversy where (as is too often the case) the difference are chiefly verbal, and the argument is interspersed with appeals to the imagination and the feelings, such vacillation is not much to be wondered at. But when the argument is grounded on ascertained facts, and when diametrically opposite principles are advocated, it must be an indolent mind which will agree with either without examination, and a weak one that will conclude each disputant to be right in his turn. It would be too much to expect every mind to be able to strip an angry theological discussion of all irrelevant matter ; or to take part at once, and decidedly, with Dr. Price or Dr. Priestley in their amicable controversy respecting Matter and Spirit : but where the dispute regards physical or well-ascertained mental facts, the mind of the reader should either be prepared to form an impartial judgment, or should let the matter alone entirely.

Such are a few, a very few, of the errors to which the un-instructed are liable. Happy he who does not, in turn, fall into them all! We have been obliged to omit all notice of those imperfections which arise from moral causes; and yet have found that we have already entered on too wide a field. If we were to point out all the intellectual perversions which arise from prejudice, all the waste of power which is occa-sioned by want of self-control, all the mental obscurity which succeeds the eclipse of that luminary which God has made to shine in the heart of every man, we should never have done.

It would be unkind to wish that the imperfections which have been described from experience should be recognised by the experience of our readers. But should this be the case, it may be of use to some to follow us in our next inquiry, into the means by which our weakness may be assisted, our errors rectified, and our love of truth duly cher-ished and substantially gratified.

ESSAYS ON THE ART OF THINKING.

IV.

Our limits allow us to offer only a few hints respecting the discipline which is necessary to the formation of habits of accurate thought. These hints must be expanded and improved by our readers, if they are to be rendered in any degree beneficial; and our suggestions must be modified according to the circumstances of those who may be inclined to adopt them.

As knowledge affords the materials of thought and the incitement to its exercise, we shall begin by offering some hints respecting the best modes of obtaining information, and shall afterwards point out the methods by which knowledge may be rendered available to the further improvement of the intellectual faculties.

We are careful to develope the power of Observation in a child, because by means of this faculty is to be obtained the most important, if not the most extensive, information which we have it in our power to acquire. In proportion to the perfect development and wise direction of this faculty will be the improvement of the intellect at large. Every human being is possessed of the power of observation, and in every case (not excepting that of the idiot) it is called into action; but how different is its operation, how various are its results, in various minds! The ignorant ploughboy beholds the changes of the seasons, the clouds and the sunshine, the waxing and waning moon, the fixed and moving lights of the sky, and gathers no new ideas from the revolutions of nature; while the fall of an apple suggests to a Newton inquiries which urge on the human intellect to the utmost limits of space and time. Such an instance is sufficient evidence that the faculty of observation cannot be too highly cultivated; and that the common belief, that the power of observation interferes with that of reflection, is founded in mistake. We may observe wrongly, but we cannot observe too much; and if the right direction be given to the faculty, if the stores which it brings in to the mind be rightly disposed and duly appreciated, those stores can never be too ample. But a small part of the external world is subjected to the examination of each individual, and it is only by means of the guidance of others that we are enabled to

8*

explore the wonders of the world within; and therefore **we**
are right to seek the instruction which may be derived from
conversation and from books.   But how little do we know
of the portion which is within our reach!   How copious a
harvest of facts might we reap, if we chose to put in the
sickle!   How multitudinous are the operations continually
going on around us, while our careless or ill-governed minds
are occupied with familiar ideas or worthless speculations!

> " Sweet music breathes,
> " Above, about, or underneath,"

for all whose ears are open to it; and the mild light of truth
is reflected from every object in nature, to the few whose
gaze is not fixed too high or too low to receive it.   We
remember a good old fairy tale (the delight of our childhood)
which carries a more admirable moral than a child can appreciate, while he envies the powers of Fine-ear, who could
hear the corn springing in the ground, and of Long-sight,
who could point out the position of every star on a cloudy
night.   The power of observation can accomplish greater
wonders than these, as children and dreamers should be
made to understand.

It can never be too early or too late to encourage the
habit of observation, nor can we ever become too wise to be
taught by the influences which all created things are designed to exert upon the mind.   The infant is well employed
when gaining new ideas by noticing new objects; and
Franklin was never more wise than when he applied himself
to learn in the same school, and thus enriched his mind with
knowledge which could never have been obtained at second
hand.   The dreamers who go through the world in a state
of apparent somnambulism, disdaining to stoop or turn aside,
are far less happy, far less wise or dignified, than the philosopher while flying his kite; and while they stumble in
darkness, he brought down the harmless lightning to play

around his head. Nature is the wisest, the only infallible
teacher, and her lore is inexhaustible. Books are but her
interpreters, and, though valuable aids when she is silent,
are never to be preferred to her lessons of wisdom. To
those teachings our minds should be ever open; and, whether
in the fields or in the streets, by the sea-shore or in the
crowded city, in solitude or in society, our observation should
ever be awake to familiarize our minds with new objects, or
to notice some novel appearance in those which are well
known. Every cloud of the sky, every blossom of the garden, every action of childhood, every change of each suc-
ceeding day, affords materials for thought and elements of
knowledge; and were all these exhausted, another world
would yet remain to be explored. The spirit of observation
requires no remission of its activity. In solitude and darkness it can still find occupation, and can gather experience
from the workings of the mind. There it can watch operations as grand and important, changes as real, and results
as interesting, as in the external world.

It is sometimes apprehended that an active habit of observation will incline the mind to be occupied with frivolous
objects, and indispose it for the reception of great truths.
But this can be the case only when its scope is limited. Its
capacity should be unbounded, that the materials which it
presents to the reflective power may be ample. We dislike
a habit of quick observation in a narrow-minded person,
because its effects are not apparently beneficial to the individual himself, and are often disagreeable to all around him.
But the evil lies, not in the habit of observation, but in the
pettiness of his mind in other respects; and if he were less
alive to surrounding influences, he would certainly be more
ignorant, and less accessible to improvement. A greater
mind does not observe less, but more; and having a wider
choice of important objects, is at liberty to dismiss those

which are frivolous and familiar, when their value has **once**
been duly appreciated.

The operation of this faculty is partial in every mind, and
is modified by the character, intellectual and moral, of the
individual by whom it is exerted; and if its exercise could
become unlimited and universal, its perfection would imply
the perfection of the whole intellectual and moral constitution. Then no influence would be wasted, and no clouds
would intervene to obscure the emanations of truth which
we may hereafter perceive to beam from every object. But
at present every mind is in part blind and indolent, and
therefore the faculty of observation varies in its operation in
every individual. In proportion as the appetite for knowledge is healthy or depraved, strong or weak, will the aliment
presented to it be salutary or hurtful, abundant or scanty.
Each provides for himself the supply he needs; the philosopher will gather philosophy, the tale-bearer will gather
materials for scandal, the artist will collect subjects for his
pencil, and the dramatist for his pen, from the new scenes
into which each is introduced. The moralist will discern
moral relations in all things, and every occurrence in the
complicated movements of society will serve as an illustration of some favorite truth; while the man whose whole soul
is animated by piety, will " see God in every thing, and all
in God." — We remember being struck by the difference
in the accounts of a grand ceremonial, given by two observers of different habits of mind; and we were thence led to
imagine how great a variety of description would be afforded
if twenty narrators had told the story instead of two. The
ceremony was the benediction of the Pope at the conclusion
of the holy week at Rome. What a field is here afforded
for a variety of observation! The architect would concentrate his attention on St. Peter's itself, regardless of the
countless multitudes which would afford a subject of obser-

vation to the statistical inquirer. Some would look on the whole as idle pageantry, while others would wait in breathless awe the appearance of the Pontiff. The natives would be engaged in remarking the peculiarities of the foreigners, and the foreigners of the natives. Many might truly mourn to behold the numerous victims of a gross superstition, while some were actually engaged in computing the value of the fine horses in the carriage of the Duke of Sussex, which were driven by himself on the occasion. — The most comprehensive mind among the observers was undoubtedly that (if such there was) on which the fewest circumstances were lost — which could, while noticing the peculiarities of the thronging multitudes of various nations, the marble edifices, the train of Cardinals, the appearance and gestures of the Pontiff, likewise remark the relation of mind to mind amid these countless thousands of beings, the darkness of some, the comparative illumination of others, and the connexion of all with the presiding Spirit which called them into being.

This habit of partial observation has been often encouraged from the idea that it is the best way to attain excellence in a particular pursuit; but its consequences (wholly escaped by none) are highly injurious to the mind. To excel in any particular pursuit should ever be a subordinate object to the general improvement of the intellectual constitution; and this object itself is eventually best promoted by encouraging the development of every power we possess. Our capacity of observation should therefore be perpetually enlarging, while the habit is strengthening. For this purpose, a classification of the facts we obtain should be an important object to us. This classification implies an exercise of the judgment.

The ideas collected by means of Observation are, in every mind, submitted to a process of Comparison and Selection. The infant, after tasting sugar, honey, and comfits, has an idea of sweetness as a quality of all these substances; and, ere long, he will perceive that the moon, snow, and a sheet of paper, have one appearance in common, and he will thus obtain the abstract idea of whiteness. These processes of Comparison and Abstraction are carried on to an illimitable extent as the mind advances; and by watching them we may discern the mode by which all attainable knowledge may be brought within the compass of a single mind; how the innumerable multitudes of facts which nature and science present may be so arranged and compacted as to lie within the grasp of an individual intellect. Towards this glorious prospect we must not, at present, even glance, but rather proceed to offer some hints respecting the processes of Comparison and Judgment.

In the beginnings of our knowledge, when the simple qualities of objects are subjected to the judgment, there is no possibility of error, provided the senses are perfect. The idiot has as accurate an idea of whiteness and sweetness as the wisest man: but when complex ideas are compared, the conclusions of the judgment will be different in various minds; and the more complex the ideas presented, the wider will be the diversity in the results of comparison. All minds will agree that $6 \times 2 = 12$; but society is even yet divided into two parties on the question of the education of the poor; and respecting various points in theology and science the diversities of opinion are endless. Yet there is, no doubt, as substantial a truth at the bottom of these subjects as in numbers, and that truth may in time be as evident to every mind as that two and two make four. Such a prospect is, however, immeasurably distant. The number of truths which may be demonstrated is very small; as we descend the scale of probabilities and possibilities their number increases, till at length we find that multitudes afford subjects for conjecture alone. They are substantial benefactors of the human race who exalt any subject of inquiry in this scale; and he who removes a single object of doubt one degree nearer to the highest probability or to demonstration, renders an essential service to his kind. There are few who, like Newton, can raise a mighty subject of speculation from the darkest recess of conjecture into the light of demonstration; but all have the power (and are required to exert it) of availing themselves of the researches already made, and of advancing their own minds towards the truth, however little power they may be able to exert over others.

For this purpose, the processes of comparison and judgment should not only be carried on when the exertion cannot be avoided, but should be vigorously urged, and watched with incessant care. All the ideas which the faculty of observation presents should be compared with those which we have already stored up on the same subject; and thus new light may be cast on a familiar object, and new relations perceived between subjects which before appeared wholly unconnected. We are all sensible how, when an engrossing subject is present to our thoughts, every object appears to bear relation to it. We meet with it in every book; every conversation has some bearing upon it. If we forget it for a moment, the next sight we see, the next sound we hear, reminds us of it, and we are astonished to perceive how close a connexion subsists among all the objects of our senses and all the associations of our minds. The connexion is, in such an instance, frequently slight, and sometimes imaginary; but this occasional experience shows us how the results of observation may be classified. In this instance, the classification is arbitrary, because the comparison was partial. Ideas were not impartially received, and then arranged according to their nature and value: but they were welcomed as supporters of some assumed truth, to which their relation was more imaginary than real. We have heard tell how, when the

apprehension of an invasion from France had risen to its
highest pitch, every distant sound was believed by those who
lived near the coast to be a signal gun, and every light was
mistaken for a beacon fire. Here a moral cause existed for
the perversion of judgment, and the process of comparison
was disturbed by fear: but an intellectual defect often occasions errors as absurd; of which Sterne's Critic with his stop-
watch is an instance in point. To such perversion of judgment all are liable who are given to a favorite pursuit, or a
peculiar mode of thinking; and though in the one case a
great deal of knowledge may be accumulated on a particular
subject, and in the other, the convictions may become comfortably strong, the mind is proportionably indisposed for the
enlargement of knowledge or the perception of truth. Generally speaking, those men who have enriched the world by
their labors in one department of art or science have not
been remarkable for enlargement of mind, and deformity
rather than symmetry has been the characteristic of their
intellectual frame. It is true we have had one Milton and
one Michael Angelo; but we have had hundreds who, to
their proficiency in a single department of science, have
sacrificed more than the object was worth. Those who propose their own improvement as their aim, will do wisely to
promote the general development of their powers, instead of
directing all their efforts to one point. To be a fine poet,
painter, or musician, an eminent mathematician, or mental
or natural philosopher, is in the power of a very few; and if
it were otherwise, the object is not worth the sacrifice which
is often made to attain it. A power of enlarged observation,
of accurate judgment, of enlightened reflection, of steady
reasoning, is worth more to its possessor than the exercise of
any single talent, however splendid or however useful, if
encouraged at the expense of the intellect at large. Believing thus, we have often grieved over the method of conduct-

ing the education of the sons of tradesmen at grammar-schools, where classical learning is the only object, and have never been able to coincide in opinion with those parents who would confine the studies of their daughters within a very narrow range, from a dread of their obtaining " a smattering of learning." Now, all agree that deep learning is better than a smattering; but surely, a smattering is better than none at all ; and if, as may easily be managed, they are guarded from the danger of over-estimating their small attainments, their minds will become enlarged in proportion to the variety of objects to which their attention is directed. Because their knowledge of many subjects must be limited, it need not, therefore, be inaccurate ; and as advancement in any one branch of science affords facilities for improvement in others, the development of the whole mind proceeds at a much quicker rate where the objects of attention are various than where they are very limited.

The more various, however, the objects of inquiry, the more cautious should be the selection from the field of knowledge. We have no superfluous time or power to waste on subjects which are unattainable, either from their own nature, or from the degrees of preparation necessary; and therefore our first inquiry should be into our own intentions in pursuing a train of thought, or entering upon a department of study. We are aware that this rule does not hold universally. The natural philosopher who proposes to devote a course of years to his studies, acts rightly in carrying on his experiments, and pursuing a train of inquiry, without proposing to himself an express object. But it is nearly certain that in that science, valuable discoveries will be elicited by protracted inquiry, though their nature and importance cannot even be conjectured before-hand. But those who, like our readers, have no other design than their own improvement, should be careful to expend their time and pains only where some calculation may be made of the probable gain. It should be their endeavour to form those habits of mind which shall be most serviceable in the discharge of their particular offices, and to acquire those kinds of knowledge which may be brought into use, and the pursuit of which may be facilitated by their situation in life. An ample field will yet be left for the excursions of the mind, while its powers will not be wasted, or its energy exhausted, by blind or ill-directed efforts after unattainable objects.

The knowledge which is to be gained by reading is, of course, infinitely more extensive than that which can be obtained by any other means; but it is worth little where the mind is unprepared to receive and assimilate it. If we passively adopt the opinions we meet with in books, or remember the facts they relate without any endeavour to reflect upon them, or to judge of their relation to other facts, we might almost as well not read at all. We may gain knowledge, such as it is; but, at the same time, that knowledge will impede instead of strengthening the operations of our intellects, and the load of facts will lie like a heavy weight, under which the motions of the reasoning power will become more and more feeble, till at length they stop. Our opinions (if they may be called our own) will be unstable and mutually contradictory; our faculty of observation will, in time, become indolent; our ideas will be deposited, as they are received, in the order of time, and the whole mind will be in a state of hopeless confusion. Far wiser is the cottager who has formed habits of quick and accurate observation, even though he may never have learned his alphabet, than the mere reader who is ever accumulating, but never gaining. The former derives valuable lessons from the experience of life, from intercourse with his kind, from notices which reach him from every quarter, of what is going on in the world of nature and of society; and the information thus obtained is ever made subservient to his further improvement, till in his mind is concentrated a higher wisdom than books alone can teach. The latter, meanwhile, can tell what this author believes, and another teaches, and a third attests; but he has no opinions of his own, and gradually loses the power of forming any. While he lends his house to be filled with other men's furniture, he suffers it to go to ruin, and sees not that it needs repair.

The exercise of comparison and judgment is as necessary with respect to the knowledge we obtain from books as to that with which observation supplies us. The ideas which we receive should be examined and arranged with equal care in both cases, and their relations with each other and with those previously received, diligently explored, and cautiously admitted. If this be done, if we meditate, compare, choose, and reject, where opinions are in question; arrange and apply where facts are the subject of inquiry, we cannot read too much for our intellectual improvement. The mind will hold all the knowledge that can ever be put into it, if it be well chosen, and properly introduced. Unlike the physical, the mental powers of digestion are unlimited; and the stature of the intellectual is not bounded like that of the corporeal frame. The capacity of the mind should be continually enlarging, so that sublime ideas may be received with less and less pain and difficulty, new and strange notions be contemplated without surprise or aversion, and a judgment be formed with a continually increasing accuracy, from a wider and a wider survey of the worlds of matter and of mind. The natural and happy consequences of such enlargement of capacity in fitting us for further improvement, we shall hereafter endeavour to show. Shadowy and bounded as is our view of the future, and awful as is the faint conception of the extent of those regions of science which remain to be explored, we may yet attain to sufficient assurance to pro-

nounce that there is not a wider intellectual difference between the new-born infant and such a philosopher as Newton, than between a man of weak and neglected mind, and
him, however circumstanced externally, whose "large discourse," whose power of "looking before and after," afford
some intimation of the ultimate destination of that being
who is empowered to became " so noble in reason, so infinite
in faculties; in action, so like an angel, — in apprehension,
so like a God ! "

ESSAYS ON THE ART OF THINKING.

V.

THE modes in which the mind may be employed upon the
information which the senses bring to it are various; and
are commonly (though improperly) included in one class,
under the term Meditation.

When trains of ideas are allowed to enter and depart,
while the understanding remains passive, the mind cannot
properly be said to be engaged in meditation, but is rather
amused in reverie.   Though this is the very lowest intellectual occupation, it is the one we all spend the most time in,
and like the best.   The most active thinkers have ever
lamented the loss of time and power which their tendency
to reverie has occasioned; and those who are less aware of
the existence of the evil, are in the habit of making yet
greater sacrifices to intellectual sloth.   We should all be
ashamed of sitting at a window, for hours of every day, to
gaze idly on what was passing without; yet we indulge our
minds in indolence of a similar kind to an awful extent,
unconscious or regardless of the danger of losing all power

over our thoughts, and of enervating every faculty we possess. By the law of association, every idea entertained in the mind introduces other ideas, which, in their turn, bring in more. This law we cannot suspend; but it is in our power to control its operation, and to make choice of the mode in which our ideas shall be combined. By voluntary power, ideas may be recalled in the order in which they were first presented, which is an act of the memory; as when we wish to fix in our minds a conversation with a friend, or the contents of a book we have been reading. By voluntary power we may combine ideas in a new series, as we never combined them before. This is an act of imagination; as when we think of our friend placed among new scenes, and plan what his conduct will be in untried circumstances. Either of these operations may be made useful to the mind by enabling it to lay a firmer hold on knowledge previously gained, or to derive refreshment from a change of occupation; but if the processes are indiscriminately mixed, or if the memory be employed on unworthy objects, or the imagination indulged to an undue degree, it would have been better for the faculties to have been suspended in sleep than thus wasted and impaired. There may be more folly hidden under a grave exterior than displayed in outward mirth; and it sometimes happens that a child is employing his mind more usefully amidst his noisy sports, than his parent while seemingly absorbed in meditation. Let it not be supposed that continual effort is requisite to make our reflections, or even our reveries, conducive to our intellectual improvement. This would be too hard a condition of excellence. The effort is unremittingly necessary only during the formation of our habits of mind, only while setting the machine in motion. The subsequent task of keeping its parts in repair, and removing the obstacles to their action, will be comparatively easy. The effort is often painful, it is true; but labor is the condition of attainment in this life; and no labor can be better bestowed than in the regulation of the intellectual powers, which are themselves the instruments by which every solid good is to be obtained. Some few are so happy as to have been early trained to intellectual as well as moral self-control; but the greater number are obliged to form the habit for themselves as they advance in life, or to forego the advantages it confers; and such are qualified mournfully to sympathize with the pious man who blushed to think that, if his very prayers were written down, and interlined with the irrelevant ideas which presented themselves in the midst of his devotions, what a crowd of incoherences and degrading associations they would present. It is probable that we are all painfully sensible of our transgressions in this respect; if not, it would be well to attempt for once the tedious task of writing down the ideas (as well as we could recollect them) which have passed through our minds during any two minutes of any reverie. But one experiment would be necessary to convince us of the waste of time and power which takes place every day from the want of intellectual control. The night affords time enough for dreaming; and the sports of imagination can be sufficiently indulged during the intervals of serious thought which every day affords. Because they are salutary, they should not only be allowed, but exalted and cherished; but, because they are so delightful as to be engrossing, they should be carefully restrained.

When the attention is fixed on an idea, or on a series of ideas, contemplating their relations and circumstances so closely that other thoughts are excluded, the mind is engaged in meditation. This act is the most efficacious by which our knowledge can be converted into wisdom. By this exercise, more than by any other, is the power of the intellect increased, and its capacity enlarged. By this exercise alone can the wealth of other minds be transferred to our own, and the extent of our mental resources be ascertained. The secret which Newton disclosed respecting his marvellous achievements, cannot be too widely known, or too carefully attended to. He declared that his intellectual power was not derived from any peculiar endowment, but from a habit of patient thought. On another occasion, when questioned respecting his method of beginning a train of inquiry, he replied, "I waited for thought." He placed the object of inquiry before his mind, and (as some degree of excitement must always precede vigorous and profound thought,) he observed the qualities and relations of the object in view, excluded all irrelevant ideas, and thus kept his mind open for the reception of all suggestions, and free from the influence of all perversions. He was not only remarkably exempt from the moral imperfections which overcloud the understanding, from selfishness, (including fear) and prejudice, but from the intellectual perversions to which almost every man is subject. His faculty of observation was perfectly obedient to his will. He could employ it on external or internal objects, excite or suspend it as he pleased. When any purpose was to be answered by observation, not a motion of a straw or a feather escaped his notice; when his business was to calculate or reason, he became, in a moment, as regardless of all external circumstances as if every sense had at once been annihilated.

The principal object which is to be attained by the exercise of reflection is the deduction of general principles from the facts which observation furnishes; and in the application of these general principles to the elucidation of new facts, we see the means by which every increase of knowledge affords the power of a further augmentation.

It is, therefore, of the utmost importance that these principles should be ascertained to be just and true; as a defect in them will necessarily vitiate all our subsequent reasonings.

Mathematicians, whose intellects have been confined to one class of subjects, have been known to cast all learning, however various, into the form of theorems, scholiums, and corollaries; while musicians have been equally expert in arranging the results of reasoning in a scale of harmony. Such inquirers have as little chance of arriving at truth, as a loaded bowl of reaching the mark. The understanding must be rectified before the observations which it takes can be true. As Dr. Watts says, " Things are to be considered as they are in themselves ; their natures are inflexible, and their natural relations unalterable ; and, therefore, in order to conceive them aright, we must bring our understandings to things, and not pretend to bend and strain things to comport with our fancies and forms."

Haste in the adoption of general principles is a serious and common error to which we have before adverted. Few persons, perhaps, are as absurd as the traveller in the east who, on entering a new country, and being entertained at an inn where the landlord was intoxicated, and his wife proud of her auburn hair, therefore noted down in his memorandum book, that all the men of that country were drunken, and all the women red-haired. But we may readily detect errors of the same kind in some department of our reasonings. We are all prone to mistake accessory for necessary circumstances, and to deduce general principles from too limited an experience, and are thus liable to lose all the time and labor employed on the subsequent reasoning, which is unavoidably defective. All deductions from the false principle that the sun moves round the earth, must be also false ; and those who argue from the assumption (founded on limited experience) that there is no such thing as gratitude among the poor, will, it may be hoped, find themselves mistaken.

The same impatience interferes to prevent our discerning in what cases we may expect to arrive at certainty, and where we must be content with a small preponderance of probability. The slightest degree of preponderance is sufficient to afford a basis for belief and for action; and we should therefore be content with it where certainty cannot be obtained. If we are bent upon establishing on all subjects of inquiry general principles, which are to be as immutable as the laws of the Medes and Persians, we shall find ourselves at length encompassed with a host of errors and absurdities, arising from principles which, instead of being founded in truth, are based upon our own ignorance and presumption.

It is astonishing how many difficulties melt away under the influence of patient thought. A subject appears at first dark and confused, and formidable objections crowd around it on every side, so that we are tempted to give up all hope of obtaining a satisfactory opinion upon it: or if we venture to proceed in our examination, our minds are cramped and perturbed by the influence of fear. While in this state, our difficulties increase; unless by becoming interested in the contemplation of the object before us for its own sake, and forgetting our hopes and fears, we discern some unperceived relation to a truth already discovered. We are then encouraged to proceed, and another and another difficulty vanishes; we perceive that here a prejudice of our own has intervened; there an ambiguity in terms has misled us. One ray of light after another breaks in to disperse the partial mists, till the truth stands forth bright and well defined, an object worthy the contemplation of an immortal intellect. No exercise, perhaps, affords a more correct or beautiful exemplification than this of the purpose and extent of our intellectual power, and of its prescribed mode of operation. The power is unlimited, its development gradual, its exercise laborious, but conducive to the most intense moral enjoyment. The modest triumphs of an enlightened and patient intellect afford a pleasure inferior only to that which attends moral conquests,—a pleasure pure, unfailing, and ever growing.

When a general principle has been satisfactorily established, it is to be applied to the elucidation of such facts as may admit of an explanation by it. If no general principles were known, the multiplicity of facts which we must register as the materials of knowledge would be too burdensome for any mind, and the examination of a very few would be the work of a life time. This limited knowledge was all that was actually obtained in the infancy of the human race; and a deficiency of general principles was the cause of the darkness of the middle ages being so protracted and profound. The method of generalization has let in light upon this darkness, and originated a well-founded and animating conviction that the meridian splendor of unclouded truth is not too dazzling for the human intellect.

By a reference of a number of facts to one principle, to which they bear a common relation, order is introduced into the midst of confusion, and the understanding is required to entertain a few well-arranged ideas only, instead of a confused multitude. When facts are thus classed under general principles, the memory is relieved, the judgment unfettered, and the imagination rendered duly subservient to the reasoning power. The commander of an army would be hopeless of preserving discipline, if the conduct of every soldier were under his unassisted charge. The forces are therefore divided into regiments, battalions, and companies, under their respective officers; and thus unity is established among a multitude of individuals, and a countless host is subjected to the control of one man.

In applying principles to the explanation of facts, care must be exercised to ascertain that the relation between them is real, and that it be not arbitrarily extended too far. Because some slight accidental resemblance exists between two facts, it does not follow that they are to be referred to the same principle. It is by their quickness in discerning resemblances, and their hastiness in classing the objects which afford them, that persons of imaginative minds are liable to wander far from the truth. The same defect leads them to multiply principles unnecessarily; so that they collect too many facts under one principle to-day; and to-morrow, being disposed to magnify an accidental difference, they apply several principles where one affords a sufficient explanation. The same young man of whom we read as laying down a rule that snow always falls on Christmas-day, because it did so for three successive years, would probably assign the fall of a guinea and that of a feather to different causes, because the one descends rapidly, and the other with a floating motion. Such a mind, while disdaining to notice the nice distinctions which mark the boundaries of the province to which each principle extends, is yet unequal to the lofty conception that the course of a planet and that of a billiard-ball is regulated by the same laws, or that the same principle which impels the first voluntary efforts of the infant's hand, is employed to form and improve the conscience, till it is recognised as

> "God's most intimate presence in the soul,
> And his most perfect image in the world."

There are two methods of reasoning from general principles, — by induction, and by analogy. The conclusions derived from a careful process of induction may be depended on as certain; but such conclusions are, from the imperfection of our knowledge, rarely to be obtained. The arguments from analogy are distinguished by various degrees of probability, some being nearly equal in force to a complete induction, while others intimate only a faint probability. It is absolutely certain that the earth moves round the sun; it is highly probable that the planets are inhabited; it is very remotely probable that the inhabitants of the moon resemble the human race in form and constitution.

According to the weakness or strength of a mind will
be its power to discern between these different kinds of
evidence, and duly to estimate their value. Some persons
of lively imagination are delighted with the discovery of a
remote analogy, and build upon it a belief which, however
hastily adopted, they determine to retain for ever; and while
thus disposed, demonstration itself is of no avail to convince
them that they are mistaken. Equally lamentable is their
condition to whom all arguments are of equal weight, whose
minds are incessantly vacillating, till reason becomes impotent, and truth is believed to be nothing but a name. If in
the one case a feather weighs down every substance that
can be opposed to it, and if, in the other, no efforts can
make the scales cease their alternating motion, the fault is
evidently in the balance, not in the weights, and it must be
condemned as utterly unserviceable.

We all, doubtless, feel how far we are from having
succeeded in rectifying (perhaps from having attempted to
rectify) the balance. We are all apt to think our reason
convinced, when our imagination alone is gratified, or our
feelings are excited; when our love of the new or the
marvellous interferes to impede the operation of the reasoning
power. By an interference of the imagination, also, are we
led to conceive a difficulty to be removed when the object
causing it is perceived to resemble another which, being
familiar to us, is supposed to be understood. But the most
familiar objects are sometimes those which we understand
the least, and concerning which our ignorance is the least
likely to be removed; as the very familiarity blunts our
curiosity, and renders us blind to the difficulties which exist.
Probably ninety-nine persons out of a hundred would have
declared that they knew why an apple falls, if asked the
question two centuries ago; and if the inquiry was proposed
why a kite comes down when the wind ceases to blow, they
would probably have answered that it must fall, like an apple,

or any thing else, when there is nothing to keep it up; and few, perhaps, would discover that the answer was unsatisfactory.

We have already offered some hints respecting the errors which arise from the imperfection of language. Those errors may be generally avoided by habits of care. When pursuing a train of reasoning in a book, we should examine whether a proposition be entangled in more words than are necessary, and also whether any irrelevant ideas are introduced. The more simple the statement can be made, the more easy is the approach to the truth. If engaged in meditation on a question proposed by ourselves, we should be careful not only to think in words, but to vary the statement of the proposition, by transposing the parts and changing the terms, if equivalent modes of expression can be found. If conducting an argument in conversation, it is absolutely necessary to ascertain that both disputants understand the meaning of the terms employed by each. It is irritating and humbling to the mind to ascertain, on arriving at some false conclusion, that the truth has been missed through the imperfection of the instrument employed to obtain it; but few misfortunes are more common, as the experience of every young logician can attest.

Frequent exercise in composition is a most important assistance in forming habits of accurate thought. Continually as this fact is insisted on in all works of education, and decisive as is the testimony of experience respecting it, it is strange that the practice is not more universally and extepsively adopted by those who desire their own improvement. If this exercise were wisely adopted and perseveringly pursued, the best ends of intellectual education would be answered by its means alone. The act of composition teaches, in the first place, to state accurately, and in the next, to think accurately. Other numerous and important

advantages arise from the practice; but the two we have
mentioned are the most closely connected with the objects
of this Essay. The student should begin the exercise of
composition by writing down the ideas of others; for
instance, a recollection of a lecture, or a conversation, or,
better still, a passage from a book with which he can compare his statement. When enabled by practice to state the
ideas of others with precision, he should frequently exercise
himself in original composition, on a variety of subjects.
Though the time thus employed be considerable, not an
hour of it is wasted; and if the labor be found irksome,
there can be no stronger proof that it is needed. If due care
be taken to vary the subjects and form of composition, all
the knowledge previously acquired will be secured, and converted to its proper uses; and every faculty of the mind
will be disciplined to a more and more faithful discharge of
its office, and an ever-increasing capacity of improvement.
If, however, the subjects be not sufficiently varied, the best
advantages of the practice will be lost. If the imaginative
write nothing but poetry, the indolent nothing but matter of
fact, the sentimentalist nothing but sentiment, ease and
fluency may be gained, but that bias of opinion and feeling
which is unfavorable to intellectual health will be continually
increasing. The truth that whatever is clearly understood
may be clearly expressed, is by no means inconsistent with
our experience of the imperfection of language, since a
comparison of two or more terms will convey an idea which
no single one is adequate to express. If this truth had
always been acted upon, or was now universally adopted,
many errors would have been stifled in the birth, or would
be presently exploded. How powerfully the practice of
composition assists to establish a practical conviction of this
useful truth, those can attest who have tried the experiment.

Some of the best advantages of this and of all the other methods of improvement which we have suggested may be secured by Conversation, if well conducted. Not only may truth be gradually drawn out by argument, and substantiated by a laborious application of facts, but by means of the intellectual excitements and moral influences which are brought into play in conversation, the circulation of intellectual wealth is indefinitely accelerated, the reasoning power receives a new impulse, the suggestions of the imagination become more lively, and its illustrations more appropriate. The mode of intercourse which can even now "reveal latent thoughts which no eye can see, and enable mind to communicate to mind its most spiritual feelings — to awake and be awakened mutually to science and benevolent exertion, as if truths, and generous wishes, and happiness itself, could be diffused in the very voice that scarcely floats upon the ear," * affords an animating presage of that higher communion which shall hereafter be sanctified by an unlimited and universal devotion to truth; in which term are embodied our highest conceptions of the substantial blessedness of our race.

The influence which this mode of intercourse enables and obliges us to exert over other minds, should serve as a prevailing motive to the utmost improvement of our intellectual powers. The time will come, if it has not already arrived, when the young, the weak and inexperienced, will look up to us for guidance, or will, at least, contemplate us as examples. The intellectual relations of the least influential of mankind are various and important; and we shall be required to account, not only for ourselves, but for the aid or hindrance we afford to those who are connected with us. If our power is to be exercised by means of example or companionship alone, we are bound to set forth to the utmost of our ability the excellence and beauty of a well-organized intellect, whose

---

* Dr. Brown.

constitution is sound, and whose immortal faculties are fitly developed. If our power is to be exercised in express teaching, a truly enlightened love for our race will urge us to impart not only what we have acquired, but the means of acquisition, and to do better than to bestow an alms on those who sit helpless at the beautiful gate of the temple of knowledge. It will impel us to strengthen the sinews, and extend a helping hand, that the suppliants may enter in by their own power, and pay homage on their own behalf.

ESSAYS ON THE ART OF THINKING.

VI.

In our observations on the Art of Thinking, we have been obliged to omit all notice of the important facts connected with the influence of moral cultivation on intellectual improvement. It is not, however, foreign to our object to observe the operation of an enlightened intellect in quickening and invigorating the moral sense.

When we declare that the practice of duty is most likely to be firm and consistent where the perceptions of moral obligation are not only vivid but distinct, and where the convictions of the understanding are not only strong but clear, we shall not, we hope, be suspected of the aristocratic bias of those minds which, if they could, would hide

> " The excellence of moral qualities
>   From common understanding ; leaving truth
>   And virtue, difficult, abstruse, and dark,
>   Hard to be won, and only by a few."

It is the delight of every ingenuous mind to spurn so degrading a prejudice as this; to acknowledge the common right of every rational being to that inheritance which the Father of lights has appointed to the whole human race. It is the delight of every uncorrupted heart to feel that the sunshine itself is not more universal in its vivifying influence than the luminary of truth; and that if the harvest of wisdom and of peace be yet scanty and immature, it is not because that influence is partial, but because it is intercepted by ignorance and prejudice. It is the delight of the benevolent mind to perceive that though wisdom is sometimes missed by those who have spent a life-time in its pursuit, it is found by multitudes whose simplicity of heart has proved a faithful guide; or, to express an important fact in the best language, that truth, while hidden from the wise and prudent, has been revealed unto babes. It is not through caprice in the distribution of the recompense of labor that protracted efforts are thus frustrated; but because the wisdom of the wise here referred to exists in their own conceit, and their prudence is the prudence of this world. Wrapt in the contemplation of their baseless visions, they have been led astray, while the babes whom they despise, in plucking the flowers of the field, have found among them the pearl of great price. Learning is not wisdom, any more than conviction is truth; and it matters not to our argument whether those whose perceptions are distinct, and whose convictions are clear, are lowly or exalted in outward rank, simple or learned in the lore of this world. They may have wrought out their convictions for themselves; or they may owe the rectitude of their intellects to wise teaching in the courts of the sanctuary, or in the wide temple of nature. The question is not now how they obtained those convictions of the understanding, but respecting their value as guides in the way of purity and peace.

From our conceptions of the character and attributes of God, arises our perception of moral obligation: and in proportion to the comprehensiveness and purity of those con-

ceptions will be the accuracy and refinement of the moral
sense.   Our ideas of moral perfection are primarily formed
from observation of the human character, and the abstract
notion is then transferred upon the Divine Being.   It is the
chief privilege of our intellectual powers to enable us perpetually to enlarge and exalt these conceptions, to purify
them gradually from the admixture of unworthy associations,
and to adorn them with new elements of spiritual beauty.
The more pure the abstraction of a moral quality, the less
unworthy will be its ascription to God.   The son of a wise
and tender parent will form a truer conception of the Divine
Being under the name of a Father, than the child who has
been subjected to capricious and unkind treatment : and the
ignorant, who look on a judge only as the dispenser of ven-
geance, will entertain a more unworthy notion of the moral
government of God, than the enlightened who regard the
laws as the safeguard of the general welfare.   If benevolence be conceived of, not as capricious fondness, but as a
regard to the general good, free from the possibility of error
in the choice of means, or of disappointment in the attainment of ends, no very erroneous notion of Divine Justice
can co-exist with so correct a conception.   It will then be
seen that the office of justice is to reward virtue and to
punish vice with a view to the happiness of all ; and that
benevolence being the sole obligation to justice, when the
purposes of benevolence can no longer be served by the
infliction of suffering, that infliction becomes unjust.   It will
be understood that justice and mercy, or that tenderness to
offenders which is authorized by benevolence, both arise
from benevolence ; for if justice inflict pain without promoting the general good, or if mercy be extended to offenders
whose punishment is necessary to the general good, it is
clear that benevolence is violated.   We speak of the Divine
perfections separately, because to our bounded faculties they

appear in different aspects; and hence arise those unworthy fears and presumptuous raptures which are alike injurious to God, and inimical to our own moral advancement. The time will come when we shall no longer thus see in part; when we shall fully understand how all the moral attributes of God merge in infinite benevolence, as the various hues of the rainbow blend into one pure and perfect ray of light. Since our obligation to allegiance arises from our acknowledgment of God as our Sovereign, since our gratitude is due to him as our Benefactor, our submission as our Moral Governor, our obedience as our Father, the more elevated are our conceptions of him under these characters, the more enlightened will be our devotion, and the less unworthy our service. When the time shall arrive that shall render our conceptions pure, our love will be also pure; that is, we shall be perfect.

It is clear that our conceptions must become refined and exalted in proportion to the advancement of the intellect: that the philosopher who explores the recesses of the human mind, and watches the operations of its delicate machinery, must form a less inadequate idea of the wisdom of its maker than the being who is scarcely conscious of having a mind: that the philanthropist who acquaints himself with the joys and sorrows of the inhabitants of every clime, must have a truer notion of Divine Benevolence than the mind, however sensitive, whose range of sympathies is confined within a narrow circle. It is true that all the knowledge which has ever been attained appears to be little more than an indication of what remains to be unfolded; but every acquisition makes us better acquainted with the wisdom which planned so vast a creation, the power which effected it, and the goodness which gradually discloses its wonders and its beauties.

Not only are our conceptions of the Divine perfections enlarged by the growth of the intellect; they are also purified by its activity. Apparent imperfections vanish, difficulties disappear, and perplexities are unravelled as our inquiries proceed, till we are enabled not only to hope but to believe that all blemishes exist in the organ of vision alone, and not in the object contemplated.

When we discover that a variety of purposes is answered by an instrument of whose use we were once ignorant, that apparent evil issues in a preponderance of good, and that the good in which we rested as an end is still made subservient to some greater good, we rise to a higher and a higher conception of our ulterior destination, and, consequently, to a more correct understanding of our present duty. While bound to obedience as strictly as when a parent's frown awed our childhood, that obedience becomes exalted towards perfect freedom; because the more justly we appreciate the relations of things to each other, the more nearly we view them as God views them, the less inconsistent will be our desires, the less opposed our wills to his. While we stand in the circumference of the world of mind, our observations must be not only obscure but partial; and the nearer we approach the centre, the more correct will be our views, and the more will they approximate to His who is there enthroned: the more clearly shall we see that to acquaint ourselves with Him is to be at peace; that toils issue in satisfaction, sufferings in repose, struggles in victory, obedience in perfect liberty.

It is clear that these enlarged conceptions are at open war with the popular notions whose prevalence yet causes so fearful an amount of misery to feeling hearts and tender consciences. The transports of the elect and the horrors of the reprobate can derive no sanctions from the discoveries of the advancing intellect, and are already subsiding into a more rational appreciation of the obligation to obedience, and of its promised rewards. It is more readily admitted than formerly, that creeds cannot effect an uniformity of belief, and that the will of God may be more clearly understood from his word, than through the interpretations of unauthorized persons. The more able we become to form our conceptions of the Divine perfections from the elements which he administers, the more willing we shall be to trace out his purposes for ourselves; to inform ourselves from the most authentic source respecting the obligations of duty, and the true spirit of the laws by which our obedience is to be regulated. By the exercise of this freedom of inquiry alone can our comprehension of his merciful designs be clear, our services be acceptable, our obedience steadfast as it is free.

Obedience may be strict, but it cannot be enlightened nor truly cheerful where the intellect is feeble and blind. The power of a sound mind is as essential as love out of a pure heart to the highest service which a rational being can offer to his Maker. Power to distinguish between the essentials and the non-essentials of duty; power to choose the best among various means of obtaining an end; power to direct the operation of those means; power to bring opposing claims to a perfect coalescence, is requisite to the most acceptable homage, — to that obedience which would pass with a single aim through every struggle and every snare, to ultimate perfection. The lukewarm philosopher may offer the fruits of his intellectual labor, and find them unacceptable, while the blind obedience of an ignorant slave is encouraged and rewarded; but he who exalts the humble devotion of the one by the enlarged conceptions of the other, is the most worthy disciple of him whose virtue was perfected by his illumination from on high; who knew God while the world knew him not.

When we look around us and observe how much moral strength is wasted by an infirmity of the intellectual faculties,

we shall wonder more and more at the low appreciation in
which the power of a sound mind is often held. What
superstitious fears cast a gloom over the homage of many a
devout spirit! What prejudices embitter the intercourses
of pious friendship! What errors of judgment neutralize
the efforts of warm benevolence! What visionary difficulties
are erected into substantial obstacles in a worthy pursuit!
What perplexity is caused by obligations apparently opposed,
but in reality not only reconcileable, but beautifully harmonious! Since action is the law of happiness, and toil the
condition of excellence, the time will never come in this
world when the performance of duty will be divested of
difficulty; but, by a careful cultivation of the intellectual as
well as the moral faculties, we have it in our power to hasten
our progress indefinitely; to walk in the straight path, re-
conciled to its toils, and to discern the clear light of the future
through the mists which are destined to melt away.

To suffer is as important a part of obedience as to act;
and the more enlarged our views of the purposes of the
moral government of God, the less rebellious will be the
struggles of our will. Those who know how the passions
grow by indulgence, who are taught by science as well as by
experience that counteraction is as necessary as stimulus to
the perfect vigor of the mind, find a substantial relief in
sorrow in the conviction that their suffering is conducive to
their ultimate good. A yet higher satisfaction arises when
self is no longer explicitly regarded, and the energies of the
sufferer are directed to the investigation of the Divine purposes in the afflictions which have befallen him, and to an
earnest endeavour to co-operate in the fulfilment of those
purposes. To submit to inevitable misfortune with humble
acquiescence, is the common duty of all: to struggle, without repining, while the issue of events is doubtful, is lawful
for all; but to welcome the dispensations of Providence,

whatever they may be, to derive spiritual vigor from every alternation of joy and sorrow, to perceive the end for which those alternations are appointed, and to aid in its accomplishment, are the privileges of a few; and those few are as much distinguished by rectitude of understanding as by purity of heart.

The alleviation which the activity of the intellect affords to the sorrow of the heart is a privilege which those only who have experienced know how to value. When the soul is sick with apprehension, or wearied with the effort of endurance, an oblivion of care more complete than that of sleep, a safe and welcome refreshment, may be found in intellectual activity. Where the power of attention has been duly cultivated, the advantages it confers are never more sensibly felt than when it is necessary for our repose to lay the memory to rest, to restrain the imagination, and to seek, in the exercise of the reasoning powers, a refuge from afflicting remembrance and mournful anticipation. While the feeble mind makes continual efforts at submission till it sinks wearied with the struggle, he who is master of his faculties as well as his passions, derives strength from the intermission of his suffering; and, without presumptuous confidence in his own resources, without undervaluing the aids of faith and the consolations of religious hope, finds a subordinate assistance and solace in the exercise of reason. The pleasures which reward that exercise are never more welcome than when other pleasures fail. The perception of order and of wise arrangement, which supplies continual satisfaction to the reasoning mind, becomes more rather than less vivid amidst the changes of external circumstances; and the opportunity which those circumstances afford for the exercise of observation, the test which they offer for the proof of principles, are received as substantial alleviations by the well-disciplined mind. Faith, however blind, and religious hope, however vague, afford a sufficient support to the mind under any infliction; while without them the exercise of the intellect affords no effectual consolation. But when faith ennobles the intellect, and the intellect enlightens and guides the efforts of faith, the mind is furnished with an inexhaustible store of consolations, and becomes possessed of power to overcome the world, — not only its temptations, but its sorrows, — not only to withstand the conflict of the passions, but to endure the wounds of the tenderest sympathies.

But as the object of enlightened self-discipline is less to secure happiness in the present life than to prepare for another, it is of greater importance to regard the prospects of the future world than to consider how the transient interests of our mortal existence may be affected by the neglect or culture of the intellect. How different must be the entrance upon another world of the enlightened from that of the perverted intellect! The one has been taught to discern the spiritual essence which resides in all material forms, and is therefore prepared to recognise them in the new heavens and the new earth; while to the other, whose views have been confined to sensible images, all will appear strange and unintelligible. The one has gradually strengthened his visual powers by loftier ascents towards the sun of truth, and is therefore prepared to encounter its unclouded lustre; while the other, on reaching the threshold of heaven, will sink down overpowered with the blaze. The one has been accustomed to interpret the melodies which breathe from the planets as they roll, and from the revolutions of all earthly things, and will therefore respond with delight to the music of the angelic choir, while the other will listen with apathy to that warbling in an unknown tongue. The one will find in every mansion of his Father's house, brethren with whom he may hold sweet converse, while the other will wander solitary through the courts, unconscious of delight, incapable of sympathy, and at length be compelled to seek in its remotest bounds some who will instruct him in the language of truth, and prepare him for the perception of realities.   He looks round for familiar objects, and finds them not; he recalls the ideas in which he most delighted, and sees that they bear no relation to his present state.   He longs for the changing light of the sun, or for the milder radiance of the moon, for an overshadowing cloud, for the gloom of night, for any intermission of the bewildering glory which surrounds him; but the sun and moon are no more, and the shades of darkness have fled away.   He desires to pay the forms of homage which he supposes to be appropriate to the place, and inquires for the sanctuary: he is told that "there is no temple therein; for the Lord God Almighty and the Lamb are the temple thereof."

If he be lowly enough to submit to instruction, patient enough to unlearn his errors, eager to divest himself of prejudice, and courageous to forego his most cherished conceptions, all may yet be well; for the gates of the heavenly city stand open for ever, and its waters flow for all that are athirst.   But it must be long before his discipline will have prepared him to enjoy, like his companion, the full delight of a spiritual existence, and before the mysteries of eternity can be revealed to his enraptured gaze.   He is not, like the wicked, banished from the regions of life and light: but neither is he enabled, by intellectual as well as moral preparation, to find in them the home of the understanding, as well as the resting-place of the affections.

11

SABBATH MUSINGS.

I.

A COVE ON THE SEASHORE.

THE bell has ceased. While it tinkled among the rocks,
my solitude was not complete, though no one is nigh.
Now may I be freely wrought upon by sound and motion,
stimulated and soothed by influences which man can only
interpret to me, and not originate.   Thou rolling sea! thou
shalt be my preacher.   Of old was that office given to thee.
Wisdom was in her native seat before the throne of God
when thy bounds were fixed ; and from her was thy commission received to be the measure of time, a perpetual suggestion of eternity, an admonition to " rejoice ever before Him."
Thine is the only unwearied voice : thy sound alone hath not
died away from age to age : and from thee alone is man
willing to hear truth from the day that his spirit awakes to
that when his body sleeps for ever.   By the music of thy gentle lapse it is thine to rouse the soul from its primal sleep
among the flowers of a new life ; blossoms whose beauty is
unseen, whose fragrance is unheeded, till at thy voice all is
revealed to the opening sense.   What tidings of the spirit
are there which thou hast not revealed or confirmed by thy
murmur in the sunny noon, or thy lonely midnight hymn, or
by thy wintry swell, rousing the rocks to answer thee, and
drowning the chorus of the blasts? Every other voice utters,
and is again silent ; men speak in vain and are weary : if they
are regarded, they still become weary.   The nightingale that
sings far inland, nestles in the silence when the moon goes down.
These winds which tune their melodies to thine, pause that
thou mayest be heard ; and yonder caverns which sing a
welcome to the winds as they enter, are presently still.   But

'if thou shouldst be hushed, it would be as if Wisdom herself were struck dumb; to me, communing with thee in this lonely cove; to the Indian in another hemisphere, now perhaps questioning thee of the departed spirits he has loved, and of the Greater Spirit whom he would fain know and love better; to the babes and to the wise who tread thy shores to learn of thee in sport or in meditation. If at noon-day thou shouldst be stilled, men would look up to the sun to see it shaken from its sphere: if at midnight, all sleepers would rise to ask why God had forsaken them. It is awful to look abroad when the gloom of the night is drawing off, and to see thee still rolling, rolling below, and to know that it is thus when every human eye is closed. But what would it be to behold thee dead! to strain the eye and ear to know if thy voice might not yet be overtaken afar! How oppressive would be the silence, how stifling the expectation, how hopeless the blank, if we should call upon thee and find no answer!

How marvellous is the relation between material things, and the things of the spirit with which they are linked, we know not how! Where any thing human intervenes, the connexion may be better understood than here, where all external things are as they would have been if I were Adam, a solitary living soul. In a churchyard the remains of humanity tell of the destinies of humanity, and thoughts of life and death rise as " by natural exhalation " from the ground we tread. Even now, the church-bell brought me tidings of the religious hopes and fears of many hearts: but, at this moment, when the wintry winds bear hither no human voices, and these everlasting rocks show no impress of human foot, how mysterious is the power by which I gather from the scudding clouds the materials of prophecy, and find in the echoes new exponents of ancient truth!

Was it not thus, at least in part, that the chosen servants of God knew Him as the world knew him not? The divine impulse being once given, was it not thus strengthened, till their souls could grasp more than we know of the past, and the present, and of that which is to come? When Christ spent the night in prayer, was he ministered unto by forms which we have not seen, or by those with which we are familiar, beheld by him in loftier grandeur and intenser beauty? That which once appeared to his followers to be thunder, was to him an intelligible voice: and was it not thus also when he was alone? When he retired from the clamor of enemies and the narrow solicitudes of friends, was not the discord of the elements music to him, because it told that his Father was with him? When the lightnings of the hills played round his unsheltered head, were not they the messengers of peace who were sent to him? If the place where Jacob rose up from sleep was to him the gate of heaven, because the Divine presence was made manifest, what must have been the mountain where Jesus watched and prayed! More hallowed than Sinai, inasmuch as the new law was better than the old. More hallowed than even the Mount of Transfiguration, because the light disclosed beamed not on the gross, outward eye, but on the inner soul.

And what a light! When was it first given? Did it come to him early, breaking afar off over the obscurity and perplexities of life, as yonder gleam touches the horizon beyond the gloom and turbulence of these waters? Did the first consciousness of his destiny come to him from above, or from within, or from a peculiar interpretation of tidings given to all? Was the mighty secret known to himself alone, or was there a mysterious sympathy with his mother? Did she, or did no one, suspect his emotions when he first distinctly apprehended the extent of his privilege, when he first said in his heart, "The world hath not known thee, but I have known thee"? There is a fullness of meaning, a fervor of gratitude in these words, of which men seem not sufficiently sensible when they dwell on the griefs of Christ, or turn to the days of his glory for consolation. It is true, he was a man of sorrows; and it is natural in his case as in others, to mourn for the sufferer as well as to reprobate the persecutors: but our sympathy ought to be regulated by the qualities of the mind with which we sympathize. While, therefore, we are thrilled with horror, or shame, or grief, as we read how Jesus was insulted, and rejected by foes, and misunderstood and forsaken by followers, we should also remember that the mind is its own place, and that to him this place was a heaven. If we know any thing of the repose of filial dependence, of the delight of divine communion; if we have felt the exquisite satisfaction of submissive endurance, and the energy of beneficent exertion; any degree of the celestial consciousness of intellectual power and spiritual purity, we must be aware that these delights, immeasurably magnified, were the daily solace of Jesus. Where there is purity, there must be peace; where there is devotion, there must be joy; and to one whose purity had reached its last refinement, whose devotion was exalted to the utmost intensity, there must have been an abundant recompence even for woes like his. It is true, that we can enter little more into his griefs than his joys: for the objects of our hopes and fears are, for the most part, the transient events of life, and our sympathies are confined within a very narrow circle of interests and expectations. It was far otherwise with him who, knowing God as the world knew him not, was able to see the issue of many things from the beginning, and to sympathize in the varied interests of humanity to the end of time. What wonder that he found none to share his burden of sympathies when, even now, the bare thought of it is overwhelming! When from an eminence he saw in vision all the kingdoms of the earth and their glory, his affections were also abroad, rejoic-

11*

ing with all who met to rejoice, and weeping with all who wept in the solitude of their homes. Knowing what was in men, their present griefs were his, their present joys were his; he felt for them more than they knew how to feel for themselves, because he knew also what was in store for them.

We could not endure such a depth of emotion, any more than we can appreciate the support which he had in a knowledge of the Divine purposes.

He looked upon children as destined to run the race of life as their parents had done before them, ignorant of their true end, rebellious under the mildest discipline, unconscious of the most unwearied benignity. How deep, how tender must have been his compassion! But more tender, more deep the joy of contemplating the issue of their wanderings, of anticipating the harvests which should spring from seed thus sown in tears. When he took the little ones in his arms, he knew that in some hearts he was kindling a flame which should not be quenched till it had consumed all impurities, and consecrated the altar on which it burned to the service of God. When he set a sinless child in the midst, how clear, how affecting a view must he have entertained of the approaching deterioration of this child's mind, and of its gradual renovation, its far-distant confirmation in purity and peace! No one else knew as he knew through what strifes, what salutary griefs, what hurtful enjoyments, what weariness, what transports, what tremblings of fear and hope the spirit must struggle in its passage to heaven : none could, therefore, feel such compassion. No one else knew the issue of this struggle, or could, therefore, adequately rejoice in the destination of human nature. To the elements alone could he confide the expression of his emotions. He came forth alone ; for there was no one to join in his petitions, or to comprehend his thanksgivings.

Jerusalem was rejoicing in the mirth of her multitudes when he wept over her. The multitudes were astonished, as they would have been if they could have known the serenity with which he looked on many forms of evil which to them seemed monstrous. Beneath the stars he had learned to see things which yet were not, as though they were, and on the sounding shore had been told that the ways of God were not as the ways of men. Therefore, when he came back into the cities, he saw with other eyes than all around him. He saw many blessings in the shape of infirmities unquietly borne and eagerly shaken off, and knew perhaps that secret tears contained a more benignant influence than the smiles by which they were chased away. The sufferers might *believe*, as we believe, that all things work together for good : to Jesus yet more was given : he *saw* it.

Under what an aspect must society have appeared to him ! The course of public affairs must have spoken an intelligible language to him, when he compared it with intimations from within. When he went up to the feast, year after year, how distinct must have been the evidence of gathering circumstances, how well-defined the shadows of approaching events as the consummation drew nigh ! To us, no employment is so delightful as to trace out the Divine purposes in past events which were once mysterious ; to mark the historical revolutions of states, and the varying fortunes of individuals ; to look back keenly through the vicissitudes of our own lot, and observe how temporal changes have wrought out spiritual stability : but this is as nothing compared with the privilege of recognising more extensive purposes in events which were, to all others, yet contingent. He saw that through the sufferings of confessors, the sacrifice of martyrs, and the evils which it was his office to to foretell, new adherents should be continually gained to the little flock who should at length outnumber the sands on the sea-shore. He saw how every impulse of every mind was appointed to carry on the grand scheme of salvation; how all outward changes, all inward workings, were to contribute to the establishment of the gospel. Yet this insight into the destinies of society was learned in solitude: surely in a solitude like this, sanctified by the sanctity of his own soul. — The winds are rising, and the caverns are thundering amidst the dash of the waves. There is a deep and holy joy even to me, amidst this turbulence. How much deeper and holier to him who saw more vividly how all things were alive with the Divine presence! When he walked the deep, tempestuous like that which tosses before me now, when he trod the pastures of the valley, or looked on the fields white for harvest, or on that glorious type of himself, the light of the natural world, he saw in these forms a signature which is not fully legible to us, and received from them promises which we cannot yet understand.

Yet though these promises are not fully comprehended, though we cannot measure the griefs, or estimate the sublime enjoyments of such a sensibility, combined with such a destiny, as that of Jesus, must not our sympathy be improved, our brotherhood with him strengthened, by studying as he studied, and resorting where he retired? The same book is open to me that he loved to look upon, and to which he perpetually referred those whom he taught. The same voice is now pealing louder and louder on my ear, to which he stood to listen by night and by day. The impulse to interpret it has to none been given in an equal degree; but yet it is given. Why, else, are men now collected in churches and on the hill-side to worship? Why is the calm of the Sabbath spread over the land? Why, else, is this mighty roar to me like the voice of the Saviour to John when he heard it as the voice of many waters? Why, else, is there a Sabbath at sea as well as on land; a gathering together to pray and praise where there is no bell to announce the day? In yonder noble vessel, now scudding, and now pitching among the winds and waters, there is, perhaps, an assemblage for worship : and if the voices should be drowned in the grander music of the elements, many there will retire where they can be alone, as I am, with God and the teachers he sends to human hearts. This impulse, if cherished, may lead to knowledge of which men yet dream not; may stimulate to vigor, of which none, but the supremely favored, have been yet conscious. Hail, then, thou voice of wisdom, shouting from the deep, and echoing from the shore! Rouse in me all the power that the world hath laid asleep! Revive in me that which I have already learned, and teach me more! While I am silent amidst this mighty chorus, breasting the storm as the steadfast rocks, speak, and I will hear !

NORWICH, 1831

SABBATH MUSINGS.

II.

A POPLAR GROVE.

WE speak of the changes of nature : but what are they compared with the mutations in the spirit of man? On such a day as this we come to such a place as this, and, while treading on the decayed leaves of a former year, we point to the bursting buds around us, and say, " How many seasons are there in the life of one man ! " But is there not a voice in this solitude which tells a different tale? Is there not here a character of stability which there is nothing in mortal life to rival ? If these trees could whisper, as they wave, the history of all that has passed beneath them, would they not speak of creation, change, and progression, such as human experience

knows not of? This aisle of columnar trees,—how long is
it since they arose side by side, and interwove their topmost
boughs, making a sanctuary where twilight may flee to rest
at noon-day? How long is it since the ivy matted the ground,
and climbed these living pillars, and hung its garlands to
the breezes on high? Perhaps the cowled devotee retired
hither to pay his debt of devotion, to transfer his prayers
from his girdle into the care of his saint. Perhaps, as he
stood beneath this shelter, some wandering breeze came to
sweep aside the foliage, and give him a glimpse of the wide
champaign studded with hamlets, speckled with flocks and
herds, and overspread with the works of man's busy hands.
Perhaps he crossed himself, and thanked heaven that he was
not like these busy men, destined "to fret and labor on the
plain below," but rather withdrawn into the stillness of
retreat, where the songs with which the reaper cheers his
toil could never come to disturb the orisons of the devout.
Perhaps the Puritan has stood on this spot, trampling the
snow-drop under foot, while looking up to the waving
tracery, lamenting its likeness to the cathedral aisle, and
wishing for power to uncover the verdant roof, and let in
dust and glare. Here, while mourning over the unconverted,
he perhaps turned away from the scent of violets, and would
fain have hushed the cooings of the wood-pigeon. Since
those days, a better homage than that of the devotee and the
fanatic has doubtless been offered; there may have been a
progression from the idol worship of ignorance to that devotion under whose influence truth springs from the earth
among the flowers, joy comes in the flickering lights, and
praise is uttered in all the stirring harmonies around. Thus
while, from season to season, Beauty has passed through this
grove and vanished, Wisdom may have made it her abode,
and may now be ready to whisper her experience from the
days of her weak childhood to this time of comparative
maturity.

Nor has she less to tell of the progression of an individual spirit than of that of generations; and her record of such a progression has she confided to these silent witnesses around me. To me there was ever a sabbath in this place: ever something awful in the invariableness of its character. It teems, therefore, with my Sabbath thoughts and feelings alone. In the winters of my childhood I loved to come when the neighbouring mansion was deserted, and the trackless snow showed the solitude to be complete; and to this alley I first bent my steps, stopping only to gather the single rosebud drooping under its little burden of snow. When the scarce disclosed entrance between the laurels was reached, when I opened my rustling way, how darkly green was the covert, carpeted and tapestried with ivy as now! None crossed my path but the startled hare; nor did the momentary alarm reveal to me what I have since learned, that the hour was to me a Sabbath, and the place a temple. In summer days, the homage was of a different kind. I came for rest from the tumult of emotions raised by the voice of the preacher. When that voice spoke things that I could understand, it was like the voice of a growing waterfall, waxing stronger till the spirit could bear no more; till the young hearer looked up to the dome to see if angels were looking in, or to watch for signs that the judgment day was come. After such an hour, welcome was the coolness which fell on me when I nestled here from the burning sun, and found all unchanged as in the wintry day: all within green and shining, whether I looked abroad on an expanse of snow, or on the sultry haze of an August noon. Welcome was rest after exhaustion; welcome were the old thoughts which came to blend with those which throbbed like keen sensations. Welcome hath been the blended influence of old and new thoughts from that day to this, when I can rejoice in the present through a clear interpretation of the past.

O how merciful is the injunction to man to pray! If there were no such injunction, who would not eagerly snatch the permission? What spirit is there that never needs rest, or can be happy without a home? And where is there a rest, where a home, but in communion — private communion — with the Father of the spirit? In sleep there is a rest for the body; in incessant change of objects there is refreshment for the intellect; but for the spirit there is or ought to be no sleep, and endless vicissitude brings weariness: and of the many refreshments which are perpetually administered by Providence, none are wholly and permanently satisfying but intercourse with itself. The natural influences of grief are strengthening and cheering when the clouds are overblown; the effects of sudden joy are often salutary as sweet; the exercise and growth of a healthful intellect affords delights which can be understood only by sympathy; and human love can fully satisfy all but an immortal spirit, can satisfy even an immortal spirit often and long together — but all these are not enough. Grief and joy come seldom, and soon pass away; the intellect sickens at times; and as for human friendship, what two minds ever were as one in their progress, their experience, their earthly destiny, their heavenly capabilities? What spirit, however purely and firmly wedded to another, has not in its bitterness sighed, "I am alone!" or in more peaceful moments breathed, "Father, there is none but thou!" Where has not absence, estrangement, or death, sooner or later, worn or snapped the bond, and left the spirit unsupported? This failure of early sympathy is a necessary consequence of that spiritual advancement which, though it confers a more than counterbalancing bliss in the formation of nobler attachments, yet cannot stay the tears which hallow the remains of buried friendships; and if, in some rare instances, minds advance together, it can only be for a while — only till the messenger, whom they know to be on the wing, appears to bear one away. In all earthly changes there is life, there is hope, there is joy; but there is no rest — and the spirit must have rest. Of even this place I should grow weary if its mutable elements were all — if the springing and fading flowers, the moving clouds, the ivy-clad trunks, which bear within the seeds of decay, were all — if there were no eternal presence pervading and vivifying all, and uniting the many parts into one whole; and in the same manner would the elements of human experience be received at times with disgust, if the same eternal presence were not there to sanctify their influences.

There are some who feel this perpetual presence a restraint; or rather who, when they remember it, imagine that a perpetual consciousness of it would be a restraint. I wonder such do not feel the atmosphere stifling, the light of day oppressive, and the motion of the life-blood a perpetual curse. Such surely imagine that the Divine presence is alike to all, uncongenial to all. They know not that it is tender to the weak, as the downy pillow to the wearied head; animating to the strong, bright to the eagle-eyed, and most awful to the high-minded, to whom the awe of purity is bliss. They know not that when a burst of song comes from young lips, as the sun breaks through the clouds, it is an acknowledgment of the presence of God. They know not that when the hands of the sleeper are folded on his breast, it is a sign that he closed his eyes amidst a blissful sense of security. They mark not on the brow of the thoughtful, in the eye of the pure, in the erect port of the free of soul, the testimony that because God is within them these are what they are. Those who fear and dislike this perpetual presence, ever conceive of God as apart though present. They compare his stability, his ultimate purity, with man's change and progressiveness. But, one and immutable as God surely is in himself, to the experience of man Deity is progressive; and hence it is that

12

the home of the human spirit is in God. The spirits of men are progressive at different rates, so as to preclude permanent companionship or lasting dependence ; but the revelation of Deity is so unintermitting, so exactly apportioned to the discernment of the worshipper, so perfectly congenial to his wants, desires, and hopes, that the repose of dependence may be as entire as the freedom of action which such congeniality inspires. Therefore is it that communion with God becomes more precious as life advances, that devotion changes its character perpetually, while the attributes of its Object are unchangeable. Therefore is it that the aspirations of piety arise in individual minds through every region, from the low desires and fears of the infant, to praise akin to that which ascended from the hills of Galilee.

The devotion which the spirit prompts in Sabbath hours, in the sanctuary of nature, may surely be taken as the highest of which that spirit is capable ; and what now seems to me that highest? It is not petition. I know not what to ask, because I know not the designs of my Father towards myself or others. I have prayed for blessings of every kind for myself and my brethren in the course of my life, and on looking back it seems to me now that there was presumption in such petitions. It will not always appear so ; and when the impulse comes again, I will again yield to it, because the desires of my spirit, from the highest to the lowest, shall ever be poured out to him ; but now, I have all things ; I feel that I shall have all things, and that all men are and shall be blessed to the utmost of their present capacities for blessedness. How full of bliss is life and the world! That child searching for violets on the teeming bank, too busily to observe me — her brother astride on the bough of that breezy tree, looking down into the nest he longs to take — the throng parting from yon distant church-door over the dewy meadows — I myself, half dazzled by these twinkling leaves, my spirit flowing like the brimmings of a mossy well — how happy are we all! I cannot form a wish for myself or them. Gratitude, deep, boundless gratitude, swallows up all desires; and the only due expression of this gratitude, the only means of tempering its fervid glow, is a joyful and entire surrender of them and myself to Him who smiles upon our joy. Truly we know not what to pray for as we ought. How low are all temporal desires to us, standing at this moment manifestly in the midst of eternity, when time is a mere abstraction of the reason, and actual existence is all with which the heart has to do! Of spiritual conditions, the apparent evil of some, and the ultimate design of all, we know yet less than of temporal. We only know that all is good. "*Let us be*," is therefore the only petition I can now offer. I know too little of the conditions of being to venture to prescribe them even to my own wishes. In this unconditional surrender merges that impulse of devotion in which a true and indispensable relief is found in some states of the spirit, but which must at some time die away. Confession of sin is the most gracious liberty which many a mourner can exercise. What ease to the oppressed, what a dawn to the benighted, is given, — what a fair and verdant way out of the tangled wilderness is opened by the condescension which invites man to confide his spiritual as well as temporal griefs to Him who alone can understand them! There is in some dark hours, in the dark hours of many years of every one's life, no other refuge from despair or from insensibility, no other support to struggles which, with this support, need never be impotent, no other way to outgrow the necessity which this permission is given to supply. But this necessity must be outgrown. If there are hours even now when we can make an unconditional surrender of our temporal lot, may there not be moments when we can exercise a similar trust respecting our spiritual state? Why not taste the perfect

peace of a joyful acquiescence as to both? Why make it a
sin to complain of the evils of the one, and a virtue to complain of the evils of the other? These evils, while evils,
we cannot but feel; we ought not to cease to struggle
against; but now — I might as well shudder at this low
black cloud that comes hurrying towards me, as mourn over
any other condition of my being.

While all here is still, as if the breezes had forgotten their
accustomed haunt, how that single elm on the lawn shivers
and stoops, as if an invisible giant were uprooting it for a
trophy! The gust is coming, lighting here and there on the
tree-tops, and rolling blackness and tempest before it. Far
off the commotion begins. How the roar swells as it ap-
proaches, rushing, driving athwart the ivied stems, and
whistling among the tossing boughs above! The terrified
birds come fluttering each from its domestic tree. How that
boy's light laugh mingles with the uproar as he rocks fearlessly in his lofty seat! He feels not more than I that these
are tokens of wrath around us, or that these heavy drops
are signs of Nature's sorrow. Human joy overflows in
tears; and why should not the oppression of her solemn joy
be removed in like manner? What a brimming shower!
and the sun already gleaming again on the thousand trick-
lings from the shining leaves which refuse to retain their
liquid burden! The whole grove glitters as if beneath the
spray of Niagara. In a moment the chill is gone, and but
for the pearls which gem those pendant crowns, the gust and
the shower might be supposed the dream of a spring noon,
the creation of preceding thoughts.

Thus may end, thus will end, the storms of the spirit;
and in bright and harmonious praise, like that which greets
my senses now, shall man bear his part when the vicissitudes
of his early day are passed. Praise, praise alone shall be
the end, as it ought to be the beginning, of devotion, though

praise must change and advance its character as the mind of the worshipper advances. The infant's first communion should be praise. He knows, or ought to know, no fear; he knows, or ought to know, no want: for what then should he petition? When he learns that others have wants, he begins to petition for them, and in time for himself. When he becomes a subject of conscience, he is led to confession and to intercession. All this time, praise should be the beginning and end of his communion: praise, first for the low good of which alone he is sensible; then for each new glimpse of glory which his opening vision reveals, till his thanksgivings reach the ends of the earth, and compass the starry heavens. Of the more sacred heights and depths which teem with realities instead of shadows, he knows not yet, nor has learned to praise creative and preserving power as manifested in the external creation for its true grandeur and ulterior purposes. Of the spiritual creation he knows nothing till long after he has been accustomed to adore the Maker of unnumbered worlds. When the rich mysteries of the sublimer creation become dimly discerned, he petitions less fervently for external good. As they wax clearer, his fears perish, his desires subside, his hopes pass through perpetual mutations till they become incorruptible, and his praise is of a kindred nature, however far inferior to that of the unseen world. He thenceforth regards the moving heavens only as they send their melodies through the soul; the forms of the earth only as they are instinct with life; and, no longer calling inanimate forms to witness his praises, he appeals from the infant on his bosom to the archangel who suspends new systems in the furthest void for sympathy in his adoration of the Father of his spirit. — Of higher subjects of praise man knows not, nor can conceive. It is bliss enough to discern the end of human worship, (in kind, if not in

12*

degree,) and in some rare moments, in occasional glimpses of a celestial Sabbath, to reach it.

O that our earthly Sabbaths could bear something of this character! But as long as so many ranks of mind join in its services, these services must be too high for some, and too low for others. Blessed is the season to multitudes, and holy its rites to innumerable worshippers. But its benefits are of a specific kind; its devotion is peculiar, and can in no degree supply the place of private communion. Alas, then, for those who join not in its rites; and alas also for those who look not beyond its rites! Strange, that any should turn away coldly from the divinely-kindled altar, where multitudes are thronging to cast in their incense, and returning with the reflection of its glory in their faces! Yet more strange that any should avoid the still solitude where the fount of this glory welleth up for ever!

Surely there shall be solitary communion hereafter as there is on earth, a peculiar devotion of the inmost spirit, to which there can be no requisites of outward circumstances. Here, while good men communicate by heart and hand, while the pure bring to the light the movements of the spirit, there is a tacit reserve, there are workings which are known by each to exist in the other, but which are testified by no sign, and could be revealed by no such testimony. Hereafter, though that which is now an intermitting refreshment shall be then the prime element of being, there will surely be, amidst the most perfect congeniality, the most entire sympathy in a common joy, a silent recognition in each of a treasure of incommunicable peace.

SABBATH MUSINGS.

III.

A DEATH CHAMBER.

THIS weary watch! In watching by the couch of another there is no weariness; but this lonely tending of one's own sick heart is more than the worn spirit can bear. What an age of woe since the midnight clock gave warning that my first day of loneliness was beginning, — to others a Sabbath, — to me a day of expiation! — At last, yonder beacon, with its revolving lights, begins to grow red and rayless before the dawn. Now it looks more like what it is, — made up of earthly fires. Waxing, waning, waxing again without intermission in the perfect silence, they have been distracting to my sense; they have seemed conscious; they have been like spies upon my privacy. — That leaden sea! If storms would rouse it, and scatter that fleet which is just visible, gliding in an unbroken line, like a troop of spirits retiring before the dawn; if the trees in the churchyard could stoop above the tombs, instead of standing like spectres, side by side; if even the hour would strike, I could cast off something of this load.

But shall it ever be cast off? All is dull, dreary, chill before me till I also can escape to the region where there is no bereavement, no blasting root and branch, no rending of the heart strings. What is it to me now that our freedom there springs from oppression here; our joy there from our sorrow here? What is it to me in the midst of this all-pervading, thrilling torture, when all I want is to be dead? The future is loathsome, and I will not look upon it. — The past too, which it breaks my heart to part with, what has it been? It might have been happy, if there is such a thing as happiness; but — I myself embittered it at the time, and for ever. — What a life of folly has mine been! Multitudes of sins now rise up in the shape of besetting griefs. Looks of rebuke from those now in the grave: thoughts which they would have rebuked if they had known them: moments of anger, of coldness; sympathy withheld when looked for: repression of its signs through selfish pride; and worse, far worse even than this. . . . . . All comes over me now. O! if there be pity, if there be pardon, let it come in the form of insensibility; for these long echoes of condemnation will make me desperate.

If it were not for this, bereavement might be borne. The loneliness would not be perpetual, for the departed would incessantly return to revive the innocent mourner with a familiar presence and animating words; — an ancient presence, and words of transient breath, but still and ever real. But are any thus innocent? Was there ever human love unwithered by crime, — by crimes of which no law takes cognizance but the unwritten, everlasting laws of the affections? Many will call me thus innocent: many will speak of consolation springing from the past: the departed breathed out thanks and blessing, and I felt them not then as reproaches. If, indeed, I am only as others, shame, shame on the impurity of human affections! Or rather, alas for the infirmity of the human heart! for I know not that I could love more than I have loved. — Since the love itself is wrecked, let me gather up its relics, and guard them more tenderly, more steadily, more gratefully. This seems to open glimpses of peace. O grant me power to retain them all, — the light and music of emotion, the flow of domestic wisdom and chastened mirth, the life-long watchfulness of benevolence, the solemn utterance of prayer, the thousand, thoughts. . . . . Are these gone in their reality? Must I forget them as all others forget?

Just now I longed for sound, and it comes all too soon. The twittering swallows are up to see the first sunbeam touch the steeple. The beacon revolves no longer: it goes out, and the sun is come. What a flood of crimson light! It mocks me, for there is no one to look on it with me. If it were any day but this, I should see life in the fields. Yesterday at this hour, the mower was beneath the window; and as he whetted his scythe, the echoes gave back the sound cheerily to the watcher and the watched after dreary hours, which yet were bright compared with this. To-morrow I shall see the haymakers in the field; but now the high grass is undisturbed by scythe or breeze. The morning breezes seem to be subject to the Sabbath. The gossamer shines, but does not gleam. I will look no more, for all is too bright for the desolate of heart.

Was it thus with the mourners who went out towards dawn on the first day of the week? Not knowing what that day should bring forth, did the golden sunrise of Judea strike into them a prophetic joy, or spread a heavy pall upon their hopes? How eloquent is the silence of that tale respecting the feelings of the mourners, and their transmutations into opposite feeling! The dreary Sabbath is passed over without notice; but how wretched must have been its uncertainty,— the utter irreconcilableness of the past with the present, the war between devoted affections and disappointed hopes, between the imperishable conviction of the fidelity of the departed, and the inexplicable failure of all expectations connected with him! The Sabbath rites must have been cold and dry, and all a blank where Jesus was not. Yet not wholly a blank; for they could mourn with one another, and search together for some interpretation of the promises of God which should restore their shaken trust.—Then, the next day, what shame that their trust had been shaken; what a bright recognition of design; what knowledge, what

wisdom to have gained in a day!—Yet I have sometimes
thought that we are more privileged in looking back on that
day,—the brightest star in the firmament of time—than
they in seeing it arise out of the chaos of their emotions.
We have a clearer understanding of the whole event, a less
tumultuous strife of passions; we are capable of a calmer exercise of faith; we have a knowledge of the results; so that, if
we loved Jesus as they loved him . . . . but we do not thus
love him: the love is of a different kind; and if I were to
see *my* departed one,—that insensible, wasted form—
standing before me as it has been wont to stand, with whom
would I exchange my joy? Strange! that I never understood the story of the Resurrection till now.

Why, knowing what I did, from the beginning, of death
and sorrow, their immediate pressure and ultimate design,
was I thus slow in understanding? Why, having been early
and perpetually warned, was I so unprepared; why were my
anticipations so utterly inadequate? Night after night for
years have we together talked of death as we stood looking
up into the blue vault; morn after morn for years have we
looked on those green mounds, and chosen in imagination
between a grave in the turf and a grave in the deep; a grave
within domestic bounds and a grave in foreign lands. Long
has each meditated survivorship: often has each acknowledged that heart-searching grief was an element of peace
which ought to be welcomed; an impulse of the spirit whose
reaction must be joy. Constantly have we watched for it:
anxiously did the one give warning that it was at hand;
faithfully did the other promise that it should be calmly
borne. But now,—how is it? The spirit is wholly infirm;
the will paralyzed; the judgment swayed from its balance.
It is either thus, or my estimate of all things has hitherto
been false. How shall strength or peace arise out of a ruin
like this?—Hush, impious doubts! Who can understand

the things of the spirit but He who made the spirit? And am I even now without evidence that my former, my firmer faith was right? Has no strength, no peace visited my thoughts since the dawn first broke? Have I not been reminded of the Resurrection?

If the remembrance of one event can thus soothe, may not a long series of experiences communicate peace? Insignificant in comparison as each circumstance may be, must it therefore be weak in its influences? God himself is the life of all influences. It is not possible then to lose all; and however the structure of happiness may be overthrown, the materials remain to be built up again. And not necessarily in a different form. If it were so, I would say, "Let them lie. I will sit for evermore among the ruins:" but the same structure may again arise, less bright, less beautiful, but a fit retreat for the remembrances and devotions of the spirit. It may be found an ungrateful mistake to suppose that there is no alternative between remediless grief and a new and uncongenial good. — What are the elements of the deepest earthly peace? Influences from one beloved, the conscious spirit on which they act, and the eternal benignant presence through which they operate. If that presence should become more evidently benignant through compassion for the mourner, if the mourner should, through a new experience, become more apt to discern invisible things, and to rely on a veiled protection, should the inner soul thus become more richly endowed, the shadows of the past may have as great power as their substance ever had, and the spirit of human love may ever be nigh, invested with a majesty worthy to succeed the lustre of its mortal days. Thus may the dreams of the night be to me instead of communings face to face beneath the stars; and the whispers of holy thoughts which breathe from those sacred walls may be as animating as the sympathies which led us to the house of God in company.

And what shall all these things be to thee who art gone to see at a glance what I must discover with pain and doubt? While my utmost hope is to attain peace through the peace of former days, what is thy hope? Shall not thy joy arise from the joy we have known together? O, if it is thus, our sympathy is not dissolved, even for a time! I will do as thou. If to thee the past and future are as one, I will not cleave to the one and abhor the other. If to thee the universe is open to go whither thou wilt, I will not refuse to learn its most thrilling mysteries; I will not grovel while thou art on the wing. I will meet thee in the deepest recesses of the conscience, where we have never yet ventured together. I will meet thee on the highest summit of hope on which we have hitherto dared to fasten our gaze. But shall we not oftenest meet in the region which lies behind? When we first entered it together, was it not with the knowledge that every future path would lead us back to it again; that, however spiritualized we might find it at each return, it would be our own familiar home for ever? Surely it must be thus with the mortal life of every one. Jesus himself must surely thus resort perpetually to the period of probation, finding the scene irradiated with the glory of his faith; his companions made meet for his friendship through the purification of his gospel; and his most deadly foes made benignant through the softening influences of his own compassion. Can I not spare thee to attain a power like this, when I myself hope to attain it also? Shall I say that I have lost thee when we are carrying on the same work, through power granted at the same time by Him who worketh in us alike? We must exalt our hope, we must spiritualize our being; thou in heaven, I for a while on earth.

What was it that I doubted so painfully a while ago? Not the fact that the dead arise. If in the moonlight I had seen a winged one couched at the foot of each of those graves; if

in the sunrise, I had seen the tombs teeming with shadowy
forms, if in the butterflies which now hover over the turfy
hillocks I had seen, not an emblem, but an embodying of a
departed spirit, I could not be more sure than I now am that
death is only an eclipse, and not an extinction; and that this,
like every other mystery of nature, shall be revealed and explained when we who survive shall be fit for the revelation.
Man has seen how, by an invisible hand, the black shadow
has been drawn over the radiant cope above, unnoticed till an
answering shadow crept over the earth; and how the sun has
ever shone forth again, according as the voice of nature promised. Man has also witnessed how a like impenetrable
shadow has stolen upon the light of his life, and cast a chill
on whatever drank in its beams; and how, from behind this
obscurity, Being has again shone forth in renewed glory,
according as the word of God had been passed. The same
hand wrought in the firmament and in the chamber of death;
the same voice spoke in the whispers of nature and in the
silence of the empty sepulchre. This has never been, this
can never be, my doubt.

Was it the benignity of Providence that I doubted? — of
that Providence which made all that I have reverenced, and
gave all that I have loved? It was benignity which so organized that now slumbering being that all influences wakened up its harmonies; that all tended to expand, to refine,
to ennoble it till, but a few hours since, it retired to await
its welcome into a new rank. It was benignity which
led that spirit high and deep, and poured over it a flood of
joy, which bathed every scene of nature, every circumstance
of life, in its own vitality. And, O! it was benignity which
made all these mine; which made to each of us the otherwise incommunicable revelation of what the human spirit is;
which sanctioned this revelation by the fact, proved to me
to-day — that what spirits are to one another they must be

13

for ever. How benign has been the superintendence of our
life!—our first meeting, our mutual pleasures leading to
mutual pains, the stirring sympathies, the calm confidence,
the incalculable aids, the peace pervading all—how benignly
have all these been ordered, while somewhat of the same has
blessed every living soul,—while they who bear the throne
of God have interchanged high thoughts, and playmates have
caressed each other in the green shade! With a touch, merciful as his who had compassion on the blind, have our eyes
been opened upon the busy world of spirits, that we may see,
at first dimly, but continually with a stronger evidence, under
what aspect all things shall at length appear when the last
film shall melt away. What benignity breathes from even
the outward forms I look upon,—the churchyard, where
repose abides in the topmost boughs of the trees as well as
on the tombs in their shade;—in the fields, where no pas-
senger comes to break the Sabbath stillness;—in the sea,
where a hundred vessels lie becalmed, as if to admonish the
troubled spirit in which anxious thoughts are tossing to and
fro! "I will give thee rest," saith the gospel. "I will tend
thy rest," saith the same voice, speaking through nature.—
I am at rest; nature shall tend my rest. I will go forth;
and beneath the shadow of the fragrant limes, within hearing
of the lapsing sea, and where human consolations are offered
so that I can accept them,—unobtrusively, in the congregated epitaphs,—I will pay the worship meet for this Sabbath of the soul.

SABBATH MUSINGS.

IV.

A HIGH HILL SIDE.

"We spend our years as a tale that is told." Such is the fact on which a voice enlarged this day in yonder church. It is a fact, as that voice proved, in pointing out the indolence, the frivolity, the perverseness, of man: but I would now regard the fact under a different aspect. Round me is the scenery, within ken are the materials, within myself is the sequence, of a magnificent tale, whose aims are higher than vain amusement, and whose catastrophe can never pass away from the mind and be forgotten. Widely, almost illimitably, the prospect spreads, and my sense is well nigh bewildered when I regard it in detail. This heathy plot on which I lie, the ravine beside me, with its pines slanting over the water course, the craggy ridge behind, which crests these hills, are of themselves enough to satisfy the meditative spirit through many a long summer's day; and what have I besides? I follow with my eye the steep chalk path by which I ascended, and see how it intersects many a sheep-track on the down, winds through many a field, diverges to farms, to cottages, and to yonder bright reach of the stream, till it is lost at the churchyard stile. And this is but a small section of the landscape. The dwellings clustered round the grey steeple show but as one abode when compared with the lordly mansion near; and many such mansions rear their graceful fronts amidst their lawns and woods, glorious beneath the sloping sunbeams. Further and yet further spreads this vast plain, with its one distant eminence, behind which hangs the smoke of the city. Its cathedral towers alone stand out from the cloud; and thus I have peaceful tidings of the inhabitants, — that they are dwellers beside a domestic hearth, and worshippers in a Christian temple. Beyond, the boundary which separates earth and sky is not discernible. Yes, that golden line which brightens every moment as the sun sinks to the horizon, marks where the eye must rest. There is Thames shedding his floods into the main, apparently losing the individuality which is elsewhere perpetually renewed. Is not this indeed the scenery of a magnificent tale? And not only the scenery, but much of the material also? Much of our life is made of matter like this. What would this scene be to an infant? A colored surface, no more extensive, and perhaps less diversified, than the carpet of his nursery. He would stretch out his craving hand to yon burnished flood as to a picture-frame on the walls. He would pass over the moving flocks that speckle the down, as smaller than the butterflies that flit above the heath blossoms on which he lies. I think I can remember something of this; something of the confused notions of distance and proportion under which the world opens upon the young sense : and I do vividly remember the days, when, having surmounted my first ignorance, and learned to guide myself, I was yet in blindness and bondage respecting external things. Then I thought motion was life; for of the spreading influences of life I knew nothing. Then all things seemed rayless, bare, and insulated. I discerned no relation between the woodbine and the bee, the dawn and the upspringing lark, the stirrings of nature and man's sabbath-hymn. Then the rose was trampled under foot when its fragrance had passed away, and the starry cope seemed like a low ceiling under which there was no more than room to breathe. No mystery then floated over the face of things. All was without form, for I dreamed not of proportion; all was void, for I conceived not of purpose; and discerned or felt nothing of spirit moving amidst this chaos. Let none say that the work of creation had no witnesses of a lower rank than the winged ones who stationed themselves round the abyss of space to gaze. Adam may have stepped forth into a formed world; but, save him, every child of humanity has been beckoned by the Creator to come and behold how all things are done, and that all things are good.

But man understands, and therefore may be said to behold this, only long after the Creator's voice has called him out of nothing. His bodily eye and ear are fitly framed; but the light is to him he knows not what, and he hears nothing of the song of the morning stars. When the second great period of his life is come — the opening age of mystery — he becomes sensible that the light must proceed from some source, and turns himself this way and that to look for it. There has till now been utter silence; but at length a wandering breath of music reaches his ear, and rouses him to a new experience. It comes again and again, and wakens answering harmonies. Must he be mute? He puts forth his voice and finds an answer, and thenceforth knows that there may be communion with what is unseen. He has now begun to prepare for his entrance upon the spiritual world. He is like the young solitary native of a prison. He wakes up and beholds bright reflections on his dungeon walls; and when he has found the crevice by which they enter, he knows by their perpetual change that there is something beyond. He turns an eager ear when melody also comes; and his response is not the less joyful because he knows not yet that his deliverance is at hand. — This is but the opening of the tale; but does it not stimulate to know more?

When the young captive comes forth into the living world, he is not left unguarded and untaught. The teachers appointed by his Maker — Man and Nature — await him at his prison door. The one seats him at the domestic board, guides him where he may witness the traffic, the strife, the coöperation,

13*

ever going on among his brethren; points out to him the sources of sympathy and the causes of contention; unveils to him
somewhat of the machinery of society; and, when he is
harassed and alarmed at what he beholds, leads him to the
sabbath-temple. There his spirit is soothed, but not satisfied.
He hears harmony, but it is in an unknown tongue. He
prefers the consolations of nature, who appoints him a couch
in her turfy vales, or brings the breezes to meet him on the
mountain top, or casts a dewy glance upon him from the
morning cloud. She calls him off from his obstinate questionings for a time by exercising him in the handiwork of
her servants. She bids him fathom her wells, and mark the
growth of her forests, and explore her echoing retreats in the
deep. Thus occupied, he is at peace for a time, but not for
long. He still asks, — and the more earnestly day by day —
"Why is all this, and what is its end?" He cannot discover this for himself. As he walks among his elders, he finds
one wiser, one richer, one more powerful than another. Some
are serene, some are troubled, some are joyous; but there
seems no ultimate purpose in all this diversity, and he soon
discerns that one lot awaits them all. They disappear, one
by one, and are seen no more. He questions nature concerning their fate, and conjures her to interpret to him the
language of the sanctuary, in which alone his other guide,
Man, will reply to his doubts. He is led to the churchyard,
where man and nature meet, — the one to shed tears, the
other to scatter flowers. He discerns a smile amidst those
tears, and sees how the motionless chrysalis comes forth
fluttering on radiant wings from amidst those flowers, and a
new hope unfolds within his breast.

His guides had often spoken to him of one who should
come to teach him greater things than any he had yet conceived; and now that the preparation is complete, this
exalted teacher appears with a commission from on high to

make all things clear. Christ comes to finish the work of
preparation for immediate communion with God. To teach
him the *history* of communion, he leads the wandering pupil
through the land of promise, — by the tents of the patriarchs,
by the tabernacle in the wilderness, over the passage of Jor-
dan, and through the cities of Israel, up to the metropolitan
throne of God's anointed, and even to the threshold of the
holy of holies; and thence to the mountain solitudes of
Galilee, and to the cave of the rock where the fount of immortality was first laid open to the day. To teach his charge
the *mode* of communion, he leads him from beholding the
infant reposing on his father's bosom to listen at the portals
of heaven to the united voices of the celestial hierarchy
which sing of immortality. And now the most perplexing
doubts of the spirit are solved. The foundling knows himself to be an heir, and has seen his inheritance, — remotely
indeed, but distinctly. He sees that he is being educated,
and to what end, and can thenceforth exercise his privilege
of coöperating with God. — The tale passes on, but does not
its interest deepen?

The pupil is now arrived at a new stage. He has learned
much, he has discovered something; he must now originate.
And here, alas! is the boundary line which our present state
of social imperfection imposes as that beyond which the
multitude may not pass. Fain would those to whom Providence has vouchsafed such privileges as from their nature
appear designed for universality, enjoy the sympathy of all
their race in their own best pleasures. Fain would the
solitary muser amid the hills believe that the dwellers above
and around him thought as he thinks, and felt as he feels.
But it cannot be. The more I watch what is doing in this
abode beside me, and the more distinctly the tones of its
inmates reach me, the more certain I am that, though
blessed, it is not with the highest kind of blessing; and that

this Sabbath eve, so full of solemn joy to some, is to them only the close of a day of rest. What an abode it is! If I did not know it to have been prepared for the luxury of those who seek the pleasures of nature in company, I should have imagined it built for the retreat of the philosopher. If I did not know it to be the charge of a peasant's family, I should have looked for an inhabitant of a different class — for a world-wearied or nature-loving recluse. How its bold front springs abruptly from the rock, while its projecting thatch is made to send the summer rain pattering among the pebbles far below! How snugly is it sheltered by the larch-planta-tion on either side, and its wall-flowers — is there any other place where they grow so abundantly? The rock is tufted with them in every crevice; they spring from every ledge, and fringe every projection. And what are the dwellers in this summer-house; the wood-ranger, and his wife and babe! They look happy, but they are heedless of what is before their eyes. They have possessed themselves of the best window, as if it were their Sunday privilege to monopolize the pleasures which their superiors eagerly seek on every other day. But what avails their privileged seat to them? That man's brow is such as should betoken high capabili-ties; yet, with this scene before him, he amuses himself with provoking the bayings of his mastiff. What mother, with her infant in her lap, can be insensible to maternal cares? Yet there is one who heeds not her babe, and who has no such intelligence in her wandering gaze as might account for the neglect. Why should not these, pupils, like the wise, of nature and of man, bred up, like the wise, in the know-ledge of the gospel, feel the full beauty and solemnity of a scene like this? Nature has been ready to do her part; the gospel can never fail; it is man who has stinted what he ought to have cherished, and perverted the energies which it was his office to control. It is through evil social influences that the eyes of such as these are turned from beholding the stars when, as now, they first glimmer through the twilight, and that their ears are closed to the soothing tones of the night winds, as they come hither from their rovings over land and sea.

It is the crime of society, also, that evils exist, compared with which this insensibility is virtue. In that shadowy wood below, there was done, but a few days since, an act whose guilt and agony made the place for the moment a hell. The murder of a child, for the sake of the purse he carried, is a crime whose atrocity and utter folly alike show that society has neglected its duty of instructing every one that is born into it in the purposes and means of living. It shows, not what some tell us, that man is disposed to guilt from birth, but that he has energies which are all-powerful for good or for evil; and thus the more daring the crime, or the more atrocious from the slightness of its motive, the stronger is the presumption that the perpetrator might have held an exalted rank in the moral hierarchy, if all its members had fulfilled their part. As it is, there is to the meditative, a strange mingling of hope and mourning in glancing over the human interests which abide within a region like that before me; — in perceiving what has been done, and sighing for what might be done, for its inhabitants. How wide their diversity of interests and occupations! There are aristocratical assemblages in these lordly abodes, and family gatherings in the farms and cottages. Wearied children are slowly going homewards through the fields; and in the city, thousands are collected for worship within their own dwellings, whose lights begin to twinkle through the darkness, or in the churches or meeting-houses, in which the gospel is spoken of according to the varying conceptions of various minds, and ever appears to the attentive observer another and yet the same. Again; there is a disagreement

between the apparent and the real occupation of many.
There are idlers in the churches, and worshippers who lie in
apparent indolence on the turfy heights.   There are world-
lings whose souls are vexed with care while they speak of
the day as a season of rest; and there are lovers of their
race who find their best repose in toilsome works of charity.
These are all pupils of man, and, to some extent, of nature;
but, alas! how bounded has been her benignant influence;
and as for the gospel, there is at least one — the murderer —
who knows nothing of it; and thousands who misconceive
its objects, and pervert its energies.   Alas! how much remains to be done before the tale which my meditation has
unfolded shall become the true history of more than a few!
How long must it be before every man may grow wise by
other means than imitation, and the mere reception of wisdom from his kind, and may have power to originate!

It is true that all wisdom is but discovery.   The sublimest
dreams of the loftiest imagination are but the exhibition of
relations which existed before.   Yet we may speak of origi-
nation when the effort to conceive is made from any other
impulse than the direct influence of man.

The ranger has left off teasing his mastiff, and is employed, as I fancy he was never employed before, gazing at the
heavens through the large telescope which he has hitherto
probably regarded merely as a machine for making visible
the vessels on the Thames.   If his own curiosity had led
him to use it by night, as he has seen others use it by day,
I should have classed him many degrees higher than I can
now do; but he has not even varied his mode of imitation.
There is a friend at his elbow, wiser than himself, who has
taught him a new application of a power with which he has
long been familiar, and has exhibited to him a vision far
more grand than the amplest meeting of the waters on which
the moon has ever shone down.   It is a fit employment for

a Sabbath eve to rouse up some fresh energy in a torpid mind, to lay open a new page of nature's radiant book. I well remember the emotions attendant on such a vision. I remember the first full view of a resplendent planet insulated in the purple depths. I remember the new perceptions, the palpable roundness, the peculiar silvery light, its evident but invisible suspension in space, and the effects of motion in perdurable silence. I remember the breathless emotions springing from the blending of old and new conceptions. I know nothing analogous to it but the discovery in solitude of a new truth; and the effect of both is alike thrilling to the spirit which discerns equally through the mental and the corporeal eye. How resplendent is the palpable reality of a mighty principle with which other principles, and systems of principles, are connected in an unquestionable but as yet undiscerned union! How stupendous is the conception that a new region of life is thus won out of nothing; and how awful the work of watching its progression in the vast circle of which the Creator himself constitutes the unity! It is my hope to be permitted, in the days of my immortality, to overtake the planets at will: and, while thrilled with the perception of the perfect fitness of their frame, to look back on worlds in the process of formation. But more vivid is my expectation that I shall pass hither and thither in the spiritual universe, empowered to apprehend truth after truth; and, on the way, to discern from afar how the elements of the moral creation are gathered together, and organized and vivified by creative power, as they are sent forth on their everlasting way.

Would that these analogous enjoyments might be speedily the portion of all, so that the eye which is made for seeing, and the mind for comprehending, should be so directed as that the spirit should be illuminated by both! This time must come. Day by day the life of the spirit is matured, as the years of man's mortality pass away, and as a heart-stirring tale proceeds to its climax. When the mind has strength to pursue its own discoveries, high revelations come more frequently and familiarly, before which its ancient ignorance stands abashed, while its new-born innocent impulses exult. Prayer becomes the equable exercise of all its faculties, holiness the habit of the spirit, and beneficence of the life. His immortality is then the primary attribute of the man. Upon it all his designs are based; from it all his actions proceed; by it his inward and outward being are alike sanctified. Then his death becomes important, chiefly with a reference to others; for the most essential part of his transit to eternity is already made. Not only is the necessary preparation completed, but its high purposes are already anticipated. He has entered on a purely spiritual life, and though he yet wears a human form, and appears among common men as one of them, he has powers which they must wait to attain, and will undergo little change but in his visible form, when he enters into the cloud which waits to receive him out of their sight.

Are there such on the earth, and where? I know not if there be; but I know that there might be. I know that it is no dream which has entranced my sense; it is a vision, and not a dream. It is a vision of that which shall be done, if, indeed, it be not at this moment fulfilled in some bright region of some Christian land. It is the winding up of that tale which the years of our life unfold. These are the messengers of God, commissioned thus to speak to such as will hear. One by one they approach to take up the narrative, and leave no pause. When their circle is completed, their swelling chorus of thanksgiving on man's behalf visits and cheers the contemplative spirit that keeps watch beside the sepulchre.

I will rejoice, therefore, not only in the holy repose of this star-lit plain, but in the destiny of those who are watching or slumbering in its dwellings. There may yet be presences in yonder wood which may sanctify it from the defilements of murder. The time may come when an infant may sleep at midnight in its shades as securely as the cushat in its native tree. The time may come when the hewers of wood and the drawers of water may prize the Sabbath repose of the body, chiefly because it aids the activity of the mind. Let me trust that even now the tumults of passion have been stilled, the intrusion of low cares forbidden, as the silent night descended upon every threshold; that there are no stirrings but those of piety and love,—of the wakeful spirit that prolongs its Sabbath devotions, or of the mother above the pillow of her child.

SABBATH MUSINGS.

V.

A DESERTED GARDEN.

MELANCHOLY ever attends upon the contemplation of transition, whether the transition relates to an external or an internal state, whether it involves progression or decay. If Paul could have seated himself on the unroofed shrine of the Ephesian Diana, sighs for its fallen grandeur might have mingled with his praises for the overthrow of its ancient superstitions. If John could have returned from Patmos to lay his bones at the foot of the holy mountain, he would have wept over the rank grass of the temple courts, and the blackened rafters of the secret chambers, while he gloried in the fulfilment of the promises. From the same cause, it is

14

natural that the bride should linger on the threshold of her native home, and that the most devoted martyr should stoop to the fading flowers at his feet, while the amaranth crown is within his reach. From the same cause, there must have been melancholy mingled with the holy triumphs of Jesus in every stage of his progression, if we may judge from our analogous experience. In the transitions of opinion and emotion by which we are instructed in our destiny, we are each led up into a solitude where we must struggle with our longings, our regrets, our fears; and however triumphant may be the issue, there is need of ministerings from above to recompense the conflict through which a state of higher responsibility is attained.

Nor is the feeling lessened when the transition is the subject of retrospect instead of present experience; and it is increased when the tendencies to change in the outward and inward world do not accord. Thus do I learn from the emotions of this hour. To stand in the same scene with an altered mind, makes us recognise the fulfilment of our child-ish desire to carry the same consciousness into alternating states of being: but this is less strange than to mark decay among the ancient materials of our thought, while the thought itself is proceeding in the growth of its immortality. If this garden had been what it was in the days when my spirit was weak in the infancy of its faith, it would have roused many emotions to look at it now with new eyes, to ponder it in another mood: but it is far more touching to feel that the external as well as the internal scene is another and yet the same, while the one tends to desolation, and the other to a richer production of its fruits.

How choice a retreat for the meditative was this place in former days! How the gay also came to enjoy its bright-ness, and how various were its charms according to the moods of the "many-sided mind!" The open plat where

the shadows of the acacias danced to the music of the breeze,
the lofty beechen covert where small white butterflies chased
each other among the smooth stems, the bank sloping to
the south where the beehives rested, and where fragrant incense went up in the sultry noon, the green walks leading,
one to a parterre, and another to the fish-pond, and a third to
a place more beloved than either, to the nook where the
murmur of waters never ceased, and the urn overflowed perpetually into the cistern below,— how beloved was all this
scene, whether the mower alone was heard whetting his
scythe in the dewy morning, or the voices of sporting children
enlivened it in the broad day, or the wood-pigeon wooed his
mate in the stillness of the evening! Hither I came, day by
day, with eye and ear intent on the beauty, and a spirit alive
to the moving mysteries of the scene, but altogether alien
from its order and repose. While my feet paced its shaven
turf, my thoughts were bewildered in thorny ways. While
I looked on the flower-beds where the glowing roses sprang
up from the dark mould, and no weeds encumbered the
growth of the meanest blossom, my understanding was like
the field of the slothful, where stones disfigure the surface,
and thistles propagate their useless tribe. Then I stood
beside the hives for hours, watching labors which I could
ascertain to be profitable, and daily sought the lark's nest in
the lawn, where I could perceive that natural solicitudes
tended to some attainable end. Then I loved to lie on the
brink of the pond, and angle, speculating on the subservience
of the different ranks of beings to each other, and, utterly
unsatisfied respecting the destiny of all, preferring this humble use of my prerogative of power to the more strenuous
exercise of it in the world. But, amidst the apparent tran-
quillity of my retirements, what tempests were working in the
deeper recesses where none could follow and mark! My
brethren would not have smiled when they saw me going

forth, rod in hand, if they could have known what conflicts
I must encounter in my solitude. The ranger's cheerful
greeting would often have been suppressed, if my countenance had been the index of my thought. I well remember
that the children once stopped to watch me when I was down
upon my face beside the cistern. They supposed me asleep,
and went away on tiptoe. If they had presently overheard
my bursting anguish, they would never again have dared to
approach. And now that the urn is broken, and the cistern
defiled, when the walks are tangled, and the last rose of the
year drops its leaves on the neglected soil, my spirit is at
peace within itself, and at leisure for the mild regrets and
finely shaded emotions which attend the retrospect of transition.

What can be the retribution of guilt, if the horrors of
doubt are what I have felt them? What can be the penalties
of vice, if those of mere ignorance are so agonizing?   And
if it be true that, through impatience of their misery, men
plunge from the lesser evil into the greater, from the flood into
the whirlpool, what voice of execration shall be found strong
enough to curse the human inventions by which the simple
are ensnared into doubt, or the human pride by which they
are despised, or the human malice by which they are condemned, when once they have entered the toils? While, in
my childhood, I ignorantly believed what men had told me
of God, much that was true mixed with much of what I now
perceive to be puerile, or absurd, or superstitious, or impious,
I was at peace with men, and, as I then believed, with God.
But when an experience over which I had no control shook
my confidence in that which I held; when I had discovered
and rejected some of the falsehoods of my creed, and when
I was therefore really wiser than before, the torment began
which was destined well nigh to wrench life from my bosom,
or reason from my brain. Why did I not observe that no

signal from above authorized the infliction? Why, while
suffering for rejecting the dicta of men, did I take their word
for it that the infirmities of the reason were deformities in
the eyes of Him who caused them, and that no better recompense awaited the struggle to see his face than exile to the
outer darkness? I had eyes to see that his sunshine was
spread before me as in the days of my youth, and that he had
written his will, and described his nature, in characters which
it was given to none to forge. I had ears to hear Him as he
called to me from the shades at noon, and instructed me from
above the stars by night. I had an understanding to compass the truths which his messengers brought from him, to
investigate their claims, and interpret their teachings, and
yet I questioned not that God was what men said he was,
and that I deserved at his hand that which I received at
theirs. It was for this impiety that I suffered, and under this
self-incurred bondage that I groaned. I revolted from the
teachings of men, and yet did not freely surrender myself to
those of God; and hence arose my perplexities, and thus is
the anguish of those days accounted for and justified.

That anguish was made more intense by the new and
vivid pleasure which had attended the first stir among my
convictions. Well do I remember the wonder with which I
first listened to a controversy respecting the required nature
and degree of Christian faith, the meditation in my chamber
which followed, and the startling question whose perceived
extent thrilled me with awe, when I witnessed, in that very
hour, the entrance of a new life into the world. I saw beneath my window-sill a swallow's nest, whence the parent
bird cast out the shell from which her young had issued.
" I have learned," thought I, " that the will of God, which
men declare to be told so plainly, is not understood alike by
all. All have the revelation before them, and yet they differ
as to what we have to do, how it is to be done, and what the

14*

consequences are to be. How do I know that I have been
rightly taught respecting the ultimate facts on which the
obligations of duty rest? What do I know more than this
young brood, of whence I came and how I exist, of who is
my Maker, and whether there be indeed a Maker? Here I
am, a living, thinking being, surrounded by forms of beauty,
and organizations of intricate wonders ; but do I really know
more than that these things are; and is it possible to learn
more?" I dreamed of no impiety in these thoughts, and I
enjoyed the first glimpse into a region of speculation whose
vastness was perceived without its gloom. I little thought
that my pleasure was but the sweetness on the edge of the
bitter cup which I was to drain to the very dregs. Yet I
would not that it should have passed from me. Far nobler
is the most humiliating depression of doubt than the false
security of acquiescence in human decisions. Far safer are
the wanderings of a mind which by original vigor has freed
itself from the shackles of human authority, than the apathy
of weak minds which makes them content to be led blindfold
whithersoever their priestly guides shall choose. The happiest lot of all is to be born into the way of truth, to be
placed among those who themselves learn of God, and only
commend their young charge to his teaching: but where,
as in my case, it is not so ordained, the next best privilege is
to be roused to a conflict with human opinions, provided
there is strength to carry it through. Though it be fought
in darkness, in horror, in despair, God is nigh to behold and
aid, and to bid the sufferer repose at length in the light of
his countenance.

Yet none could be found to encounter the conflict if they
had the slightest prescience of its horrors. My former Sabbaths in this place — what infliction in all the records of condemnation could aggravate their misery? The same bell
which now brings the young worshipers tripping over the

green, and calls the old man from among the tombstones, rang then as now; but how differently to my ears! I looked out then from this very alley upon the church porch, where sober greetings are exchanged as the people enter; but with what an agonizing mingling of contempt and envy, of compassion for them and loathing of myself! I might have been among them, but I would not; and yet I coveted what I thought their ignorant repose. I thought of them in prayer, and longed to pray: but how could I? I could not make to myself an idol, and then believe it was a God: and I was as yet unsatisfied that there was One who heareth prayer. I followed with my eye the gay insects that flitted round me, and longed to be, like them, alive and active, but without wish or want. I listened for the song of praise, and felt that I also would adore if I knew whither to refer my adoration, and if I could offer it unmixed. I was oppressed with a sense of the marvellous beauty of the face of things, and the immeasurable might of that which organized them. But what and where was this principle? Could it be reached; could it be worshipped? And how could I adore when I felt in every nerve that all this mighty, this delicate, this beautiful assemblage of creations, was to me but an apparatus of torture? Then I envied the lark as, hushing its warblings, it dropped from its heights into its grassy nest. I longed, like it, to delight in the crimson cloud, and in looking abroad ever the earth at sunrise, without questioning whence came those hues, or to whom belonged the praise of that transcendent architecture. Then I looked on the unfinished labors of the fields and orchards: the shocks in which the sickle was left, the ladder and basket beneath the tree, the remainder of whose burden was to be stripped tomorrow. "Vanity of vanities," thought I. "Other harvest-fields besides the churchyard bear this inscription. Men labor, and gather, and consume, and then labor again till they are themselves consumed. Thus is it with the bee, save that to it labor is thoughtless pleasure, and it has no perception of the aimlessness of its toil. It knows not, as I know, that the best which can befall it is to consume the golden store which it has taken so much time and labor to collect, and to begin with a new season the same round of activity. The toil of men, in like manner, only produces food; food only sustains the life: the life returns to the production of the means of life, till other means are wanted to sustain it which cannot be found; and thus is toil vanity, the fruits of toil are vanity; life is vanity, and death is the vanity of vanities. Why then do we live?" No wonder I then sighed for death, hoping as I did to find by some unknown means a satisfying of my doubts, or a refuge from them. No wonder I dreamed of death by night, and strove to realize the conception of it by day. No wonder I hid my face from the light, and closed my ears to the murmuring waters, while I revolved every imagination I had ever formed of the darkness, and stillness, and immeasurable vastness of death. Yet then was I, perhaps, the most wretched. I could not divest myself of the conviction that my doubts were so many sins. Men told me, and I could not but in part believe, that to want faith was a crime; that misery like mine was but a qualification for punishment; and that every evil of which I now complained would be aggravated hereafter. Alas! what was to become of me, if I could find no rest even in the grave, if the death I longed for was to be only apparent, if the brightness which I found so oppressive here should prove only like the day-spring, in comparison with the glare of the eternal fires amidst which my spirit must stand hereafter? In such moments, feeling that there was no return to the ignorance of the child, or the apathy of common men, I prayed, to whom I knew not, — for madness.

Blessed be God, I was led by another way out of my torment, — a long, and dark, and rugged way, but one on which
are perpetually echoed back the thanksgivings of a spirit
now at peace. If it were not for the mementos around me,
I could not credit how weak had been my reason, how perverted my imagination, or at how low a depth of ignorance
it has pleased the Father to fix the starting point whence the
interminable career of the spirit must begin. I daily feel
that I am still but beginning; that realities are discerned
only in their faintest outlines, and the language of truth
only caught in the most remote of its reverberations. I daily
feel that God is yet to me less than the wisest and tenderest
parent is to the infant who can barely recognise his presence,
— who can rightly refer the voice and the smile, but knows
nothing of any nobler attribute. I feel daily that Christ
has but opened his mission to me, that Life and Death have
only told me whence they come, and that I can but dimly
discern whither they are leading me. But yet, infantine as
is such a state, how much has been achieved, and how intense is my joy in the achievement, and my gratitude for the
discipline under which it has been accomplished! Bear
witness to this, all ye records of the feelings of my darker
time, — of the time when the order and beauty was yours,
and the desolation mine! While nature is drawing a veil
over the ruins of art, and plying her work the more diligently
the longer man is absent, take from me another record of
the things of the spirit. I now see no vanity, though there
is much decay. Though the urn is overthrown, the spring
welleth up to feed the life which flourishes around, and the
foxglove and the bindweed grow where nothing blossomed
before. The cistern is broken, so that the waters escape to
diffuse themselves in the grass; but a new region of life is
opened among the mosses on its brink, and in the damp
nook whence yonder blue dragon-fly came forth. I see not

that there is less beauty in these alleys, because the periwin-
kle has strewed the way with blossomed shoots, or because
the hollyhock has fallen from its support, or because the
decaying leaves are not, like other mementos of mortality,
removed from sight.   The fruit-trees drop their degenerate
produce, to be carried away by the field-mouse or devoured
by birds, and the vine trails its clusters among the rank
grass; but in all this there is no vanity, — no failure of purpose, — no breach of a tacit promise.   According to our
present conceptions, there may be less beauty, — though
even this is doubtful, — but there is more life, and an all-
sufficient end in the influences at work on the human spirit.
I come not here for analogies from which I might derive a
presumptive belief in the truths which I could not formerly
admit.   Those truths I have learned elsewhere on far superior evidence, and by a large variety of means.   This is the
place in which to rejoice in the comparison of what is now
given with what was then withheld : in the conviction that
the Father has nowhere declared his children guilty, because
they have not truly known him, while struggling to obtain
the knowledge, and mourning their own ignorance.   This is
the place in which to retrace the progress from despair
through the various degrees of doubt to hope, to belief, to
assurance, to perpetual rejoicing and devout thanksgiving.
Here, where I once doubted whether I had a Maker, and
whether, if there were such an one, men did any thing but
mock themselves in calling him Father, are the best witnesses of my avowal that I have found these doubts to be
the result of human creeds, as far as they are impious,
and that I have reached, through the very severity of
the discipline, a refuge whence I can never again be
driven forth into the chaos of the elements out of which
my new life has been framed.   Human life has passed away
from this one of its abodes, and the regrets which linger

serve but to confirm my faith in Him who led its dwellers to a far distant and better habitation. And if I could behold the entire earth made into one bright, beautiful garden for the whole race of men to dwell in, and if I could return when all were gone, and wander through its untended shades, I trust I should feel a thoughtful rejoicing in each record of past conflicts, and a solemn gratitude that the passing struggles of an earlier existence are appointed but as an introduction to the vast and indestructible privileges of a maturer state.

SABBATH MUSINGS.

VI.

A HERMIT'S CAVE.

This, then, is the cell consecrated by tradition to the service of God. Around the walls of this cave hangs a sanctity akin to that which hallowed the fastnesses of Judea, after the Saviour had been seen to issue from them. — So think the dwellers below, who gaze with awe when the misty curtain of the morning is drawn up from its shadowy entrance: and if they come hither to see where their saint spread his heathy couch, or shed for half a century his penitential tears, it is with somewhat of the same reverence that the youthful Hebrew convert must have felt when he overtook the Teacher, reposing himself in the clefted rock from the noonday heats, or watching the thunder cloud as it descended upon the valleys. — The feeling is not to be derided in the one case more than in the other, since it is only misplaced, and not factitious or absurd. The error relates to the object, and not to the emotions with which it is contemplated. If I believed, like the priest-ridden flock below, that their saint was as lofty in soul as Paul, and as pure as John, I would come in the calmness of reason to worship where he had worshipped, and meditate where he had reposed. As it is, the difference between them and myself is, that the same emotion flows in another direction, and that I discern a kindred sanctity where they look not for it.

The place was not ill-chosen by the holy man, if the circumstances could but have been adapted to that highest worship — the service of the life. All the natural objects around breathe praise; and the chorus might have been complete if the mighty voice of the affections had not been dumb. The ceaseless dash of the waterfall on a wintry day like this, the bleating of the flocks in spring, and the shepherd's call coming up from beside the fold, the flapping of wings when the eagle darts into the summer sky, and the anthems of the autumn winds, these are all praise; but they are no more than inarticulate melodies till the concords of human spirits are joined to them, converting them into the native language of angels. The lamps of this temple are also many and beautiful; the icicles that glitter in the cave's mouth; the rainbow that comes and goes as the sunbeams touch the spray and vanish; the mists of the valley that roll beneath the silver moon, and the tinted clouds that sail around her — these in their turn light up this temple; but they are shifting, flickering, expiring flames; and there is yet wanting the altar of the human heart, on which alone a fire is kindled from above to shine in the faces of all true worshippers for ever. Where this flame, the glow of human love, is burning, there is the temple of Christian worship, be it only beside the humblest village hearth: where it has not been kindled, there is no sanctuary; and the loftiest amphitheatre of mountains, lighted up by the ever-burning stars, is no more the dwelling-place of Jehovah than the temple of Solomon before it was filled with the glory of the Presence. The devotee who retired hither to extinguish his human affections was therefore like that son of Aaron (if such there were) who took up his abode in the courts of Jehovah when their doom was sealed, vainly trusting that the " Let us go hence" had not been said; for ever building himself an abode among the crumbling ruins; for ever collecting on the altar the ashes which the bleak winds must for ever disperse. How impious such unbidden service! How mournful such fruitless toil!

Yes! Love is, worship, authorized and approved: and various as the degrees of love, is the appointed nature of the service, and the proportionate intensity of the devotion which man owes to God. The infant who cherishes the fledgling in her bosom, may claim sisterhood with the wakeful Samuel: and they who see the sportive boy with his finger on his lips beside the cradle, are slow of heart if they perceive not that he is "about his Father's business." Many are the gradations through which this service rises till that is reached on which God has bestowed his most manifest benediction, on which Jesus smiled at Cana, but which the devotee presumes to decline. Not more express were the ordinances of Sinai than the divine provisions for wedded love; never was it more certain that Jehovah benignantly regarded the festivals of his people, than it is daily that he appointed those mutual rejoicings of the affections which need but to be referred to Him to become a holy homage. Whence arose the passion, if He did not bid it spring to birth? Why is there happiness in it, if He has not smiled upon it? Whence is its might, for good or for evil, if it did not derive its vigor from Him? And why does its matchless power ever achieve the loftiest and purest aims, if it be not guided by His hand, and obedient to His voice? Yet, in the face of these evidences of divinity,

15

in the absence of all the intimations which here and there undoubtedly exist, that service of a different kind is required of individuals, in the midst of the proofs which every where abound of what love can do and bear for the sake of God and man, there have been many who pronounce common that which God has purified, and reject or disdain that which He has proffered and blessed. — How ignorant must such be of the growth of that within! How unobservant of what passes without! Or, if not so, yet worse; how mistaken in their views of the Father of spirits, and of the providence by which he ministers to them! Could such have been with me at the scene of which my heart is yet full, could they have watched as I have the course of that love which, after many troubles, has found its rest in marriage, they would no longer — and yet perhaps they would still doubt; for similar evidence has — blessed be God! — always been before men's eyes, to convince the teachable of the wisdom of His purposes through the benignity of His ordinances.

Marriage is an occasion on which none refuse to sympathize. Would that all were equally able and willing to understand! Would that all could know how, from the first flow of the affections till they are shed abroad in all their plenitude, the purposes of their creation become fulfilled. They were to life, like a sleeping ocean to a bright, but barren and silent shore. When the breeze from afar wakened it, new lights began to gleam, and echoes to be heard; rich and unthought of treasures were cast up from the depths; the barriers of individuality were broken down; and from henceforth, they who choose may "hear the mighty waters rolling evermore." Would that all could know how, by this mighty impulse, new strength is given to every power; how the intellect is vivified and enlarged; how the spirit becomes bold to explore the path of life, and clear-sighted to discern its issues. Higher, much higher things than these are done

even in the early days of this second life, when it is referred
to its Author, and held at his disposal. Its hopes and fears,
some newly-created, some only magnified, are too tumultuous to be borne unaided. There is no rest for them but in
praise or in resignation; and thus are they sanctified, and
prayer invigorated. Thus does human love deepen the divine; thus does a new earthly tie knit closer that which
connects us with heaven; thus does devotedness teach devotion. Never did man so cling to God for any thing
which concerns himself, as for the sake of one he loves better than himself. Never is his trust so willing as on behalf of one whom he can protect to a certain extent, but
no further. None can so distinctly trace the course of
Providence as they who have been led to a point of union
by different paths; and none are so ardent in their adoration
as they who rejoice that that Providence has led them to
each other. To none is life so rich as to those who gather
its treasures only to shed them into each other's bosom; and
to none is heaven so bright as to those who look for it
beyond the blackness and tempest which overshadow one
distant portion of their path. Thus does love help piety;
and as for that other piety which has humanity for its object — must not that heart feel most of which tenderness has
become the element? Must not the spirit which is most
exercised in hope and fear be most familiar with hope and
fear wherever found? How distinctly I saw all this in those
who are now sanctifying their first sabbath of wedded love!
Yet how few who smiled and wept at their union looked in
it for all that might be found!

There was occasion for kindly smiles at this happy fulfilment of a betrothment which had brought with it many
cares; and the family parting called for tears; but
there was a deeper joy, and tears from a higher source,
in some who understood the manly gentleness of the

one, and the trustful peace of the other of those who were
now sanctioned in a companionship which had begun long
before.   There was no need for surprise at a mood in each
so different from what had once and often been their wont.
The change was natural and right, and accountable to those
who knew them.   The one was at peace with all that world
which had appeared so long at war with him.   He feared
nothing; he possessed all; and of the overflowings of his
love he could spare to every living thing.   The other thought
of no world but the bright one above and the quiet one before her, in each of which dwelt one in whom she had perfect trust.   If there had been heedlessness of the guidance
of Providence, or ignorance of any thing in the heart of her
husband, there must have been a mingling of apprehension
with her trust, of trouble with her peace.   But there was
none such; and if there be steadfastness in the laws of the
affections, none such will there ever be.   In her the progression has been so regular, and the work so perfect, that
any return to the former perturbations of her spirit seems
impossible.   Well may I who watched over her remember
it all; — the early days when she was wholly engrossed, and
sickened at all that could not be brought into connexion
with him, — the days of ample diaries and solitary walks,
and social abstraction, and fitful devotion; — the later times
when, ceasing to be engrossed herself, she was jealous of the
very mention of his name by any but the few whom she
admitted to private confidence, and when she was looked
upon as one set apart by the possession of a mysterious joy
with which none might intermeddle; — the still later season
when her benevolence flowed forth again, enriched and
solemnized, when she smiled not the less for others because
she bore traces of a tearful solitude, when the flush and
the start were controlled, and a dignified patience filled up
the intervals of those vicissitudes which we all mourned,

but could not prevent; and lastly, the short period of smooth expectation which seemed too bright to be real, but which only vanished in the sober certainty so long looked for in vain, — the period of daily-growing tenderness to parents and sisters, and of regretful love of persons and places which had been looked upon almost with disgust when there was no prospect of leaving them. How increasingly solemn were her devotions in the church and the family all this time, from the alternate tears and coldness of the early days, up to the lofty calmness of her worship the last time she went with her family to the house of God! How vivid became her sensibility to nature, how generous her friendship, how melting her charity! What wonder that her father's voice trembled when he gave her his blessing, and that her weeping sisters looked on her scarcely as one of themselves, when she commended them to the love of her husband? She entered upon a new life when her love began; and it is as easy to conceive that there is one Life-Giver to the body and another to the spirit, as that this progression is not the highest work of God on earth, and its results abounding to his praise.

No such progression could have gone on in this cell, — dark, while open to the summer's sun, and dreary, though encompassed with the glories and beauties of heaven and earth. How listless, how vacant must have been such a life! How little holy the longing for companionship, or the nervous dread of the human face, one or the other of which is the torment of all recluses. There, where a few yellow leaves lie to be the sport of the wintry winds, was the couch of the holy man. There, when the first crimson ray of morning beamed upon him, he covered his face that he might sleep again, and defer for a while the weary day. When he came forth at length, far different were his orisons from those of the first dwellers in a paradise, who worship-

15 *

ped the more fervently because they knelt hand in hand.
He looked with a dull eye upon the purple hills and shadowy
lake, and the gemmed herbage of the rock. He listened with
a languid ear to the plash of oars when the early fisherman
began his toil. With a slow step he went to fill his bowl from
the dripping ledge, or to gather herbs from the moist crevices.
When this was done, and all his petty, selfish wants supplied,
there was only to lie watching how the goats sprang from
one point to another of the grey rocks, or to mark the signs
of busy life below, or to listen for human voice or footstep,
possibly with a pang of jealousy lest his sanctity had not
preserved him from being forgotten, or with an aching envy
of those whose lot he strove to despise.   Thus wore the long
day, idly but not peacefully ; for I doubt not there were
struggles for devotion, for penitence ; a perpetual endeavour
after meditation, (which cannot be forced upon a troubled
spirit,) an incessant missing of the aim for which all was
sacrificed.   Then there must have been a haunting consciousness that shadows were creeping over the understanding, and apathy benumbing the heart ; that the messengers
of God with whom in the days of his enthusiasm he had
claimed brotherhood, were fading away from their substantial
existence into mere images of the memory ; that Christ
himself was falling back into the ghost-like procession of
historical pageantry, and that the Presence was being gradually withdrawn, leaving nature, which had promised to be
immortal, cold, silent, and corpse-like.   If it were so amidst
the living and moving beauty of a summer's morn, what
must it have been in a day like this, when the tufts of snow
which a breath might dislodge lie glittering on the sprays of
the larch, and the fleecy rack shifts not its place in the
heaven ! How desolate the going down of the mute day !
How hateful the approach of the chill, stealthy night, when
repose was neither earned nor wished for !   If ever a gleam

of joy passed over his soul, it must have been when the storm
came striding over yonder peaks with his train of echoes in
full cry : then might the recluse join in the din, and not
fear the hollow tones of his own voice. It is said that he
once descended to the village in the night-time, to hallow
every threshold with his blessing. If it were so, he must
have learned there how he was accurst. What a pilgrimage
of woe ! — to traverse the silent street, and see every where
the tokens of labors to be resumed, and enjoyments to be
fulfilled ; to linger beneath the chamber window where the
taper was burning, and sigh to share the solicitudes of the
watcher ; to hasten away from the bayings of the mastiff
with the feeling that he was indeed an intruder where he
had no part nor lot; to wander round the star-lit churchyard,
envying those that were laid side by side, and shuddering
that he had doomed himself to be an outcast even from
among the dead ! Yet if the fountain of his tears was un-
sealed by this descent into the warm region of humanity,
his must have been a kindly grief. If it were not so, he
would scarcely have remained till dawn ; he would scarcely
have been seen by the early laborer to loiter on his rocky
path, to turn and look from every resting-place, and to send
down a long, lingering gaze before he disappeared within
his cave. It was after this that he employed himself in
carving the epitaph which was to consecrate his lonely cell,
— the sepulchre of the living man ere it was that of the
dead. Before the inscription was complete, the epitaph was
wanted. There, standing as now at the head of his couch,
it was seen by those who, coming for the holy man's blessing, found his lamp burnt out, the embers of his fire extinguished, his bowl of water upset within his reach, and his
glazed eyes unclosed in death. What were his latest prayers ? If he uttered from the abundance of his heart, they
were for such things as the dreariness within and without

would suggest; — for help and mercy from God, shown
through the offices of a human hand, the light of a human
eye, the whisperings of a human voice. O! may he not, in
an unwise endeavour to anticipate the peace of hereafter,
have marred that peace!

Not less watchful, and far more diligent, will be the devotion of those who are this day passing their irrevocable vow
to serve God in their household with a perfect heart. By
the vigor with which they will attempt the performance of
untried duties, by the reverence which they will be seen to
entertain for each others' aims and powers, by the jealous
guarding of each other which that reverence must prompt,
by their unconscious manifestation to society that they are
under a solemn sense of responsibility and a serene enjoyment of spiritual blessings, they will glorify God in instructing
man. By the new soul that shines through their eyes, and
the diffusive tenderness which flows from their presence, by
the images of repose which their mutual confidence exhibits,
they will give life and stability to our conceptions of what
peace on earth may be. By the growing vividness of their
emotions, they will be ever learning more of the capabilities
of the spirit, while the full exercise of these capabilities will
be insured by the conjunction of their deepened sympathies
for man with their mutual reference of all they have and
hope for to God. By doing and bearing all things for each
other, they will learn a better endurance than religious ambition or enthusiasm ever sustained, and a higher zeal than
has ever animated an unbidden and aimless service. Whether
they are seen refreshing themselves in the evening sunshine
after the toils of the day, or the centre of a society on which
they shed perpetual blessing, or suffering together in dignified patience under the chastisements of their Father, or
bearing testimony in his temple to the fulness of his benignity, while, in all changes, they identify the interests of

humanity with their own, they cannot but show how they have been educated by God himself to an obedience to his two great commandments. To those who know them as I know them, they appear already possessed of an experience in comparison with which it would appear little to have looked abroad from the Andes, or explored the treasure-caves of the deep, or to have conversed with every nation under heaven. If they could see all that the eyes of the firmament look upon, and hear all the whispered secrets that the roving winds bear in their bosoms, they could learn but little new; for the deepest mysteries are those of human love, and the vastest knowledge is that of the human heart. It must be so; for by the one is revealed all that the affections can learn of Deity; and in the other are its highest workings displayed. Why else did Christ refer thither all his teachings, and his appeals to be heard and credited? If it were not so — if he had sought the wilderness otherwise than as a place of deposit for his human sympathies, and for the purpose of refreshing and exalting his benevolence, I, for one, could not have regarded him as charged with the whole counsel of God. He would then have ranked with those inferior messengers of a temporary dispensation who dwelt in dens and caves of the rock; and we should still have looked for one who, although himself necessarily unfettered by earthly ties, would yet offer his bosom as a resting-place for devoted friendship, and gladden with an act of benediction a marriage-feast.

MORAL ESSAYS.

ON MORAL INDEPENDENCE.

MAN is made for sympathy. It is the deepest want and the highest privilege of his nature; a want by which in his most apathetic state he never ceases to be stimulated; a privilege of which, in his most degraded condition, he can never be wholly divested. An idiot has been found attempting to warm and feed the dead body of his mother: the insane wipe one another's tears, and soothe each other's terrors; and murderers are haunted by the cries of their victims. Every one is introduced into new states of feeling, each hour of his life, by glances of the eye, tones of the voice, or by the mere sight of the works of human hands, or the record of human thoughts on the printed page.

This sympathy, though actually one in its nature, is commonly supposed to be of various kinds, because it acts in different directions. Sympathy with God, — that is, the love of Truth, — is separated in our language, and is therefore too liable to become separated in our thoughts, from that love of our race which acts with the force of an instinct within us. There is no real ground for such a distinction. Our God-ward sympathy is with that which is real and unseen: our man-ward sympathy is also with that which is real and unseen ; with the thoughts and feelings of our fellow beings. But though this unity of nature in the two sympathies is a truth which ought not to be lost sight of, there is no objection to speaking of them as distinct, according to their direction.

When this one sympathy is kept true to its object, or, (according to the other mode of expression) the two sympathies are kept in harmony, all is right with us. We are in a state of rectitude towards God, and love towards our race. When the two are not in harmony, we are falling away, and disappointing the purpose of our being. Either failing is so fatal to peace and progress that it is impossible to say which is the most to be dreaded. It is only too easy, however, to show which is the most enticing, in the present age of the world and state of society.

When the fullest revelation of himself which God has given to the world was still fresh, and the memory of his signs and wonders was recent, men were in danger of regarding him too exclusively, as apart from his Providence. They thought of cultivating their sympathy with him by contemplation, instead of by action. These were the days when hundreds of thousands of anchorites dwelt in as many caves or cells, watching for visions which, if they came, came only from the nerves ; and trying to become the depositories of his confidence, when they did not even attempt to explore the course and purposes of his government. The opposite error prevails at present. God has become almost hidden behind his works : and men act with a regard to one another quite irreconcileable with the profession that in God they live and move and have their being.

All do not do this. In every age of the world, there have been some, — salt of the earth, — who have been true alike to God and man : and there is now a sprinkling of such in every community ; men who in the equal love of their Father and their brethren, learn how to purpose and act; and purpose and act according to their convictions. But there are very many more who learn one thing, and purpose and act another; or who learn and purpose one thing, and act another; or who take no pains at all, but are borne along with the multitude, to do evil or good, as may happen, making human opinion their god, and human sympathies their guide. Not incessantly, perhaps, are any thus borne along; not without occasional struggles to free themselves from the wearying pressure of human authority; not without yearnings for some more kindly stimulus than tyrannical opinion. If some apparent chance should plunge one of such deep into forests which the hand of God had planted ages before, he cannot but rise to some freedom in the largeness of his own thoughts. He sees here how God, with time for his sickle, is mowing down the growth of a thousand years; and he feels that there is a higher bidding than that of the weak being who could not, without God's leave and help, cut down the grass of his meadow to-day, and to-morrow cast it into the furnace. If some unaccustomed circumstance should place such a man on a mountain top, whence he could view some considerable section of a continent, and stay to see how human dwellings are brought out by the dawn from beneath the shadow of the night, and again vanish in their littleness when the stars come forth, he rises for a time to sympathy with him who made man appear thus minute in the midst of creation, while actually putting him in possession of a domain in comparison with whose vastness this earth is but as one of the bright points in the arch of the sky. For the hour, his sympathies are balanced, his life is rectified: the voice of God comes to him from " above, about, and underneath," and the voices of men subside into the distant murmur which harmonizes with, instead of overpowering, the music of nature. For the hour, he loves truth and

16

despises authority, and resolves to carry this love and this contempt back with him into society. All probably feel thus at times. The danger is, lest these higher sympathies should be overpowered by those which have become more familiar. The actual misfortune is, that very few retain their forest convictions, when they come back among the stubble of human prescriptions and decisions; and that still fewer maintain the freedom of their mountain top, when they reënter the scenes of strife and competition below.

It is, however, a great weakness to suppose that God's truth is not as evident, that our sympathy with him is not as much a want and a luxury in society as in the most retired scenes of nature. The littleness of all minor regards is as palpable in the presence of high principles as beneath the burning stars. However hurried and jostled we may be in the throng of men, we may repose as serenely in the bosom of Providence, (if only our affections be fixed above,) as if we were alone in the wilderness. Wherever there is a principle to be acted upon, however minute may be the occasion of daily business which calls it up, — there God is. Wherever there is a truth to be set forth and vindicated, there God is acting with us. Wherever there is a human right to be asserted and maintained, there our filial sympathies unite with our fraternal as entirely as in our Elder Brother, when he gave thanks for all of us who were to be admitted into his joy. Indeed, it is only by regarding our fellow-beings in the light of God's truth and love, that we can have any permanent sympathies with them at all. It is only by taking our stand upon principles, and keeping ourselves free to act, untrammelled by authority, that we can retain any power of resolving and working as rational and responsible beings.

For, what is Authority? If the strongest minded of men were to tell the truth about the processes of their own minds, what a scene of vacillation and infirmity would be laid open! A meditative philosopher there may have been here and there who, like Bentham, may have shut himself up with a few clear principles, and have carried them out without a thought of modification, without a suspicion of question, without a moment's embarrassment of doubt. But such instances are rare; and such a course of action is not, taking men as they are, commonly desirable. Most strong men have to share with the weak a much less easy discipline. They know what it is to rise in the morning with a strong persuasion of something; to be shaken before noon, to perceive a troublesome amount of evidence on the opposite side before night, and perhaps wait days, weeks, and months, for a mood of equally strong assurance with that from which they set out. They know what it is to feel their cheeks tingle at the recollection of the presumptuous decisions of their youth, while mourning over the less dangerous but more painful uncertainty of their riper age. They know what it is to be called upon for an opinion on a subject considered, or a book read five years before, when the judgment then formed rises up suddenly in absolute incompatibility with some other decision, now confidently held. They know what it is to mix alternately with the friends and foes of some institution, and have their sympathies engaged by each, till they begin to wonder whether there are any bounds to the conflicting evidence which may be offered, any unity of principle in the case, or any power of judgment in themselves. They know that the only hope of rational and steadfast conviction, lies in diligent study, patient thought, and a faithful comparison of new facts with old principles; a process which few are able, and still fewer are willing to carry out with perfect fidelity. —If such be the weakness of the strongest, such the difficulties of the most resolute, what *is* authority?

The most careless must sometimes find this question forced home upon them when they compare the opinions of the same man at different periods of his life, and perceive the contradictory movements of the society in which they live. The most indolent and blind must sometimes be struck with the absurdity of a multitude, each one of whom is too weak to stand erect, leaning each against his neighbour for support, instead of getting strength. The most indifferent must occasionally shudder at the abyss of uncertainty which is yawning beneath them, at the storms of circumstance amidst which they are tost, if they are destitute of principle to guide, or a refuge to which to betake themselves. What is authority to them, shipped as it is in the same bottom with themselves? All who are men must feel at times, that as man is made speculative, authority cannot be meant to be his God; that as man is made timid, authority cannot be his fit refuge; that as man is made active and responsible, authority cannot be made his permanent rule, stimulus, and sanction. Better be a dweller in a mud hut, on some hillside of Judea, in the season when the rain descends and the floods are abroad, than spend life in the dark cave where all the winds of heaven are at perpetual war.

Not only does individual peace depend on freedom from authority, but the very existence of society rests on individual rectitude. Society would have been dissolved ages ago in every civilized country, but for the rectitude of the few who have thought for themselves, and acted to God, instead of yielding to, or augmenting the force, by which the mass would otherwise have been whirled away from the eternal principles on which its security depends. These few have constituted the centripetal force by which the centrifugal has been checked. Their's has been a glorious lot on earth, and they must hold some of the highest places in heaven. Though their human affections must have been often lacerated here, there must have been an incessant healing, by an effusion from their divine sympathies; and, if they now look down on the abodes of mortals, they cannot but gloriously remember that their own blood and tears are the bond by which men are united in families and in citizenship.

The wonder seems that there are not more to covet the honor and blessedness of such rectitude; especially as its exercise would become more safe, while no less blessed, in proportion as the number of the upright increased. The wonder seems that so large a majority should prefer uncertainty to assurance, danger to security, darkness to light, insignificance to the most glorious of distinctions.

The wonder would indeed be great, if every individual man were a perfect sample of man in the abstract,—man, as Hamlet conceived of him;—man, as originated by the functions of Deity, and framed to act in infinity, and for eternity. But every man is not such a sample, such an equal component part, such a white ray from the luminary of humanity. In the intellectual and moral inequality of men lies their deficiency of intellectual and moral independence. If their sympathy with God,—their love of truth,—were perfect, this would rectify the balance, and preserve their virtue, though it could not equalize their privileges. But this sympathy with God is not perfect: and earthly regards, whether to others or to self, ruin the gradation which would form a perfect state of society.

Some fall through an unmodified acceptance of what has been said above of the greatness of man in the abstract. Their own individuality shrinks before the mighty abstraction, and they submit to Authority, under the notion of doing homage to Humanity. They forget that God is yet greater than this Humanity; that its mighty voice has never yet been put forth in unity and strength; and that if it could, it would

16*

be only an echo of that which is resounding for ever in the recesses of every human spirit.

Moral feebleness is, however, seldom owing to error of so high a character as this. Moral perversion of some kind is usually answerable for it, whether it goes under the name of selfishness, timidity, mistake as to the right objects of pursuit, or any other term by which a deficiency of sympathy with God may be expressed.

What a lack of this sympathy must there be when men relinquish their moral independence for want of nerve! When we think what pleasure is annexed to the very exercise of the faculties, what calm satisfaction there is in decision, what ever growing strength in action, what exultation in freedom, what repose on the maternal bosom of Truth, what ample life in the presence of God, it is scarcely to be conceived that any child of the race should fear to encounter the petulancies of his companions in the school of Providence. But so it is. Men take pledges which they believe they shall forfeit, deny principles which they know to be true, hide truths which are confided to them to be revealed, uphold institutions which their Maker's hand is pulling down, hold their peace when they should speak, shut their eyes against the light, and banish themselves from their Father's presence, because they cannot meet the questioning eye, or bear the pointing finger, or contemplate the petty instruments of man's persecutions. The airs of heaven cannot brace their nerves, the music of heaven cannot compose their spirits, the hand of their Father cannot uphold their faith to encounter the storms and troubles of an hour. Let such be left to the retribution of their own contempt.

Nothing can be expected from one who lives for wealth, but that he should get wealth. No one will speak to him of loving truth, or of sympathy with either God or man. He will be found to be with the multitude, or standing aloof, according to the probable effect upon his purse. He will uphold with clamor a barbarous institution, if only it keeps up a demand for his merchandise; or declare his belief in any thing which is countenanced by his customers. He is perpetually harassed by ugly visions of being homeless and hungry; thoughts almost as fearful to him as the saying he cannot but hear sometimes at church, about our bringing nothing into this world, and its being certain that we can carry nothing out. Such an one contributes his share to public opinion, and derives his sole importance from being an opponent of God's purposes:—an opponent, because influence which is given on the side of money is usually against truth.

Little is also to be expected of the office-seeker. There is nothing in the discharge of office which is necessarily unfavorable to moral independence. If the servants of Society could not also be friends of God, we must hesitate to believe society to be a divine ordination. It is the seeking of office which is perilous to freedom. An office-seeker puts himself into a position of dependence upon human opinions. He professedly refers his desires to his brethren, and not his Father; he assures them that his welfare is in their hands; that, in short, he is their property. Whether they accept or reject him, the words 'moral independence' had better never pass his lips, the conception of individual freedom had better never enter his mind, till his hour of repentance arrives; for the words have become cant, and the conception the cup of Tantalus. It is a god-like privilege to do the work of society: it is a reptile degradation to prey upon its honors.

The case is yet worse with those who act for fame; for the circumstances imply the possession of some kind of power, by which the aspirant is distinguished from the many: power which is given to be sanctified in the service of truth, and not to be profaned by the breath of men. When a man has once thus desecrated his holiest gift, bartered his true for a spurious immortality, put his manhood up to sale, actually begged for a place in the grand slave market of society, it is folly to look for him among those who go to and fro under the free heaven of truth. He has doomed himself to drudge in the yoke and under the lash, with few to pity his bondage.

Those few have thus a hard, though not an unequal struggle to maintain for God and the right. Against them are the careless, the timid, the sordid, the ambitious, the vain: with them they have their Father.

It may be asked how the conflict should be hard to those who have God on their side. The very words appear almost blasphemous. This would be true if God revealed himself as clearly and immediately on the side of truth in present struggles as in past. If he did so, there would be no struggle. It is because he reveals himself only to watchful consciences, speaks only through principles, works only by men's hands, that faith is necessary to rectitude. The reason why so few are ready to do his work is, that few are vigilant in conscience, intent upon principles, and diligent in the labors which they prescribe. The heart of man yearns so for sympathy, the voice of the multitude is so stunning, the pressure of outward circumstances is so strong, as to be fatal to all but those who have long found that the righteous are never alone. It is easy, in the solitude of the closet, or amidst the sympathy of a church, to conceive of the faithful as passing serenely through the storms of opinion, possessing their souls in peace in banishment, and disregarding death, in prospect of what is beyond. It is easy to be in a mood of bravery amidst such a contemplation. But the actual experience is as little like this as the toils of the pilgrim, fainting and stumbling amidst the burning sands of the desert, are to his anticipations, when he dwelt on the bubbling springs and palm shades that were to refresh him on his way. We are apt to think of martyrdom as of no very difficult thing; and perhaps it was easier than some kinds of confessorship in the present day: but we must remember that we do not realize the whole of martyrdom. We can realize its supports, but not its trials: the martyrs realized its trials, but with difficulty its supports. The wheel, the fire were before their eyes; and yet worse, the scorn of the ignorant, the ridicule of the worldly, the pity of the reputed wise, the reproaches and tears of the nearest and dearest. These mists rising up before their eyes could not but often dim the truth; these clamors could not but sometimes almost drown the voice of principle; and the yearnings of natural affection nearly over-power the higher sympathy which called upon the sufferer to perish. If the most god-like of martyrs found this cup almost too bitter to be tasted, we must be wrong in supposing that the conflict with nature and man is easy to be borne.

Neither must we make light of the obligation to confessor-ship in our own day, nor join too readily in the chorus of thanksgiving that the days of difficulty are over and gone. It is not so, and it never will be so. Men are now subjected to trial, not, as formerly, for calling themselves Christians, but for being Christians. It is creditable to be seen going to church on Sunday, but as disreputable as ever to follow out Christianity completely every day of the week. It is still dangerous to life, liberty, and property in some Christian countries to espouse the very primary principles of Christianity; difficult and painful in every spot on the globe to set about the grand project proposed to us of being perfect as our Father is perfect. The barest practical assertion of the brotherhood of men sets a man at enmity with society; the simplest token of paramount sympathy with his Father, alienates his brethren. Some of the noblest spirits of this age

who have found their home in truth are therefore driven out
of every other; their employments are taken out of their
hands; their steps are compassed about; their purposes are
baffled; their affections outraged; and nothing is willingly
left them which the world can either give or take away.
Such is the lot in this our day of those who resist the en-
croachments of tyrants on thrones, or assert the rights of
slaves under the yoke. Such is the lot of those who bring
forth any thing new and strange, as if it were something
real and practical, from the old repository of principles to
which it is creditable to assent, but on which it is disreputable to act; — who, for instance, prove that they cannot serve
God and Mammon, and that they esteem it the greatest of
dignities to be a servant.

Impossible as it is, however, to realize in conception the
perils and pains which fidelity to principle has to encounter,
it is good to contemplate its aids and its career. We obtain
thereby a clearer conviction of its nobleness and its beauty :
we learn thereby where most eagerly to resort for strength,
where most confidently to look for solace. It is good to
conceive both of what the faithful have to expect for their
fidelity, and how they will endure it; and also of what their
lot may be, if to their fidelity be added equal meekness, love,
and a faith in man corresponding to their faith in God. It
has perhaps never been proved how far the exercise of these
graces may modify the lot of the faithful. It is time that
this should be proved; and the conception must be prepara-
tory to the proof. Till our Father shall be pleased to grant
us the spectacle of one of ourselves in whom the Divine and
human sympathies are perfectly combined, let us cherish
within us the conception of such an one. Can we not conceive of one who lives in freedom, transparent in character,
simple in manners, strenuous in action, while living in
intense repose; with a telescopic view of principles, and a

microscopic observation of sympathies; planting his foot fearlessly in the highest regions of storm, and welcoming the faintest breath of love which wanders through the low places of life; having no concealments but of his solitary troubles; resenting no offences except inroads upon human rights; conscious of no fears but such as every hour is overcoming; of no desires but such as each moment is fulfilling; rejoicing wherever rejoicing is; never weeping but with those who have cause to weep; laying hold upon nothing but truth, possessing nothing but life; awed before the faintest presence of holiness on earth; awed by nothing but holiness in heaven? If such an apparition of life and love should pass through one generation of society, not shrouded in fears and follies, but disrobed in its divine purity, and majestic in its meek wisdom, it is scarcely conceivable that men should turn away from it, or rise up against it. "It would command all minds; it would touch all hearts." The sage would bow before it, and the infant spring to its embrace. And if there should still be any blind, desperate, and impious enough to lay violent hands on its mortal existence, its advent would be not the less a sign of a new era of blessedness to its race.

Who knows but that such an one is dwelling among us? What hinders that any one of us should be he?

THEOLOGY, POLITICS, AND LITERATURE.

IT seems strange that a people so advanced as our own, favored, as a nation, with so many and clear indications respecting the right direction of human inquiry, and the comparative value of human pursuits, should at this day be so indisposed as it is to a union of the two great departments of

research, — Moral and Physical Science. Is it not true
that the main body of thinkers is employed in investigating
the various combinations of material substances, in exploring
the wonders of chemical, and displaying the powers of mechanical science, while the great ends for which these in-
vestigations are pursued, are left almost unnoticed? Is
not physical science made the first object in all our associations for promoting the enlightenment of the lower classes?
Is any thing comprehended under the name of useful knowledge, but the facts which belong to this kind of research?
Do the great body of the people ever hear, out of church, of
any other kind of knowledge which would be good for them,
than that which relates to sensible objects? And is there
any counterpoising influence in such of our institutions, as
either from their long standing, or from their congeniality
with the spirit of the age, are supposed to exercise power
over public opinion? What are our universities doing, and
our schools, and our pulpits, and our periodical press? Are
they aiding or counteracting the bias? They are not directly
aiding, but they are much further from counteracting it.
They profess to be the organs of moral science, some exclusively, others in union with physical research. But, falling
far short of their profession, they injure the cause they profess
to espouse. The three great paths of research by which
moral truth may be approached are not explored by them
with a diligence proportioned to their comparative importance. Theology, Politics, Literature, the three phases of
illuminating truth, are not watched and philosophized upon,
like the greater and lesser lights of the material firmament.
Literature, the lowest in the gradation, has the greatest
attention paid to it. Our universities have, for the most
part, no higher aim; and such as have, fail to make it good.
Classical learning is all in all within their walls, and our
very bishops are chosen from out of them for their accom-

plishments in Greek. The partial pursuit of physical science forms the only exception to this general character; for, what is the political attainment of our universities, and what their theological enlightenment? The classics are the one great object in our public schools. Our periodical press is at work upon politics as well as literature; but in what way? — stumbling on amidst a dark accumulation of facts, or finding an uncertain and perilous way by the light of passing events. Political science, as taught by our periodical press, is in as crude a state as physical science two centuries and a half ago; and though the existence of a regenerator among us gives us hope of a rapid and certain advance, the Novum Organon with which he has furnished us, will not be in full use till his grey hairs have descended to the grave. Few as yet, in our free and enlightened nation, know any thing of broad political principles and fundamental political truths; and those few have reached them by so many individual processes of induction. Providence is, by its own methods of education, teaching us politics; but we do not yet come to politics to teach us of Providence.

As for theology, — who can pretend that it is a national study? Who can look at its present state, and believe that a multitude of intellects have been guided towards it by any steady impulse, or fixed upon it by any prevailing energy? If it has been pursued as a science, never before was science pursued so unavailingly. It has not been so pursued; for the primary dogma of its professors has been that theological truth differs essentially from all other truth in not being an object of induction, a subject of reason, a matter of research. We wonder that in so teaching, they have ventured to speak of *truth* in relation to theology; for we have no clear conceptions of truth otherwise than as an object of reason arrived at by a process of induction. But, it may be said, there has been research — there has been induction. Wit-

17

ness the vast libraries of theological learning which our institutions can boast. We reply, if an age of the world should come, when physical science shall be at such a stand, that the philosophers of the time shall be wholly occupied with ascertaining the authenticity and credibility of our Philosophical Transactions, will any criticism or controversy on the records alone, merit the name of research into physical science? Such labors may be very valuable in their way, and infinitely preferable to those of some contemporaries, — if such there should be, — who would neglect or pervert facts, for the sake of building irrational theories on insulated expressions; but neither set of inquirers would do much for the advancement of science. They would leave unsought the grand principles, capable of indefinite development, of consistent application, of unbounded coöperation, which are precisely what is wanting in the popular theology of our day.

Such then is the state of inquiry among us. Physical science is advancing steadily, and with an accelerating rapidity, under the guidance of philosophical principles. Moral science is lagging behind, blinded, thwarted, led astray by a thousand phantoms of ancient ignorance and error, which would have disappeared long ago, if the dawn of philosophy had not arisen as cloudily upon this region as brightly upon the other. What is to be done?

Let it be ascertained what are the true objects of research, and what is their natural connexion, instead of proposing to split men into parties whose object shall be, — not a division of labor which shall benefit the whole, — but to magnify one science at the expense of another, and to persuade as many novices as they can to pursue one to the exclusion of all others. Let it be ascertained whether material science, useful, wonderful, beautiful as it is, be not meant to derive its fullest lustre from its subservience to the science of mind; and whether moral science, in its turn, may not supply new principles to physical research, and important aids to its prosecution. The natural gradation, the true proportion of all the sciences, must be understood before the value of any one can be estimated; and nature, not prejudice, must be the demonstrator.

Place man on this globe with a perfect frame, and full of unperverted intelligence — what will he wish to learn? He will seek to know how he came there; and this discovered, for what purpose, and under what law. His most direct path to the first aim of his inquiries may be physical research; but he is not satisfied with it, till it leads him to the point he seeks. He may reach his theology by means of physical inquiry; but it is theology which is his aim. He next asks, for what purpose he is made? He explores the past and the actual state of nature, and especially of man, and his inquiries again lead him back to the Fount of Being. Then he must know under what law he lives? He traces the manifestations of Providence in all that exists around him, and yet more in the home of his own consciousness; and as these things can be understood only by a reference to his great first principle, he is once more led back to Deity as his primary study, and that through which, and for the sake of which every other is to be pursued. Henceforth, moral and physical science are to him connected in an indissoluble union. He studies Man, his nature, his interests, his destination; but it is with a reference to the First Cause; in other words, he studies theology through politics. He also studies Nature, the sky above, the sea around, the earth beneath, the passing winds, the changing lights, and the fathomless mysteries which dwell within them all; but he studies them for the sake of Him who made all; or, in other words, he enriches his theology with the treasures of physical science. Theology is, with him, the beginning, middle, and end of his researches. Not the theology of the schools, or of the dark ages, or of any who would lord it over God's heritage; but the theology which is chanted by the waves, aud illuminated by the stars, and pictured forth in the history of his race; the theology which, having hovered in peerless majesty over the peculiar people, sprang, strong in its immortality, from the fires of their holy temple. Next to God, his study is Man; next to man, his study is Nature.

Look back and see whether such is not the natural order of inquiry. Observe whether the great lights of the world, of whatever age and nation, have not united the things of the spirit with those of the senses in their contemplations. Zoroaster made the study of the elements subservient to worship. Pythagoras came down from contemplating the starry skies to expatiate on the immortality of the soul. Solon founded his moral on natural law; and Moses used the learning of the Egyptians as a qualification for the service of the God of the Hebrews. It was his broad gaze over the expanse of nature, and his penetrating glance into the intimate connexion of things, that made Socrates the sun of the heathen world, and enabled him to declare what invisibly exists from what visibly· appears. Plato studied geometry and poetry in conjunction, — travelled into Sicily to examine its volcanoes, and into Egypt to master its mathematical sciences, — and then returned to discourse of the realities of which these were the shadows, — of the eternal principle which dwells alone, and sends its emanations hither and thither, through the universe. His stern pupil, at whose feet the world lay for centuries, founded his logic on his search after "every star that heaven can show, and every herb that sips the dew." The Stoic philosophy was based on the observation of the immutability of the laws of the universe; and it was the harmonious flow of the tide of being, which filled the soul of Epicurus with serenity and love. Archimedes united metaphysics with his deepest researches into matter. The service which Bacon rendered to mankind, was the furnishing philosophical principles to the pursuit of physical science; and Newton spiritualized his mighty discoveries by a perpetual reference of all that is to Him who made it. Thus far, experience confirms reason in her decision respecting what ought to be the objects of human inquiry, and in what order they should be pursued.

Nor is this contradicted by the fact that revealed religion has, thus far, been held as a truth severed, by an original difference of constitution, from all other truth. If it be so, if Christianity have thus far done nothing for any truth but its own, it still does not follow that such aid is impossible, or not designed by its Author to be eventually afforded. Is it not clear that Christianity has been long and widely misapprehended? Is it not clear that, while our religion is held separate from our politics, separate from our literature, separate from our science, it no more puts forth its full power, than if it were held separate from our daily actions and thoughts? If our religious teachers are right in telling our artisans that their faith should go with them into their workshops, — as well to animate the hand as to control the spirit, — it must also be right for our naturalists to carry theirs into the fields, and along the caverned shore; for our scientific men to infuse theirs into their researches, and to let it preside over their experimental philosophy. The one may perchance find illustrations that he dreamed not of, among the roosting birds, or the recovered treasures of the deep; and the others may be struck by relations they could not anticipate between truths which had appeared unconnected. There may be something in the silent motions of the firmament, or in the unvarying and multitudinous relations of number and quantity, or in the illimitable extent and mighty power of transmutation and affinity, which may suggest new and high thoughts of the administrations of Providence, of

17*

the share which man has in them, and of the modes in which the most marvellous of its wonders, and the most precious of its promises, have been and shall be fulfilled. It is at least certain that there is an everlasting relation between the highest stimulus to exertion, and the modes and results of that exertion, whatever be its nature and direction.

If it be a fact that the balance of truth is so unequal as we have represented it, it is high time that something was done to restore it. It is time that the students of moral science were preparing themselves to become masters. It is time that they were gathering disciples about them. It is time that they who would learn should at least be offered a choice as to what they should learn. If we cannot at once form societies, and send forth libraries, and diffuse through the kingdom a spirit of research, whose object shall be the promotion of moral science, we can, each in our way, show what that science is, its high obligation upon the race, its benignant influence upon nations, its attractiveness to individuals. There are few who, like Milton, can recognise and display this truth in all three of its great manifestations — who can " reconcile the ways of God to man," — who can reason on the rights, and defend the liberties of his race, and, retiring to " behold the bright countenance of truth in the quiet and still air of delightful studies," woo others with the " soft and solemn-breathing sound " which issued from his retreat, to come and join him in his worship. Long will it be before we shall meet with an individual who can do this ; but by a combination of powers, much may be effected to which individuals are unequal. Let it be shown what there is true and beautiful in the study of

THEOLOGY,

which teaches the existence and attributes and providence of Deity, not only by cold abstractions of the reason, but by the living facts which are ever stirring within and around

every rational being. Theology is not understood till it is
seen to comprehend all that relates to the cause of all. It
teaches the purposes of creation; it leads to the study of the
laws of mind, and reveals the operation of Providence in the
history of the human race and of individuals; it shows how
Providence has now guided nations by a uniform impulse to
a certain point of enlightenment, and now startled them into
perceptions of a higher truth by the passing gleams of some
new philosophy; now uniting them in the profession of a
general faith, more or less pure, and now breaking them up
into parties of adherents to different schools. It shows how
individuals are led on by vicissitudes acting upon their springs
of thought and feeling, and opens a prophetic view into the
future of another world as well as this. In displaying the
workings, it shows the will, of God; and comprehends the
study of the eternal principles of morals; and — ever blending the exhibition with the perception, ever furnishing the
illustration with the truth — presents to us the holy, the benignant form of him, the moral image of the Father, whose
name it is our high privilege to bear. Theology has ever
included whatever belonged to the highest interests of man:
since it became Christian, it has been the depository of the
best treasures of the human spirit, where its hopes are stored
up, where its joys are renovated, where its griefs are soothed,
where its fears are annihilated, where it may find that all
things are its own, as surely as itself is Christ's, and Christ
is God's.

Let it be shown what there is true and beautiful in

POLITICS:

in that science which treats, not of this or that measure, as
if its results concerned only the parties expressly contemplated in it; not of this or that statesman, as if his influence
was bounded to a certain tract of country, and to the period
of his ascendancy; nor even of this or that country, discon-

nected from the rest of the world. Let the grand principles be ever reverted to on which hang, more or less, the destinies of every man that breathes; and by these principles let every decree of the legislatures of Europe and America, every act of the executive, every movement of the people, be watched and tried. Under the pervading spirit of philanthropy, let the advances of society be stimulated, its errors exposed, its sins mourned, its triumphs hailed; and this, not only within our own borders, but wherever men and brethren exist. Let it be felt as a degradation when the negro kisses the feet of his white tyrant, and commemorated as an era when he sails away to establish himself in freedom on the shore of another continent. Let it be mourned as a general calamity when a patriot council dissolves at the nod of a despot, whether a narrow sea or a broad ocean intervene. Let the cry for reformation be echoed, whether it come from the streets of our own metropolis, or from the prisons of Lisbon, or from the charnel-houses of Juggernaut. Let philanthropy be watchful and meditative and active; secure of observing and thinking and doing aright, while guided by the two great principles of the equality of man's rights, and the progression of his destiny.

Let it be shown what there is true and beautiful in

LITERATURE.

Let its influence in working out and consolidating opinions, and in refining the taste, be amply exhibited and carefully guarded. Let the resources of various nations, the treasures of many languages, be laid open to general use. Let philosophy be honored in this mode of her manifestation; let criticism be gentle in its integrity; let poetry be worshipped as a concentration of all intellectual power, and cherished as an incarnation of all moral beauty. Let this be done with a view to higher ends than temporary purposes; and it may be found that the necessities of the lower ranks may be reached through the luxuries of the higher; and that in feeding the imagination and taste of the mortal, we are strengthening the embryo faculties of the seraph.

NORWICH, 1832.

ON THE AGENCY OF FEELINGS IN THE FORMATION OF HABITS; AND ON THE AGENCY OF HABITS IN THE REGENERATION OF FEELINGS.

I. *On the Agency of Feelings in the Formation of Habits.*

THOSE who have been accustomed to observe with attention the processes of their own minds during the passage from childhood to youth, and from youth to mature age, will be readily disposed to sympathize with the complaints of the ingenuous minds which perceive with wonder and dismay that as their intellects become enlightened, their feelings grow cold, and that added years take from the depth and strength of their sensibility. The experience of this change of feeling is one of the severest trials to which the mind is exposed in the progress of life, and there are probably few who are wholly exempt from it. Happily, it is only temporary, easily explained, and (like most other processes of our moral being) satisfactorily justified. It may be useful to point out the purposes for which our feelings are bestowed, and the reasons why they are more vivid in childhood than in an after period, and by what means they are renovated and purified in the progress to old age.

When the age of enthusiasm and romance is passing away, when the realities of life press on our attention, we perceive, by degrees, that our sensibilities are less easily acted upon by circumstances, and that impressions from external objects are less deep and permanent than formerly; and are apt to im-

agine, with a kind of horror of ourselves, that the sources of
feeling are dried up, that the world is gaining an undue
dominion over us, that the forms and hues of the spiritual
creation are gradually fading away, and that they will soon
disappear for ever from our mental eye.   We turn from the
books which used to afford a full measure of excitement,
lamenting that we can no longer find " thoughts that breathe,
and words that burn : " the breezes of spring, though soft and
sweet, no longer fill us with the intoxicating delight which
formerly allied us with the carolling birds and sporting lambs :
we no longer spring from our light slumbers, at an untimely
hour, to welcome the rising sun, and worship him as a God.
The tale of distress which formerly would engross every
faculty, causing tears to flow from our eyes, and sleep to fly
from our pillows, now excites a more moderate sympathy,
and leaves our attention at liberty for other cares and interests ; and even our devotional feelings are less ardent, and
the promises and threatenings of religion no longer produce
emotions of ecstasy and despair.   This change ought, undoubtedly, to stimulate us to inquiry into the state of our
minds.   If we find, on examination, that we have gained no
equivalent for what we have lost, if we are convinced that
feelings, innocent and virtuous in their nature and tendency,
have passed away and left nothing to supply their place, it is,
indeed, time to tremble ; and we may well fear that there
is a canker at the root of our affections.   But if we can
satisfy ourselves that evanescent feelings have given place to
permanent principles, if we can acknowledge to ourselves
that our employments are of a more useful nature than formerly, and that our piety, though less ardent, is more influential, our benevolence, though less warm, more active and
equable, we may dismiss all fear, and, without apprehension,
leave our feelings to take their course, while we exercise our
cares on the preservation of the good habits which have
sprung from them.

The chief value of good feelings arises from their being instruments in the formation of good principles and habits. Children begin life without a bias towards any course of action, but with a large capacity for pleasure and pain, and a lively sensibility to them. It is the work of a good education to engage these sensibilities on the side of virtue, and to make them act as a stimulus to virtuous actions. The misery which a kind-hearted child feels at the sight of a starving family, (and which is more acute than that which is experienced by the most benevolent person of maturer age,) supplies the place of that good principle which time has not allowed to grow up into strength, and prompts him to bestow all that he has in order to impart relief. His sensibility is no less wounded by the sight of a nest of unfledged birds, deprived of their parents' care, or of the writhings of the fish upon the hook ; and this vivid emotion tends to confirm his newly-formed habits of humanity towards the brute creation. These feelings are, in themselves, evanescent, and if not connected with action, are worse than useless ; as excitement causes a waste of energy which can only be repaired by increased vigor of action. But if they be made the immediate impulse to some effort of benevolence, they have answered the purpose for which they were bestowed, and in departing, have left behind something more than equivalent to themselves in their utmost intensity and depth. A frequent repetition of these feelings produces a series of actions, till, by the unfailing power of association, the emotion and consequent action become inseparably connected ; and the feeling, rising in dignity and importance, becomes a principle.

How much more valuable, as a guide and stimulus, principle is than feeling, it is needless to show; but principle itself, in its earlier operations, is wavering and uncertain, and still craves the aid and companionship of those vivid emotions which may long continue to impart strength, and to cherish its purity. This aid, this companionship, is granted for a while, and principle goes on from weakness to strength, till, by a constant succession of single efforts, a habit of action is formed, and the great end for which feelings were bestowed is attained. Now that they have done their work, they hold a subordinate place in our moral being; from being our masters, they descend to become our servants; and happy are we if we exact from them reasonable service, and know how to direct their agency for the promotion of our own peace, and the purification and strengthening of our virtue. They do not expire — they have immortalized themselves in the principles which are their own work; but, having passed through one stage of their existence, they retire for a while into some recess of the soul, from whence they shall issue again in a more exalted and beautiful form, fitted for an intenser enjoyment of the light of heaven, and strengthened for a lofty flight above the objects of earth. Of this renovation we shall hereafter speak; let us now consider how we are to console ourselves for their temporary retirement.

We are not responsible for our feelings, as we are for our principles and actions. They are not so directly in our own power, and are not the subjects of exhortation, approbation, or reproof, in the rule by which we are to govern our lives. Self-reproach is therefore misplaced in respect of our feelings, if our actions are right. Our emotions depend so much on circumstances wholly beyond our own control, on the variations of our bodily state, on the changes of external events, and the unavoidable predominance of one set of associations over others, that we should be severely tasked indeed if we were required to maintain them at any given degree of intensity, or to keep them in any particular state at any appointed time. As far as we can, by the aids afforded us, command our associations, and govern the actions which are connected with certain feelings, it is in our power, and it is our duty, to cherish or repress those feelings; but over the variety of accessory circumstances which may intervene to influence our feelings, we may have but little control. Our care, then, should be to look to our principles, and to avoid all anxiety about our emotions. Their nature can never be wrong where our course of action is right, and for their degree we are not responsible. If to this it be objected, that we make states of feeling the subject of praise and blame in our judgments of others — that we regard with love and approbation one whose devotion appears warm, and his sympathies unbounded, while we shrink with dread and dislike from him who listens with apathy to the groans of the sick and the complaints of the sorrowful, and who looks with a dull eye on the most glorious works of nature — it is enough to reply, that we regard their sensibility as it affects their course of action; or, if we do not, our approbation and dislike are misplaced. If the piety of the one consists only in frames and feelings, and his benevolence exhausts itself in smiles and tears, his emotions are absolutely worthless: and the reason why we dislike the apathy of the other is, that his feelings are dead-because he has neglected to cherish them by efforts of duty, and has defeated the purpose of his being. The one ought not to be the object of envy, nor the other of compassion, because they are possessed or destitute of warm emotions, but because those emotions have been rightly fostered or impiously annihilated.

If it can be proved that the vivid, undisciplined emotions of youth are not only useless when principles have once been formed, but are actually a hindrance to the purification and exaltation of these principles, no further consideration will be needed to reconcile us to the diminution of their vigor. If not made subservient to principles, they would overpower them: and of this truth we may see abundance of illustra-

18

tions, if we look abroad into the world. There we behold
beings once innocent, amiable, and well-disposed, happy in
the full flow of youthful sensibility, and attractive from the
simplicity of their minds and ingenuousness of their hearts;
but now, tainted by the contagion of vice, or corrupted to
the heart's core; some, victims to a morbid sensibility which
makes their life one lingering sickness of the soul; others,
hardened to the most awful degree of indifference to the
welfare of their species, or to their own peril. At the critical
period of life when principles should, if ever, be formed, they
surrendered themselves to the mastery of their passions and
sensibilities. Their passions being nourished by gratification, gained an unlimited ascendency; their sensibility,
amiable still, but undisciplined, misled them day by day,
weakening their intellectual and moral powers, and reducing
them through one stage of disease to another, till they stand
on the brink of the grave of their best hopes and noblest
endowments. The rake, the drunkard, the gamester, the
brutal murderer himself, have all experienced in their day
emotions, perhaps, as warm, as pure, as exquisite, as those
whose temporary decay we mourn: and what have these
emotions done for them? Had they been willing to submit
to the natural and salutary process by which these feelings
become converted into habits of piety, benevolence, and
obedience to conscience, they might now have been as angels
of light compared with their present state: but they disturbed
the process, and their strength has become weakness, and
the milk of human kindness, the appropriate nourishment of
their spiritual frame, is changed into a corrosive poison. —
Let us be careful, then, to yield our obedience where it is
due, and to follow Principle wherever she leads, without
casting a lingering look on the flowery paths in which we
have hitherto trod. The blossoms must fall off before fruit
can be produced; it is the part of folly to weep because they

fade, and that of wisdom to tend the ripening fruit, without regretting the transient beauties of the spring, which, having afforded their due measure of delight, and fulfilled the purpose of their creation, have passed away.

In our religious services, we should be more careful to pay our tribute of reverent gratitude and praise regularly, calmly, and cheerfully, than to kindle flaming raptures, or excite thrilling fears. We should endeavour to have God in all our thoughts, to acknowledge his hand in the daily events of our lives, to study his word, and to glorify him by our actions; and not to wait for some particular emotion before we venture to approach him, or neglect prayer because we find our hearts too cold for so sacred a service. We may, we must, sometimes feel deep concern at the deadness of our devotional feelings; but the stream, though stagnant, is not frozen, and the way to restore its purity, and hasten its course is to open its accustomed channels to light and warmth from heaven. If we find our sympathies with our brethren less vivid than formerly, we must not sit down to ponder our troubles; for this is the sure way to concentrate our attention on ourselves, and to perpetuate the evil. We should not wait till some object of misery presents itself to our gaze, to awaken the sensibility which has hitherto been the spring of our actions; but, remembering that what our hand findeth to do we are to do with all our might, we should relinquish our inactive meditations, exclude selfish regrets, and hasten to the performance of some active duty. Some may ask, "Are we then to forego without a murmur the dearest privileges and most exalted enjoyments we have ever known — the sensibilities which have been the delight, the ornament, the very element of our being?" I answer, "No. Submit but for a time to the guidance of principle, and your feelings will revive with added vigor: the offspring of virtuous habits, they are endowed with immortality, and if duly cherished, they will accompany you from strength to strength, and at length appear with you before God."

How the generating process is performed, we will hereafter consider. In the mean while, it is right to bear in mind, under all discouragements, that He who called us into being knows our frame, and has himself appointed its periods of weakness and of strength. It is our duty to acquiesce in these appointments, and, with respect to spiritual as well as temporal endowments, to bless his hand, whether he gives or takes away.

NORWICH, 1829.

II. *On the Agency of Habits in the Regeneration of Feelings.*

HAVING formerly ascertained the cause of the temporary deadness of the sensibility which sometimes attends the formation of habits, we now proceed to the pleasanter task of describing its renovation, and of tracing the progress of its purification.

It is well worth while to undergo the painful struggle which we have described as appointed to many ingenuous young minds, for the sake of experiencing the ever-growing delight which attends the development of emotions far more pure in their nature, and exalted in their character, than the intense, but short-lived, feelings of youth. Devotion, in the purest state in which it can be cherished, previous to the formation of habits of piety, yields but little enjoyment, compared with that which attends the further advancement of the mind. The high excitement which is felt by the inexperienced soul while undergoing the rapid changes of its emotions, the alternations of sunshine, lightnings, and thick clouds, may gladly be resigned for the calm delight of watching the day-spring from on high, as it increases more and more unto the perfect day. The steadfast hope, the cheerful trust, and still improving satisfactions, which are the natural rewards of devotional habits, far transcend, in their influence on our happiness, the highest fervors of an undisciplined piety. The manner in which these satisfactions spring up and grow within us may be easily explained.

When we are led by a sense of duty, rather than by inclination, to offer the services of devotion, that degree of pleasure which ever attends upon obedience to conscience will neutralize, and perhaps overpower, the pain arising from the consciousness of our deadness of feeling. Prayer is (as it has been no less truly than beautifully expressed),

> "A stream which, from the fountain of the heart,
> Issuing, however feebly, nowhere flows
> Without access of unexpected strength : "

and the aid thus granted to our efforts (not a supernatural aid, but no less welcome from its being the offspring of association) affords encouragement and pleasure. Our pleasurable feelings become connected with the time, the place, and the service, and are easily excited again in similar circumstances: so that, if there were no hindrances to the process, our pleasures would increase in a rapid proportion with every act of devotion. There are, however, drawbacks, many and great; and worldly thoughts, consciousness of guilt, and a thousand adverse circumstances besides, intervene to check the flow of our devotion, and render our efforts painful, and sometimes almost fruitless. Yet, if we steadily persevere, our advancement in piety will be sensible, and on the whole satisfactory. Our pleasurable emotions will overbalance the painful more and more continually: and as we become more able to see God in every thing, all the events of our lives, all the circumstances of our being, will lend their influence to feed "this calm, this beautiful and silent fire," which is destined at length to consume all that is earthly and impure within us. Surely there can be no comparison between the devotional excitement of our youthful days, whose excess was invariably followed by a proportionate depression, and which in its best state was flickering and uncertain, and that confirmed state of habitual piety in which the soul is endowed with a heavenly strength to endure, and a boundless capacity to enjoy: when every object glows with sunshine from another world, and every voice speaks in the music of a higher sphere.

In no instance is the influence of habit more evident in the renovation of feeling than in the exertion of benevolent principle. When the selfishness natural to childhood has so far given way as to allow of the exertion of benevolent principle, we sometimes feel dissatisfied with ourselves, because we perform acts of kindness from an impulse of conscience only, having our own peace of mind in view more than the good of the object of our care. This is assuredly a very imperfect kind of benevolence, yet it is one which all must practise before they can attain to any thing higher and better. Here, also, steady perseverance will overcome our difficulties. Various pleasures will arise from the gratitude of the object, the new interests thus opened to us, the consciousness of useful employment; and, perhaps, a large portion from the society and coöperation of friendship; and these pleasurable feelings, becoming associated with the act and the object, will render a repetition of such offices of kindness more an impulse of the inclination, and less an effort of conscience continually, till we come to do good naturally, and without any express regard to our own peace of mind. By the same means we have transferred our personal interests to the ob-

jects of our care, and they consequently awaken in us the
same sympathies which were formerly expended on ourselves.
The pleasures of benevolence, however faint and imperfect
at first, afford sufficient inducement to us to seek their continuance and extension; new objects are found, and these
introduce others, and so on; we are led to think less of ourselves, and more of others perpetually, till we gain a glimpse
of that glorious prospect which to some exalted spirits seems
to have been realized even in this world, when the joys and
sorrows of others become matters of as intimate concern to
the mind as ever were its own, in its most selfish days; and
every thing that lives and breathes finds ready access to the
open heart, and a secure asylum in the expanded affections.
Such was Howard: in childhood, selfish, no doubt, like other
children; in youth, impetuous and precipitate; in mature age,
calm, persevering, inflexible, in action; ingenuous and disinterested in character; simple and mild in manners; in feeling, sensitive in the highest degree.   In his career of benevolence, he set out from the same point as other men: by
constant adherence to principle, by perseverance in virtuous
action, his affections became enlarged, and his sensibilities refined, till this part of his character became divine,
purified from all corruption, and incapable of deterioration.
What further encouragement do we need than an example
like this? What further instruction? What more abundant
source of pure and grateful hope?

If any further exemplification of our leading fact were
needed, it might be found in a variety of instances, whose
moral import is not so great as those already adduced, or
where the process tends to deteriorate the mind. If the fine
arts were not cultivated, our emotions would be incapable of
excitement, if the most perfect specimens were to drop from
the clouds; and it is by the study of them alone, that any

individual mind can derive more than a low degree of pleasure from the contemplation of their grandest achievements. To a child, one picture or statue is as good as another, except from causes foreign to the excellence of the work, as a resemblance to some beloved and familiar object, &c. But after a due degree of study, his feelings become warm and vivid to a remarkable degree, so that one piece excites' disgust or contempt, while another awakens emotions of rapture, and he can gaze upon it hour after hour, and day after day, with renewed pleasure. Bring a sculptor and an Otaheitan savage together, to take a first view of the Apollo Belvidere, and compare the depth and extent of feeling which is excited in each. The one will gaze with mute delight till the evening darkness has veiled every limb and feature, while the other will, after a slight and careless survey, gladly transfer his attention to a bunch of peacock's feathers, or a string of gaudy beads. Transport both men to the island home of the savage, and he will bend with awe and delight before his uncouth deities, while the artist feels nothing but disgust and contempt at the hideousness of their form, and the absurdity of their proportions.

How remarkably bad habits tend to cherish malignant feelings, it is needless to point out; and where all sensibility appears to be extinguished by vice, it will usually be found that some outlet exists for the baleful fires which make a hell of the corrupted heart. And should it be objected, that men of depraved habits sometimes afford examples of a refined and exalted sensibility, it is replied, that, in such men, sensibility is usually morbid, and always partial; that it leaves the heart from which it sprang, and takes up its abode in the fancy, where it grows more and more sickly, and would, in course of time, expire. The poet who rouses our passions, awakens our sympathies, opens to us the hidden recesses of the soul, and unveils the secrets of nature, may, by the cultivation of pure habits of thought and action, obtain a still increasing power over the hearts of men. But if he should live in the frequent violation of moral laws, if he should habitually disregard the interests of others, concentrate his desires on the attainment of his own ends, and exercise his powers solely for the gratification of his pride, and with a view to the increase of his fame, his friends will soon discover that his sensibilities become less and less like those of other men. They will be disappointed to find that the affecting incidents of life which stir up emotions in their hearts, are regarded by him with carelessness and indifference; at the same time that he sends forth from his closet strains which cause many tears to start, and which kindle flames in many hearts more ingenuous than his own. In course of time, a change will be as evident to distant observers as to surrounding friends. Notwithstanding all the advantage he has gained over the public mind — the favorable prepossession, the long-standing admiration and affection — the power and the fame for which he has sacrificed so much, will melt away; for his appeals no longer reach the heart, and his illustrations are found to be too overstrained to engage the imagination, or to please the taste. If he live long enough to undergo the full punishment which here awaits the perversion of intellectual and moral powers, how awful is the warning! Yet all this might be as distinctly foreseen by an accurate observer of human nature, as that the vine would yield no golden clusters while its root was mouldering, or that the waters of the fountain would not retain their sweetness when the source had become bitter.

On the contrary, the powers are ever-growing, the sensibility still becoming more pure and lively, of the poet who has trained up his thoughts in unceasing devotion to God, and the diligent service of his race; and who has so carefully associated his emotions with reason and principle as to refuse the indulgence of them when no purpose of improvement or usefulness sanctions their excitement.

> " It were a wantonness, and would demand
> Severe reproof, if we were men whose hearts
> Could hold vain dalliance with the misery
> Even of the dead ; contented thence to draw
> A momentary pleasure, never marked
> By reason, barren of all future good."

And he is right; for if we wish that our actions should be inseparable from virtuous feeling, we must be careful that emotions, however innocent, should not be encouraged to arise and pass away, without tending to the accomplishment of some moral purpose. When, by no agency of our own, emotions are excited, it is therefore our duty to refer them to some principle, to bring them to the support of some habit. The glories of a sunrise, the sublimity of the stormy ocean, the radiant beauties of the night, awaken spontaneous emotions : but it is our duty to perpetuate their influence by looking "through Nature up to Nature's God." In like manner, we should convert every pang and glow of conscience, every excitement of sympathy, into the nourishment of our moral being : and for the result we may take the word of one who, in his address to Duty, shows that he has obeyed her call, and received her rewards.

> " Stern Lawgiver! yet thou dost wear
> The Godhead's most benignant grace ;
> Nor know we any thing so fair
> As is the smile upon thy face.
> Flowers laugh before thee on their beds,
> And fragrance in thy footing treads."

Having traced these facts back to their principles, there is a strong temptation to anticipate the operation of these principles on our future being, and their influence on the happiness of another state. But this would lead us into too wide a field. It is sufficient, for the present, to reflect that all beings and all circumstances may be, must be, made to minister to our spiritual life, for good or for evil. We are subject, during every moment of our existence, to influences which we cannot reject, but which will work good or harm within us, according to the dispositions with which they are received. If well received, this world of matter will gradually become to us a spiritual universe: if the contrary, our own nature will become more abject than that of the brutes that perish, and infinitely further removed from happiness. In the one case, all things will minister to our peace ; in the other, to our woe. In both it may be said, that "all things are ours :" let us be careful "that we are Christ's" and that, through him, we are God's.

ESSAY ON THE PROPER USE OF THE RETROSPECTIVE FACULTY.

I.

"Forgetting the things which are behind."

THE faculty of memory is of such prime importance in the formation and improvement of mind, that no progress whatever can be made without it. This faculty supplies the materials on which all the others work ; and in proportion to its original strength or weakness is the approximation to intellectual power or to idiotcy. It becomes of less importance as the other faculties are developed, as they supersede its office by supplying to each other the elements on which they are to be severally employed : and hence we perceive the cause, and recognise the purpose, for which the memory becomes less tenacious as years advance. The other faculties being brought into play, the essential strength of the memory becomes of less and less importance to the general intellectual improvement; while the correctness of its discipline should be made an object of perpetual attention.'|

A powerful, undisciplined memory is so wearisome a qualification in a companion, that it is only necessary to have known such an one to be aware how its vagaries delay the progress of the mind, and impede the steady advance of its improvement: while instances of a defective memory in eminent men of every class and degree, are so common as to prove that a great tenacity of facts and impressions is not a primary requisite of excellence. It was by applying his extraordinary power of abstraction to the materials furnished by memory, as well as observation, that Newton wrought out stupendous results from a very scanty assortment of facts. While observing that an apple falls, and remembering only that a feather floats, and that rain was once vapor, he was advancing much more rapidly towards his theory of gravitation, than if his mind had been crowded with remembrances of all the circumstances which happened at the time he was observing feathers and showers. To him the art of forgetting was as serviceable as an unreflecting person would predict it to be disastrous. To have a strong memory under command is an inestimable advantage; but to have a weak one under command has been proved to be sufficient for all needful purposes, while the other faculties are vigorous.

This view of the instrumentality of memory, in promoting or delaying the improvement of the intellect, is universally allowed; but most persons appear to act upon an opposite theory in their spiritual concerns. Whereas, not only are the instruments identical in the two cases, but their operation is strictly analogous. All the powers of the intellect are engaged in spiritual processes, and precisely according to their usual method of operation. The only difference is, that in the one case they are employed upon facts; in the other, on impressions.

This difference, it is true, involves an important distinction
— but a distinction which only serves to corroborate the convictions we are about to offer.   Both facts and impressions
are important only in their results ; as they afford knowledge
or exert influence.   The results of facts are not necessarily or
often immediate; those of impressions are so.   The agency
of memory is, therefore, more important in the first case than
in the last.   A fact may lie in the mind, like a seed in the
ground, for days, months, and years, preserved by the memory, as the seed by the surrounding soil, before the fit season
shall arrive for it to put forth its manifestations of use and
beauty ; but an impression exerts its influence immediately
or not at all.   When, for intellectual purposes, the memory
recalls facts, their intrinsic value may remain the same, however frequently they may be placed before the mind; but
when for spiritual purposes, the effect is different.   Impressions become weaker, and their influences more and more
impaired or perverted, the more frequently they are acted
upon by memory.   Though, in their own nature, they are,
like all moral influences, imperishable, they are peculiarly
susceptible of corruption and perversion ; and it is far better
that they should subsist (though individually lost to consciousness) as wholesome elements of our moral being, than that
they should pass under a change which is injurious to them,
and can answer no good purpose whatever.

The great object of earthly discipline being to invigorate
the spiritual nature, it is clear that whatever causes useless
exhilaration on the one hand, or depression on the other,
ought to be avoided.   The habit of dwelling on the past
does both.   It needs not a moment's consideration to perceive that the contemplation of past achievements, (as
achievements, and not for the sake of their results,) must
occasion an elation of heart ill becoming those who are only
entering upon the path of spiritual life.   It is as if the infant

19

should glory in having put his foot to the ground, and sit down to congratulate himself on the feat, when perhaps his destiny may hereafter call him to traverse the globe. While we employ the memory in presenting and embellishing our own good deeds, we are indulging in the most degrading kind of spiritual voluptuousness, and insulting Him who bestowed our faculties for higher purposes.

Many who agree with us, as to the folly and danger of this species of spiritual intoxication, advocate an extreme quite as pernicious, though, as it is less alluring, it is less common. They would depress and debilitate the soul by the indulgence of remorse. Confounding remorse and repentance — things as different in their nature as Memory and Hope — they impose on themselves, and enjoin on others, the injurious penance of recording past sins, and reviving past sorrows, which, having yielded their results, are fit only to be forgotten. They flagellate and macerate their souls as monks of old did their bodies; and the punishment has the analogous effect of weakening the powers which need invigoration, and of superinducing disease to which the penitent is not constitutionally liable. If our meaning be here mistaken, if we be supposed to countenance levity and carelessness in spiritual concerns, or any contempt of the discipline of life, the misapprehension must arise from the error we are endeavouring to expose.

Remorse, by which we understand the bitter feeling arising from the belief that in a situation precisely the same we might have acted differently, cannot be rationally indulged by those who maintain that all the circumstances of their external and internal life are foreseen and ordained by God. The sorrow, shame, and fear, which are the elements of repentance, have no necessary connexion with Remorse, which is altogether a fallacious feeling, and like all other fallacies, hurtful to those who entertain it. In its operation it is wholly retrospective, and in its influence as debilitating as it is agonizing. It resembles the malignant tortures of the tyrant, and not the salutary and tender inflictions of the physician. Of the emotions which combine to form repentance, shame is retrospective, sorrow relates to the present, and fear is prospective. United, they produce a change of mind from vice to virtue, making use of the past only as subsidiary to the future. Thus and thus only should the past be used. Our contemplation should be fixed on the results of circumstances rather than on the circumstances themselves : i. e. on the present in preference to the past. Having found that in certain situations of temptation we have fallen, our proper use of our experience will be in avoiding such situations if we can, or in strengthening the principles which may uphold us ; and not in mourning because, being placed as we were, with infirm principles, we did not act as it was impossible we should have acted.

The Scriptures are our warrant for thus using our experience. They exhort sinners to sin no more; they supply support to virtuous principles, and incentives to holy feelings. They appeal to our experience of the misery of vice, and they also reproach the sinner. But nowhere do they blame any one for not having acted differently, his principles and habits remaining the same. They denounce his principles, they reprobate his habits, and all their exhortations tend, not to unavailing lamentation over the past, but to newness of life. It seems strange that while we advise one who has sustained a misfortune to turn his attention from it in search of a remedy, and one who has committed an error to repair and forget it, we should prescribe a different course for the guilty. We bid him be sorrowful, not that his motives are corrupt and his habits depraved, not that he is too weak to resist the impulse of his passions, but that, all this being the case, his conduct is not upright, pure, and moderate. On the same principle we should lament, not that some of our brethren are poor, and miserable, and blind, and naked; but that, being so, they are starved, and shivering, and in darkness. If they really feel sorrow and shame for their condition, and fear of its consequences, the best, the only account to which they can turn these painful emotions is as incentives to improve their state. As deep a feeling of shame as is consistent with a due independence of other men's opinions, as large a measure of sorrow as can consist with a sensibility to surrounding blessings, as awful an emotion of fear as is compatible with filial trust, are the proper constituents of repentance; but they should be used as prompting to present action, and tending to future good; and, therefore, as entirely disconnected with remorse.

It is universally allowed that means are valuable only as instrumental to an end, and that they should, therefore, be discarded when the end is obtained. If this maxim were acted on as generally as it is admitted, earth would become almost a heaven. We should have no misers, no profligates, no tyrants, no slaves; few, very few sufferers by what are called natural evils, and, what is more to our purpose, no self-tormentors. Guilt and sorrow having wrought their work of regeneration, would cease to be painful in the retrospect, if not forgotten. Of such a state of things we have at present no prospect in this world; but the nearer we can approach to it, the better for ourselves and others. The sooner we can get rid of the swathing bands of infancy, the more rapid will be our growth to maturity. The sooner we can with safety drop the outward forms which are but adventitious helps to essential things, the sooner we can rise above the external bondage and internal conflicts which beset and waylay and hinder the immortal spirit in its pilgrimage, the greater will be our vigor and fitness when entering on a better state of being. This was Paul's conviction when he described himself as forgetting the things which were behind, as well as pressing forwards to those which were before. He had, like other men, been guilty of faults and follies; but how did he revert to them? Not with any wish or imagination that they could be undone, or that they might have been avoided; but as warnings to himself and others; as testimonies of the moral providence of God, as healthy stimulants to a purer and more vigorous course of action. These results being obtained, these influences being realized, " the things which were behind" were consigned to oblivion.

The habit of dwelling on the past, has a narrowing as well as a debilitating influence. Behind us, there is a small, — an almost insignificant measure of time; before us, there is an eternity. It is the natural tendency of the mind to magnify the one, and to diminish the other; for the one we have measured step by step; the other is so foreshortened by the situation from which we view it, that we are unable to measure it. However steadily the reason may set about instituting the comparison, the imagination is first baffled by the infinite inequality, and then, turning for relief to the familiar space already traversed, is easily led to estimate its comparative by its positive magnitude. So false an estimate must impair both the rectitude and speed of our career. What chance has the helmsman of steering his course aright, if he contemplates only the shore he has left, the breakers he has traversed, and the clouds which have blown over? To the ocean before him he may discern no limits, and there may be no familiar object on the horizon which can help him to measure the intervening space; but he knows that something more than a waste of waters is before him; and if he be wise, he will strive to reach it by the shortest and safest track. With a similar intentness should we look into futurity with a perpetual reference of our observations to our present

19*

guidance. The conflicts of our youth were of an ignobler kind than those we shall henceforward have to sustain; our temptations meaner, our errors grosser, our fears more abject, our guilt more debasing; the contemplation of them can therefore only tend to contract the mind, and vitiate the moral taste.

It may be asked, how, if all this be true, we are to render the duty of instructing others compatible with our own spiritual improvement?

We answer, that while engaged in such a task, there is a perpetual reference of our own experience to the interests of others, which deprives the act of retrospection of all its injurious influences. In such a case, we are instituting vigorous, present action, and not lost in an enervating reverie on the past. We are actuated by an invigorating impulse, instead of sinking under a selfish temptation.

It may further be asked, whether in heaven there will be this forgetfulness of the things that are behind, — whether, among the secrets of the heart which shall there be revealed, there will not be a display of all the fostering and ripening influences which have nourished the soul to maturity? There probably will be such a display; according to our conceptions, there must be such an one exhibited to the intimate consciousness of every individual; but in a manner widely different from any which can take place here. Here we are apt to conceive external things as of a substantial, their influences as of a shadowy nature. There we shall apprehend exactly the reverse. All things of which we here take cognizance are but attributes and manifestations of an essence which now eludes our search, but which we shall hereafter recognise as a manifest existence. These external things will then have passed away as shadows, and will be immortalized in their influences. These influences, of which so many are here misapprehended through the imperfection of our faculties, or forgotten from their multitude, or unnoticed from their subtlety, will there be presented in completeness of number and proportion, as an epitome of the life which has been passed. They will not be summoned by memory, but recognised by consciousness. They will not pass before the mind in procession, like ghosts clad in earthly vestments: they will be presented in one vast, living group. It is evidently impossible to anticipate its magnitude and beauty; but we may predicate what some of its elements will be. The scenery will consist of all that is fairest in the visible frame of the universe, presented in essential and not material beauty, — forests, lawns, girdling mountains, and the illimitable ocean, bathed in an atmosphere of warmth and fragrance, and enveloped in an ether of light. All of the human race who have ministered to the spirit, however separated here by time or space, will be there assembled; patriarchs will be encamped among the pastures, and the chosen people in the wilderness: savage nations may bend before the lights of heaven, and our own kindred and friends compass us round. The Athenian sage may be seen instructing his pupils to listen to the harmonies of nature, while his own attentive ear catches faint echoes of a voice, unheard by all besides, rising above those harmonies to interpret them to listening souls. In the midst is He who points out to the universal race the approach to that presiding Presence which has created, sanctified, and immortalized this spiritual universe.

If the past should live again in some such mode as the imagination can only faintly shadow forth, it will be, strictly speaking, by a revivification and not by recollection: and for purposes totally different from those which we vainly hope to fulfil by mourning over irremediable evils, whether natural or moral, or by traversing again the field of experience, where we have already reaped all the produce which the season will yield. While time is the measure of our life, and vigor its noblest attribute, any habit by which the one is wasted, and the other enervated, must be irréconcileable with our destination, and incompatible with our lasting peace.

Norwich, 1830.

ESSAY ON THE PROPER USE OF THE PROSPECTIVE FACULTY.

II.

" Reaching forth unto those things which are before."

The perfect adaptation of the external and internal world to each other affords an evidence to which no one can be blind, that a perpetual reciprocation of influences is the purpose which they are designed to fulfil. It is not more certain that the materials afforded by nature are those by which the immortal spirit is to be built up, than that the stirring soul is to exert a reciprocal action upon those outward things which minister pleasure and pain to itself and others. Our recognition of the existence of any substance is coincident with our reception of influence from it; and it is a condition of happiness that a reciprocation, as certain, though sometimes less immediate, should take place between the faculties of the mind and the external objects on which their activity is to be employed. A faculty which moves without producing any result, no more fulfils its general purpose than a sunbeam darted on the eyes of the blind. It is made for action; and exercise is the condition of its health and vigor. This is true of all the intellectual faculties, and of all the moral powers generated by them. The one to which our attention is now more immediately directed is hope, one of the most powerful of spiritual agents.

The elements of hope are furnished by the memory, selected by the judgment, and combined and embellished by the imagination. This agent is, above all others, designed for an active, and not a contemplative existence. It can see nothing fair which it does not long to approach, nothing grand to which it does not aspire; nothing good which it does not strive to grasp. If fettered and imprisoned by the tyranny of any adverse power, it sickens at the sight of unattainable good, like the captive at the gleams of the morning sun; and, like him, if long stinted in the elements of its life, it pines and dies. But it is no more able to obtain for itself the objects of its desires than any other single faculty. All need coöperation; all fill an appointed office; all act upon one another while employed also on external objects. The office of hope is to stimulate the faculties to the attainment of some good of which it has a clear discernment. The mere perception of the existence of that good is not hope; the estimate of its value is not hope; the desire to possess it is not hope. With the perception and desire must be combined a stronger or weaker conviction of probability; and that probability depends on the employment of action, — of the appointed means to secure the desired end. Whenever the anticipation becomes disconnected with action, hope resigns its place to the imagination, and the substantial approaching good fades into a retreating, intangible vision. Thus the energy, the very existence of hope depends on action; and in proportion to the vigor of the hope will be the energy of the action.

Hope is not, like some other faculties, regularly progressive in the human mind during the period of its mortal existence. In childhood, its power is overweening; in youth, disproportioned to the judgment; in manhood, it sinks to its lowest rate of influence; but from that time, if the spirit be well disciplined, it becomes more and more refined and

vigorous till the close of life. Its omnipotence in childhood
is owing to the total deficiency of judgment. The infant
stretches his hands to the moon with the evident expectation
of reaching it; and the higher he is held, the more vehement
is his desire, and the more grievous his subsequent disappointment.

The infirmity of the judgment in youth is the cause of
the still disproportionate strength of hope; and it is not till
the experience of life has fostered the judgment, and chastened the hope, and yoked them into companionship, that
their pursuit of the highest objects can become enlightened,
and their advance equable and rapid. Thenceforward, their
natural destiny is to go from strength to strength, till all
obstacles shall be overcome, and all infirmities have vanished.

In this heavenward career was the Apostle far advanced
when he described himself as "reaching forth unto those
things which are before." Forgetting all that had no reference to present action, he made the future as well as the
past subsidiary to the present. Not idly gazing into futurity
any more than indulging in fruitless retrospect, he was perpetually *reaching* forwards, *pressing* towards the mark, so
that the recognition of higher objects became an immediate
impulse to their pursuit, and the seeing of the eye infallibly
originated the effort of the soul.

In this path (the brightest and shortest to heaven) the
rejoicing pilgrim meets with perpetual encouragements to
persevere, and infallible assurances that he is in the right
way. If the vigor of the action corresponds with the strength
of the hope, a larger scope will be gradually afforded for the
exercise of both, and the happiness to which they are designed to minister will be perpetually on the increase. There
is no comparison between the pleasure arising from the gratification of young and undisciplined desires, and of those

which are chastened by wisdom. There is likewise no comparison between the impetuous, ill-sustained activity of the
soul in youth, and its equable and vigorous exercise in a
healthy maturity. The two kinds of gratification are also
as different in nature as in degree. The greatest positive
pleasure which life affords is in a sense of development; and.
this is enjoyed to its utmost extent when the spiritual capacities, formed from strong intellectual faculties, are perpetually
exalted and enlarged; when hope comprehends views of
increasing sublimity and beauty, and prompts to the grandest achievements of which a growing nature is capable.

This sense of development, though not immediately occasioned by the prospective faculty, could not exist without its
agency. It springs immediately from the expansion of the
principles of action; and that expansion corresponds with
increased vigor of action; and that increased vigor of action
is caused by the elevation of the hope. For this expansion
of principles, provision is made in the revelation which is
our guide and teacher, and in the nature which God has
given us. It is sanctioned by the testimony of him who
knew what was in man, and by the experience of life. Yet
is such a development practically, if not speculatively, dis-
allowed by many who know not the evil consequences of
contracting and corrupting the influences of religious hope.
Such persons (Christians perhaps, though unenlightened)
provide themselves, and would fain furnish others with a set
of principles (which they believe to be set forth by the
Scriptures) for the guidance of the heart and life. These
principles they believe to be divine and perfect, unsusceptible
of change, and incapable of improvement. They set out
safely on their spiritual course, and, as long as they make
progress, all is well. But there is in all immortal things a
tendency to growth and increase; and the mind becomes
capable of higher desires and achievements than the princi-

ples on which it has acted can originate, unless they also are
allowed to expand with the growth of the mind. But here
the prejudice intervenes, against which we protest. Because
the principles are rightly believed to be divine in their origin,
and immortal in their nature, they are wrongly supposed to
be already perfect in their development, and immutable in
their form. It would be as reasonable to argue that the
principle of filial fear, by which the young child is properly
actuated, should continue to be his guiding principle through
life; as that the motives which influence the infant Christian
should serve the same purpose when his spiritual capabilities
become apostolic. The consequences, not alas! imaginary,
of this fatal mistake are, that the growth of the soul is
stunted, the range of the faculties is contracted, and hope,
whose divine office it is to present objects of nobler attainment, being baffled in every attempt to lead upward and
onward, sinks dispirited and feeble.

The truth is, and we have gospel authority for our conviction, that all influences must be modified to suit the changes
of the thing influenced. There were divine and eternal
principles involved in the institutions of Judaism; yet those
institutions have long been outgrown. There are divine and
eternal principles involved in the theism of many savage
nations, in the first religious notions of a child, in the various forms of civil government, and in the obscure dawn of
every science. Yet all these things are destined to overthrow or decay. The principles, being divine and imperishable, remain; but renovated, expanded, embellished. And
so it is with the principles of spiritual philosophy. Our
reverence must be given to their essence, not to their forms,
— forms often changed, and ever perishable. It has ever
been a benevolent employment of moral philosophers to
frame systems of ethics for the information and guidance of
inferior minds. In their day, such systems are the instru-

ments of important good; but if they could be rendered
permanent they would be rendered injurious. The most
exalted philosophy of one age is too mean for the capabilities of another. Let the principles of morals be, as they
undoubtedly are, destined to outlive the heavens and the
earth, still they must, like all other principles, be perpetually
modified by the results of experience, expanded so as to
occupy the growing faculties, and embellished, that they may
stimulate the exertions of religious hope; embellished, not
by earthly decorations, but by growing manifestations of that
celestial beauty which is ordained to be gradually revealed,
lest our weak vision should be "blasted with excess of
light."

It cannot be for an instant supposed that we are advocating laxity of principle, or independence of its guidance. It
is because we wish the principles of spiritual philosophy to
be strict and undeviating in their operation, that we contend
for their being allowed full and free scope. We would dis-
entangle them from fetters; we would pull off whatever mask
may disfigure them, and beseech them to show us the way to
life: and having done so, we would follow them, cheerfully
and undeviatingly, delighted to watch their growing radiance, and not afraid to recognise them amidst the glory of
their successive transfigurations.

Thus only can hope become to us the agent of heaven,—
the medium of infinite good. Thus only can our natural
sense of the insufficiency of present objects to satisfy the
soul be made the incentive to larger attainments; and the
consciousness that we are not already perfect, impel us to
follow after, to reach forward, to press on, till holiness and
peace be won.

The importance of the agency of hope in promoting our
spiritual advancement, leads on to the inquiry whether such
agency is to be exerted for ever. We think probably not.

20

We shall doubtless be for ever reaching forwards to higher
objects, but not under the same influences which are necessary here. Even here, our insight into futurity becomes
more distinct as well as more excursive, as the soul grows
in vigor; and if we should, as we may rationally anticipate,
so far participate in the attributes of divinity as to see things
that are not as though they were, the future will, like the
past, be embodied in the present, and the office of hope will
be ended. "Hope that is seen is not hope." Let us not,
however, shrink at the supposition that this guide of our
lives, this soother of our sorrows, this friend of our souls,
shall be annihilated. Her existence will merge in that of a
superior power. Her union with faith even here becomes so
close that the same attributes may be ascribed to each. In
heaven they shall be one, till another change shall pass upon
them, and they shall stand forth in sublimer dignity and
more radiant beauty, in the form of one whose name we yet
know not, but whose office will be to convince our glad
spirits that the same law which constitutes us the property of
God, makes all things ours, nature and providence, life and
death, things past, present, and to come.

THE HANWELL LUNATIC ASYLUM.

It is commonly agreed that the most deplorable spectacle
which society presents, is that of a receptacle for the insane.
In pauper asylums we see chains and strait-waistcoats, —
three or four half-naked creatures thrust into a chamber filled
with straw, to exasperate each other with their clamor and
attempts at violence; or else gibbering in idleness, or moping in solitude. In private asylums, where the rich patients

are supposed to be well taken care of in proportion to the
quantity of money expended on their account, there is as
much idleness, moping, raving, exasperating infliction, and
destitution of sympathy, though the horror is attempted to
be veiled by a more decent arrangement of externals. Must
these things be ?

I have lately been backwards and forwards at the Hanwell Asylum for the reception of the pauper lunatics of the
county of Middlesex. On entering the gate, I met a patient
going to his garden work, with his tools in his hand ; and
passed three others breaking clods with their forks, and
keeping near each other, for the sake of being sociable.
Further on, were three women rolling the grass in company ;
one of whom, — a merry creature, who clapped her hands
at the sight of visiters, had been chained to her bed for
seven years before she was brought hither, but is likely to
give little further trouble, henceforth, than that of finding
her enough to do. A very little suffices for the happiness of
one on whom seven years of gratuitous misery have been
inflicted ; — a promise from Mrs. Ellis to shake hands with
her, when she has washed her hands, — a summons to assist
in carrying in dinner, — a permission to help to beautify the
garden, are enough. Further on, is another in a quieter
state of content, always calling to mind the strawberries and
cream Mrs. Ellis set before the inmates on the lawn last year,
and persuading herself that the strawberries could not grow,
nor the garden get on without her, and fiddle-faddling in
the sunshine to her own satisfaction, and that of her guardians. This woman had been in a strait-waistcoat for ten
years before she was sent to Hanwell. In a shed in this
garden, sit three or four patients cutting potatoes for seed,
singing and amusing each other ; while Thomas, — a mild,
contented looking patient, passes by with Mrs. Ellis's clogs,
which he stoops to tie on with all possible politeness ; finding

it much pleasanter, as Dr. Ellis says, " to wait on a lady than be chained in a cell." In the bake-house, meanwhile, are a company of patients, kneading their dough ; and in the wash-house and laundry, many more, equally busy, who would be tearing their clothes to pieces if there was not the mangle to be turned, and a prodigious array of linen in the drying closet to be ironed. A story higher, are coteries of straw-plaiters, and basket-makers, and knitters, among the women, — and saddlers, shoemakers, and tailors among the men. A listless or moping one may be seen here and there; and the greater number can think of nothing but their own concerns; but certain curious arguments and friendly discussions may be perceived going on in corners ; kind offices are perpetually exchanged. The worst grievance, for the time, is a good deal of senseless chatter; while here is the actual fact of a large company of lunatics, clean, orderly, sociable, busy, and useful. When the dinner-bell rings, what a cheerful smile runs round ! and how briskly they move off to the ward where their meal awaits them ! feeling, perhaps, what one of them expressed, — " However little intellect we may have, we all know what the dinner-bell means." There is another place where the greater number of them go, with equal alacrity; to the chapel, where they may be seen, on a Sunday evening, decked out in what they consider their best, and equalling any other congregation whatever in the decorum of their deportment. Where are the chains, and the straw, and the darkness? Where are the howls, and the yells, without which the place cannot be supposed a mad-house? There is not a chain in the house, nor any intention that there ever shall be ; and those who might, in a moment, be provoked to howl and yell, are lying quietly in bed, talking to themselves, as there is no one else present to talk to. They will probably be soon ready to make a rational promise to be quiet, if they may get up

and join their companions. A few, who are not to be
trusted with the use of their hands, but who are better in society than alone, are walking about their ward, with their
arms gently confined ; but, out of five hundred and sixty-
six patients, only ten are under even so much restraint as
this. Almost the whole are of the same harmless class with
the painter in the hall, who hastens to remove his ladder and
paint-pot to let us pass, and politely hopes to see us all in
London very soon; or the self-satisfied knitter, who con-
cludes me to be a foreigner, because I do not know Mrs. A.
B——, of C——, who is a great friend of hers, and because
I have nothing to do with the Bank of England.

This institution is for pauper lunatics alone. Here —
thanks to Dr. and Mrs. Ellis — we see at length, an instance
of the poor receiving from society as much of their rights
as the rich, and more. Here, if Dr. and Mrs. Ellis had their
will, we should enjoy the animating spectacle of the most
dependent class of society receiving their due of enlightened
aid as well as support. That Dr. and Mrs. Ellis have not
their will fully gratified, is owing far less to any fault of individuals, than to circumstances of society hitherto uncon-
trollable. These circumstances will be, must be, over-ruled,
so that the rich shall be raised to an equality of advantage
with the poor, in the single instance in which they are at
present sunk below their pauper fellow-sufferers.

The inferiority of condition of the rich lunatic, will not
be questioned. It is only in circumstances of subordinate
importance that he is more favored than the most wretched
patient in the worst cell of a bad workhouse ; and, in all
that is essential, his situation is not to be compared with any
one of the paupers under Dr. Ellis's care. What matters
it how his meal is cooked, and of what delicacies it may be
composed, if he must eat it alone, and be reminded that he
is not to be trusted with a knife and fork? He would be

20*

happier sitting at one of Dr. Ellis's long tables, enjoying his
dumpling with the rest, and plying the knife and fork which
answer his purpose, while they are so contrived as to be as
harmless as a spoon.　What is it to him that his bed is of
down, if he cannot sleep?　He might envy Dr. Ellis's patients in their clean and quiet wards, sleeping through the
night, because they have been busy through the day.　What
is it to him that his chair is of damask, if he is to be strapped
down in it, because in his restlessness he is destructive?　He
would be far happier painting Dr. Ellis's hall, or patching a
shoe-sole, with hands shaking with eagerness.

Of course, it is not meant that the occupations of the rich
lunatic should be like those of the poor; but only that the
rich should have occupation, and the blessings which accompany it, — free action, variety of scene, and social sympathy.
The chance of the rich lunatic for recovery, or for happiness, if he be not recoverable, is undoubtedly much better
than that of the pauper, if it be duly improved.　Being educated, he takes cognizance of a much wider range of objects; his sympathies are more numerous, as well as keener;
and the arrangement of external circumstances has much
more influence, over him.　He is infinitely more susceptible
of moral influence, and of intellectual occupation.　Yet it
is the ignorant, gin-drinking pauper whom we now see entertained with constant employment, and governed by a look
or a sign, while the educated gentleman and accomplished
lady are left helpless, to be preyed upon by diseased thoughts,
and consigned to strait-waistcoats and bonds!　This is bar-
barity, this is iniquity, whatever may be done for them besides.　Let their secret be ever so carefully kept, let their
physicians have their forty or fifty guineas a week, every
week of the year, let heaven be wearied with prayers and
tears on their behalf, they are each still as oppressed and
injured beings as any wretch for whose sake the responsible

shall be brought into judgment. There is far more truth and reason in the perpetual complaints of such sufferers, "I ought not to be here," — "It is a barbarous thing to treat me in this manner," — "They have no more right to use me in this way than others have to use them so," — there is far more truth and reason in these complaints than in the excuses of those who inflict the confinement. Where is the right to conclude that because disorder is introduced into one department of the intellect, all the rest is to go to waste? Why, because a man can no longer act as he ought to do, is he not to act at all? Why, when energy becomes excessive, is it to be left to torment itself, instead of being more carefully directed than before? Why, because common society has become a scene of turmoil and irritation to a diseased mind, is that mind to be secluded from the tranquillizing influences of nature, and from such social engagements as do not bring turmoil and irritation? In this case, it is clearly the insane who have the best of the argument; their guardians are in this case the irrational. These guardians will not be justified in their arguments on this head, till their charge is placed in some such public institution as that at Hanwell, where the inmates shall compose a cheerful, busy, orderly society; where there shall be gardening, fishing, walking, and riding, drawing, music, and every variety of study, with as many kinds of manual occupation as the previous habits of the patients will admit. Till all insane persons are admitted into such public institutions, under the care of official guardians, the almost universal complaint of the lunatic will be justified. He may believe himself made of glass, but he is justified in his complaint. He may speak in the character of the Great Mogul, or of the angel Gabriel, but he is justified in his complaint.

Why must such institutions be public, and under the superintendence of official guardians? some will ask: and then

they will tell us of private asylums, where gardening and
study go on, and which are fitted up with turning lathes, and
musical instruments.   But the question is not whether any
private asylums are so conducted, but whether all are.   It is
not enough that, by a happy accident, two out of four lunatics, (or, more probably, two out of fifty,) may belong to
families who will not sacrifice them to their selfish desire of
secrecy, or to their pecuniary interests, or to their horror of
renewed intercourse with one who has been insane; while,
by an equally accidental happiness, their physician may be
fully qualified to "minister to a mind diseased."   It is not
enough that two out of four should be thus protected, if the
other two are left to the tender mercies of selfish relatives,
and interested physicians.   The other two have a claim to a
home, where they cannot be thrust out of sight, because
their family are ashamed of their misfortune; where they
will be permitted and assisted to recover, instead of being
treated in a manner which would upset the strongest brain;
where their remaining will be no source of gain to their
physician; and whence their return to society cannot be
impeded by the fears and interests of their relatives.   If it
be thought malignant to suppose that relatives and physicians
are apt to oppress their unfortunate charge, let it be remembered how strong are the temptations, and how feeble the
counteraction of circumstances.   Let it be remembered that
insanity is still considered as more disgraceful than crime,
and that it is therefore made the immediate interest of the
family of the insane to bury him in oblivion.   Let it be remembered that to bring him forth again, and reinstate him
in society, is to revive a family stigma, and involves a sacrifice of good things enjoyed in consequence of the sufferer's
affliction.   Let it be remembered that the physician feels it
a thankless office to restore his patient, and knows that his
emoluments will cease with the cure of his charge.   Let it

be remembered how much easier it is to go on in the old and undisputed way, which brings credit and profit, than to begin with anxiety and labor, a new method which will cause opposition, censure, and loss. Let it be remembered that the subject in whose behalf this new method is to be undertaken, is singularly helpless, and absolutely defenceless. Let all this be considered, and then who will say that the case of the opulent insane should be left to the chance of the perpetual victory of unsupported moral principle, over a host of ever-active temptations? If any one still doubts, let him compare the proportion of rich lunatics restored to society, with that of cures of recent cases in the Hanwell Asylum; let him inquire of conscientious physicians engaged in private asylums, whether they find it easy to dismiss their cured patients; and let him, moreover, ascertain whether there are no instances of a long struggle of disinterested affection, before certain sufferers could be released from the most exasperating bondage, to enjoy the free gifts of Providence, from which they had been for a long course of years iniquitously debarred. There is but one available precaution against iniquities like these; and that is, having the officers of asylums placed above the influence of the families of the patients, rewarded otherwise than in proportion to the hopelessness of the cases under their charge, and made responsible to some disinterested authority.

The attempts at secrecy in cases of insanity are already generally useless. There is no occasion to waste words in showing that they are selfish and cruel. Every one knows that it is for their own sakes that families consign an afflicted member to forgetfulness. Every one knows that the chances of recovery are incalculably lessened by the patient being withdrawn from congenial occupation and companionship. The only question is, Whether the secret is any better kept now than it would be if the sufferers were placed under a new kind of guardianship. Now, the family, the physicians, the intimate friends, the dependants, the lawyer, and other men of business with whom the sufferer is connected, and his companions, if he have any in his retreat, all know his state. If he were placed under official guardianship, his official guardians would also know. This is all the difference. No one dreams of such institutions being laid open to the gaze of curiosity, of their being subject to the visits of any but the friends and legal protectors of the sufferers. It is only meant that, instead of a jail under an irresponsible jailer, such an institution should be a retired colony under the protection of law, — an infirmary for a kind of disease which cannot be cured at home, and which experience has shown will not be cured in private hospitals. The case is just this. The disease may be kept secret at home, but it cannot be cured. It may possibly be cured at a private asylum, but cannot be kept secret. It will not be kept secret at an institution under official management; but it will, in all probability, be cured. What, therefore, does duty to society and to the sufferer require? That the attempt at secrecy should be given up, and the cure sought by the most promising means.

If proof of this strong probability of cure be desired, let the inquirer go to Hanwell and see what has been done there. If he wants enlightening as to the philosophy and fact of secrecy about cases of insanity, let him go and hear what is known at Hanwell. "Learn what is doing at Hanwell," is an entreaty which may fairly be addressed to every member of civilized society. It is the duty of the great number who are connected with the insane. It is the duty of every one who is interested, first in the diminution, and then in the extirpation of a disease which is known to be rapidly on the increase. It is the duty of all who desire that the fallen should not be trampled on. It is the duty

of the rulers who are guardians of the public welfare;
and especially of any one who may have official influence over the lot of any of the wretched class of opulent
lunatics. If they would but go and see with their own eyes
what may be done, there would be a prospect of the staying
of this great plague, and of the deliverance of not a few who
are now groaning under it.

The proportion of cures in a lunatic asylum must always
depend very much on the circumstances under which patients are admitted. In a Quaker asylum for instance, the
proportion of cures is not likely to be great, because Quaker
lunacy, being seldom caused by drunkenness or the violence
of the passions, usually proceeds from some deeper and more
unmanageable cause. The proportion of cured in the Hanwell Asylum must also hitherto be small, because very few
of the cases now there were recent. The malady of
the greater number was brought on by gin-drinking, and
rendered irremediable by a long infliction of chains and
idleness. Subjects originally so bad, and then kept in a state
of exasperation for years, cannot be expected to yield a good
proportion of curables. But, taking the recent cases, (which
is the only way of estimating the treatment fairly,) it will
be found that Dr. Ellis cures ninety in a hundred. It should
be remembered, too, that cases which are commonly called
recent, (that is, in which absolute insanity has been manifested for three months or so,) are not what enlightened
medical men would call recent. They know how long —
how many months or years — the evil must have existed,
though the patient may have been unconscious of it, or have
been driven by fear to conceal it. If, under this disadvan-
tage of concealment, ninety out of a hundred are yet cured,
who will say that any kind of insanity is incurable, if its
beginnings be but watched?

These beginnings would be watched if the guardianship of the insane were placed in proper hands. The pernicious desire of secrecy being put an end to, proper methods of management would be adopted in an early stage. At present, when the nerves begin to be affected, the patient's first object is to keep his uncomfortable feelings from his friends — a notion which would never have entered his head, if he had not been educated in it. The agonies of his sleepless nights, his dreamy feelings by day, his failure of memory, his unaccountable agitations, are all kept secret, with more and more pain, till his eccentricities can be self-restrained no longer. His horror-stricken family then pursue the same plan. They try to fancy him rational to the last moment, and keep him shut up from everybody but his physician, till he becomes too ill to remain longer at home. Scarcely a beginning is yet made in overcoming a prejudice, and consequent custom, which would all along have appeared absurd enough if applied in any other case. It is difficult to see why an inflammation of a little portion of the brain should be more disgraceful than an inflammation of the throat; yet how absurd would it have been called, any time within this century, for a man with a quinsey, to have struggled to conceal it, in the hope that it would go away of itself, before any body found it out, — struggling to speak and swallow as if all was right about his throat, — and in perpetual agony lest the unlucky choke, which must come at last, should happen to betray him. There is all possible certainty that inflammation of the brain may be stopped as easily as any other inflammation, if it is attacked in time; and when people have learned to consider it in the same light as any other ailment, (except in as far as the importance of its consequences should induce a greater watchfulness,) they will first train their children, as wise parents do, to give a simple account of any uneasiness that they may feel, and then be ready to put them, with like simplicity, under the management most likely to effect their cure. When those days come, insanity will probably be no more of an evil than the temporary delirium of a fever is now; and those days will be at hand whenever a blameless disease shall cease to be considered a disgrace, and the absurdity of concealment shall be abandoned. That this delusion should be surmounted, will be found the heart's desire of every enlightened and benevolent physician of the insane. If there be any who help to maintain it by humoring the prejudices of the friends of their patients, they expose themselves to a violent suspicion of caring more for their gains than for their science or their duties.

The commonest objection to the true method of managing lunatics, — treating them as nearly as possible like rational beings, — is the supposed danger of letting them be at large. What is to be learned at Hanwell about this?

It is nearly twenty years since Doctor and Mrs. Ellis began to treat lunatics as much as possible as if they were sane; and in all that time *no accident has happened.* This was, of course, the point of their management most anxiously pondered by them, when they took the charge of the Wakefield institution, which was conducted by them with high honor and success for many years. The question of confinement or liberty was that on which the whole of their management hung. They decided for liberty; determining that the possible loss of a life, perhaps of their own, would be a less evil than the amount of wo inflicted by the imprisonment of a great number of irritable persons for a long series of years. They threw open their doors, were lavish of air, sunshine, liberty, and amusement to their patients; and have been rewarded by witnessing the happiness they proposed, without paying the possible penalty. It should be remembered that the irritable are exasperated by opposition, and not by freedom. How much of the safety of Dr. Ellis's

21

patients may be owing to the recognition of this principle,
and how much to the system of classification to which he has
been led by his adoption of phrenological principles, it is for
himself to declare; but no one who witnesses the results can
doubt the wisdom of his methods. I saw the worst patients
'in the establishment, and conversed with them, and was far
more delighted than surprised to see the effect of companionship on those who might be supposed the most likely to irri-
tate each other. Some are always in a better state when
their companions are in a worse; and the sight of wo has
evidently a softening effect upon them. One poor creature,
in a paroxysm of misery, could not be passed by; and while
I was speaking to her as she sat, two of the most violent
patients in the ward joined me, and the one wiped away the
scalding tears of the bound sufferer, while the other told me
how "genteel" an education she had had, and how it grieved
them all to see her there. Why should it be supposed that
the human heart ceases its yearnings whenever confusion is
introduced among the workings of the brain? And what is
so likely to restore order, as allowing their natural play to
the affections which can never be at rest? For those who
cannot visit Hanwell, it may be enough to know that no
accident has happened among Dr. Ellis's many hundred
patients, during the twenty years that he has been their
guardian; but there is a far higher satisfaction in witnessing
and feeling the evident security which prevails in the establishment, where the inmates are more like whimsical children, manageable by steadiness, than wretched maniacs,
controllable only by force. "O, do let me out! Do let me
go to my dinner!" wailed one in her chamber, who had
been sent there because she was not "well enough" for
society in the morning. The dinner-bell had made her wish
herself back again among her companions. "Let me out,
and I will be quiet and gentle." "Will you?" was the

only answer when her door was thrown open. In an instant she dispersed her tears, composed her face, and walked away like a chidden child. The talk of these paupers often abounds in oaths when they first enter; but the orderly spirit of the society soon banishes them. " I cannot hear those words," Mrs. Ellis says. " I will hear any thing that you have to say in a reasonable manner. I am in no hurry. I will sit down: now let me hear." No oaths can follow an invitation like this; and the habit of using them is soon broken.

An observation of what is passing within the walls at Hanwell may be found to throw much light on what is done in the world; and, on this account, it is to be desired that all who have any share of the welfare of humanity in charge, should visit the place for higher purposes than those of curiosity. They may gain even much more than guidance towards the true principle of treating insanity. Let them inquire the chief cause of all this mental disease among the women who compose the majority of the society, and they will be told, " gin-drinking." Let them next inquire what led to gin-drinking, and take the answer to heart. Let them mark the direction taken by the sorrow and anger of the murmurers. " How do I do?" said one, in answer to a gentleman present, who had once incautiously promised to see what could be done for her. " Pretty well, only pretty well. How else should I be in this place? It is a barbarous thing to keep me here when you said, long ago, you would do something to get me to London. You are like all the rest. You are a delusive man." It is as true of these help-less sufferers, as of the proudest among the wise: that not a word of their lips is forgotten before God. Alas, for those against whom the idlest of those words is rising up in judg-ment!

One blessed consequence (among many) must ensue from
the Hanwell institution being more visited and becoming
better known.   There could not but be a speedy abatement
of that popular horror at the inmates, which, when they
arrive at the stage of convalescence, is an affliction and an
injury, from which their benevolent guardians are wholly
unable to protect them.   Mrs. Ellis's efforts to procure for
them a gradual and safe re-admittance into the world have
failed, though her wishes were complied with by the com-
mittee.   She petitioned for a pony chaise, in which the
convalescent patients might go backwards and forwards
between Brentford and Hanwell, when a messenger went to
Brentford on business ; and every one must see the advantage
to the patients of witnessing a little of the bustle of the world
before they were called on to engage in it for themselves.
The pony chaise was granted ; but, alas ! the people in the
neighbourhood were frightened, and the permission to go to
Brentford is withdrawn !   For the same reason, no patient is
now permitted to show himself in the parish church, however
well he may be.   The trial was made, and the patients conducted themselves perfectly well ; but it disturbed the devotions of their neighbours that they should be there, thanking
God for their relief from the worst of calamities ; and at that
church they are to be seen no more.   This popular prejudice
seems to render necessary the fulfilment of Mrs. Ellis's
anxious desire that there should be a liberty asylum, an
intermediate resting-place, for these poor people, between
their present quiet home and the bustling abodes to which
they must return.   These people are paupers.   They cannot
command leisure when they feel troubled, or rest when their
new strength fails them.   However they may feel overcome
during their first weeks of re-entrance upon life, they must
seek for work, and do it to get bread.   This is their happiest
lot.   Few of them escape being wounded by some shyness,

some intimation that, having been in a mad-house, they will never again be on equal terms with the rest of the world. They are well aware of this beforehand, as is shown by their falling tears when Mrs. Ellis's last benevolent smile is upon them. Her parting blessing *is* a blessing. She invites them to come "home," whenever they find themselves uncomfortable; and the feeling that they can do so, supports them when they go forth from their safe and kindly retreat, to shift for themselves in the cold world. The use made of the invitation shows this. A painter, who had long experienced the kindness of Dr. and Mrs. Ellis, at Wakefield, was grieved to leave them. Sometime after he had returned to his business in the world, he had a typhus fever; and when he was recovering, his first desire was to get back into his old quarters. "I will go up to the asylum," said he; "I am sure they will give me a nursing till I get strong." And so they did. But no invitation to return, no possible ordering of circumstances with respect to them in the Hanwell institution, will serve the purpose of a liberty asylum, where all will be rational, and at perfect liberty to go in and out, in pursuit of their daily labor, and other business in the world. It is to secure them quiet nights, and a clean and orderly home, and a refuge from wounding treatment when first resuming labors and anxieties, which are quite enough for a delicate brain to bear, that this liberty asylum is desired. Till such an establishment exists, there will be a failure of justice towards Dr. and Mrs. Ellis, and of mercy to their charge.

But there is another arrangement even more desirable than this. In witnessing the results of this splendid philanthropic experiment, nothing painful was intermingled with my delight but the thought of how much hangs upon two lives. This is too frail a dependence for a scheme which involves so vast an amount of human happiness. The best acknowl-

21 *

edgment which society in its gratitude can make to Dr. and
Mrs. Ellis is to take care that their work shall be perpetuated
when they rest from their labors.   They have still the sorrow,
after their long and intrepid toils, of finding themselves unaided, even in their own institution, by the services of hearts
and minds like their own.   How is it possible that servants
should be fit for so peculiar an office as that of tending the
insane, when no pains have yet been taken to train them?
By common consent, lunatics have hitherto been treated as
babes, or as wild animals, soothed by falsehoods, kept in awe
by harshness, or controlled by violence.   The race of servants is not likely to be the first to perceive the folly and
iniquity of these methods, and to set about speaking nothing
but truth, and uttering nothing but mildness, through all the
temptations and provocations they must meet with in the
discharge of their office.   It is high time that some arrangement was adopted for training governors for their responsibilities, and servants for their work.   Mrs. Ellis truly says,
that there is little to be taught, — good sense and kindness
(unteachable requisites!) being the life and soul of the system : if system it may be called.   But there is much to
be unlearned ; and people are disabused of their prejudices
by example, not by precept.   Dr. and Mrs. Ellis ought not
to be left to pick out the best assistants they can select from
the multitude of ignorant mercenaries who apply for service.
It should be the care of the benevolent to be on the watch
for persons worthy to assist and succeed them, and bring
those persons under the operation of the benignant examples of the governor of the Hanwell house, and of his lady.
We may then feel certain that the social benefit originated
by them is made fast and safe, and that future generations
will have cause to bless their names.   ,

Some future generation will perhaps be more sensible
than we are of the remarkable circumstance which this

institution presents to us, in the equal participation of a
woman in one of the most magnificent achievements by which
society is served in this age of magnificent achievements.
The grandest philanthropic experiments which have hitherto
proved undoubtedly successful, have been the work of men;
and it has been thought enough for women to be permitted
to follow and assist. Here is an instance, unsurpassed in
importance, where a woman has, at least, equally participa-
ted; an instance, too, where more was required than the
spirit of love, patience, and fortitude, for which credit has
always been granted to the high-minded of the sex. A
strong and sound intellect was here no less necessary than a
kind heart. The very first act was an intrepid stripping off
of prejudices, and an enlightened discernment alike of the
end to be attained, and the means to be chosen. The instrument has been proved perfectly equal to the work, and
the sex is placed in a new state of privilege. Some will be
doubtless found to perceive and make use of it. Women
who are dejectedly looking round for some opening through
which they may push forth their powers of intellect, as well
as their moral energies, will set Mrs. Ellis's example before
them, and feel that the insane are their charge. They may
wait till the end of the world for a nobler office than that
of building up the ruins of a mind into its original noble
structure. Not the faithful Jews, restoring the temple of
Jehovah by night, with arms by their sides, were engaged
in so hallowed a task. It involves some few perils, and a
multitude of irksome toils; and the weight of the sympathies
which it puts in action, are at times as much as can be sustained: but the spirit rises to meet its responsibilities; and
it has never yet been proved to what peril and what toil the
bravery and patience of woman are unequal. They will not
fail in an instance like this, where it is known that the contest is with an evil which has only to be fairly met, to give

ground, day by day. If it is true of woman that she can
hope against hope, and toil against unceasing discourage-
ment, there is no question what she can and will do towards
a work whose completion is, if she will believe it, in her
own hands.

LONDON, 1834.

LETTER TO THE DEAF.

MY DEAR COMPANIONS,

THE deafness under which I have now for some years past
suffered, has become, from being an almost intolerable grievance, so much less of one, to myself and my friends, than
such a deprivation usually is, that I have often of late
longed to communicate with my fellow-sufferers, in the hope
of benefiting, by my experience, some to whom the discipline, is newer than to myself.

I have for some time done what I could in private conversation ; but it never occurred to me to print what I had to
say, till it was lately not only suggested to me, but urged
upon me as a duty. I adopt this method as the only means
of reaching you all; and I am writing with the freedom
which I should use in a private letter to each of you. It
does not matter what may be thought of any thing I now
say, or of my saying it in this manner, by those who do not
belong to our fraternity. I write merely for those who are
deeply concerned in the subject of my letter. The time
may come when I shall tell the public some of our secrets,
for other purposes than those which are now before me. At
present I address only you ; and as there is no need for us to
tell our secrets to one another, there may be little here to
interest any but ourselves

I am afraid I have nothing to offer to those of you who
have been deaf from early childhood. Your case is very

different from mine ; as I have reason to know through my intimacy with a friend who became deaf at five years old. Before I was so myself, I had so prodigious a respect for this lady, (which she well deserves,) that if she could have heard the lightest whisper in which a timid girl ever spoke, I should not have dared to address her.   Circumstances directed her attention towards me, and she began a correspondence, by letter, which flattered me, and gave me courage to converse with her when we met, and our acquaintance grew into an intimacy which enabled me at last to take a very bold step ; — to send her a sonnet, in allusion to our common infirmity ; my deafness being then new, and the uppermost thing in my mind, day and night.   I was surprised and mortified at her not seeming to enter into what I had no doubt in the world must touch her very nearly ; but I soon understood the reason.   When we came to compare our experiences, we were amused to find how differently we felt, and had always felt, about our privation.   Neither of us, I believe, much envies the other, though neither of us pretends to strike the balance of evil.   She has suffered the most privation, and I the most pain.

Nothing can be more different than the two cases necessarily are.   Nine-tenths of my miseries arose from false shame ; and, instead of that false shame, the early deaf entertain themselves with a sort of pride of singularity, and usually contrive to make their account of this, as of other infirmities, by obtaining privileges and indulgences, for which they care much more than for advantages which they have never known, and cannot appreciate.   My friend and I have principles, major and minor, on which our methods of managing our infirmity are founded ; but some of the minor principles, and all the methods, are as different as might be expected from the diversity of the experience which has given rise to them.   Nothing can be better for her than her own management; and, of course, I think the same of my own for myself, or I should change it. Before I dismiss this lady, I must mention that I am acquainted with several deaf ladies; so that no one but herself and our two families can know whom I have been referring to.

I am afraid some of you may be rather surprised at the mention of plans, and methods, and management,—for, alas! we are but too apt to shrink from regularly taking in hand our own case. We are left to our own weakness in this respect. We can have but little help,—and we usually have none, but much hinderance. I do not mean by this, to find any fault with our neighbours. I have met with too much sympathy, (as far as sympathy is possible,) with too much care, and generosity, and tenderness, to have the least inclination to complain of any body connected with me. I only mean that this very tenderness is hurtful to us in as far as it encourages us to evade our enemy, instead of grappling with it; to forget our infirmity, from hour to hour, if we can; and to get over the present occasion somehow, without thinking of the next. This would be considered a strange way of meeting any other kind of evil; and its consequences in our case are most deplorable. If we see that the partially deaf are often unscrupulous about truth, inquisitive, irritable, or morose; suspicious, low-spirited, or ill-mannered, it is owing to this. It is impossible for *us* to deny that if principles are ever needed, if methods are ever of use as supports and guides, it must be in a case where each of us must stand alone in the midst of temptations and irritations which beset us every hour, and against which no defence of habit has been set up, and no bond of companionship can strengthen us. What these temptations and irritations are, we all know:—the almost impossibility of not seeming to hear when we do not,—the persuasion that people are taking advantage of us in what they say,—that they are discussing us, or laughing at us, — that they do not care for us as long as they are merry, — that the friend who takes the pains to talk to us might make us less conspicuous if he would, — the vehement desire that we might be let alone, and the sense of neglect if too long let alone; all these, absurd and wicked fancies as they are seen to be when fairly set down, have beset us all in our time; have they not? For my own part, though I am never troubled with them now, I have so vivid a remembrance of them all, that I believe a thousand years would not weaken the impression. Surely that degree of suffering which lashes us into a temporary misanthropy when our neighbours are happiest, which makes us fly to our chambers, and lock ourselves in, to hide the burning tears which spring at the mirth of those we love best, which seduces us into falsehood or thanklessness to God and man, is enough to justify and require the most careful fixing of principles, and framing of methods. We might as well let our hearts and minds — our happiness — take their chance without discipline in all cases whatever, as neglect our own discipline in this.

The first thing to be done is to fix upon our principle. This is easy enough. To give the least possible pain to others is the right principle. How to apply it requires more consideration. Let me just observe, that we are more inexcusable in forsaking our principle here than in any other case, and than the generality of people are in the generality of cases. Principles are usually forsaken from being forgotten, — from the occasion for them not being perceived. We have no such excuse while beginning to act upon our principle. We cannot forget, — we cannot fail to perceive the occasion, for five minutes together, that we spend in society. By the time that we become sufficiently at ease to be careless, habit may, if we choose, have grown up to support our principle, and we may be safe.

Our principle requires that we should boldly review our case, and calmly determine for ourselves what we will give up, and what struggle to retain. It is a miserable thing to get on without a plan from day to day, nervously watching whether our infirmity lessens or increases, or choosing to take for granted that we shall be rid of it; or hopelessly and indolently giving up every thing but a few selfish gratifications; or weakly refusing to resign what we can no longer enjoy. We must ascertain the probability for the future, if we can find physicians humane enough to tell us the truth: and where it cannot be ascertained, we must not delay making provision for the present. The greatest difficulty here arises from the mistaken kindness of friends. The physician had rather not say, as mine said to me, "I consider yours a bad case." The parent entreats to be questioned about any thing that passes; brothers and sisters wish that music should be kept up; and, what is remarkable, every body has a vast deal of advice to give, if the subject be fairly mentioned; though every body helps, by false tenderness, to make the subject too sacred an one to be touched upon. We sufferers are the persons to put an end to all this delusion and mismanagement. Advice must go for nothing with us in a case where nobody is qualified to advise. We must cross-question our physician, and hold him to it till he has told us all. We must destroy the sacredness of the subject, by speaking of it ourselves; not perpetually and sentimentally, but, when occasion arises, boldly, cheerfully, and as a plain matter of fact. When every body about us gets to treat it as a matter of fact, our daily difficulties are almost gone; and when we have to do with strangers, the simple, cheerful declaration, "I am very deaf," removes almost all trouble. Whether there was ever as much reluctance to acknowledge defective sight as there now is defective hearing, — whether the mention of spectacles was ever as hateful as that of a trumpet

is now, I do not know; but I was full as much grieved as
amused lately at what was said to me in a shop where I went
to try a new kind of trumpet: "I assure you, Ma'am," said
the shopkeeper, "I dread to see a deaf person come into my
shop.   They all expect me to find them some little thing that
they may put into their ears, that will make them hear every
thing, without any body finding out what is the matter with
them."

W ell, what must be given up, and what may be struggled
for ?

The first thing which we are disposed to give up is the
very last which we ought to relinquish — society.   How many
good reasons we are apt to see, — are we not? — why we
should not dine out; why it is absurd to go into an evening
party; why we ought to be allowed to remain quiet up stairs
when visiters are below!   This will not do.   Social communication must be kept up through all its pains, for the sake of
our friends as well as for our own.   It can never be for the
interest of our friends that we should grow selfish, or absorbed
in what does not concern our day and generation, or nervous,
dependant, and helpless in common affairs.   The less able
we become to pick up tidings of man and circumstance, the
more diligently we must go in search of the information.
The more our sympathies are in danger of contraction, the
more must we put ourselves in the way of being interested
by what is happening all about us.   Society is the very last
thing to be given up; but it must be sought, (and I say it
with deep sympathy for those of you to whom the effort is
new,) under a bondage of self-denial, which annihilates for
a time almost all the pleasure.   Whatever may be our fate, —
whether we may be set down at the end of a half circle,
where nobody comes to address us, or whether we may be
placed beside a lady who cannot speak above her breath, or
a gentleman who shouts till every body turns to see what is

the matter; whether one well-meaning friend says across the room, in our behalf, "do tell that joke over again to ———," and all look to see how we laugh when they have done; or another kind person says, "how I wish you could hear that song," — or "that harp in the next room," or "those sweet nightingales," if we happen to be out of doors, — whether any or all of these doings and sayings befall us, we must bravely go on taking our place in society.

Taking our place, I say. What is our place? It is difficult to decide. Certainly, not that of chief talker, any more than that of chief listener. We must make up our minds for a time to hold the place that we may chance to be put into, — to depend on the tact and kindness of those near us. This is not very pleasant; but if we cannot submit to it for a while, we cannot boast much of our humility, nor of our patience. We must submit to be usually insignificant, and sometimes ridiculous. Do not be dismayed, dear companions. This necessity will not last long, and it is well worth while undergoing it. Those who have strength of mind to seek society under this humiliation, and to keep their tempers through it, cannot long remain insignificant there. They must rise to their proper place, if they do but abstain from pressing beyond it. It is astonishing how every thing brightens, sooner or later. The nightingales and the harp will be still out of the question : but they will be given up almost without pain, because it is a settled matter to every body present that they are out of the question. Friends will have discovered that jokes are not the things to be repeated; and that which is repeated will be taken as coming in due course, and will at length consist of all that has been really worth hearing of what has been said. Other people may laugh without occasioning a nervous distortion in your countenance; and it is quite-certain that if your temper have stood your trial, you will never pass an evening without meeting with some attention which will touch, some frank kindness which will elevate your feelings, and send you home wiser and happier than you came forth.

This can only be, however, if you have stood your trial well, if you bring an open temper and an open countenance. It is a matter of wonder that we are addressed so much as we are; and if, in addition to the difficulty of making us hear, we offer the disagreeableness of (not a constrained, that will be pitied, but) a frowning countenance, we may betake ourselves to the books or prints on the table, but may as well give up all hope of conversation. As a general rule, nothing can be worse than for people to think at all about their coun- tenances; but in our case it is worth while, for a time, and to a certain extent. I was kindly told, a few years ago, that many people wished to converse with me, but that I looked as if I had rather not be spoken to. Well I might; for I then discovered that in trying to check one bad habit, I had fallen into another. I had a trick of sighing, to cover which I used to twist my fingers almost out of joint, (and so do you, I dare say,) and the pain of this process very naturally made me frown. My friend's hint put me on my guard. Instead of twisting my fingers, I recalled my vow of patience, and this made me smile; and the world has been a different place to me since. Some such little rule as turning every sigh into a smile will help you over a multitude of difficulties, and save you, at length, the trouble of thinking about either smil- ing or sighing.

It has always been my rule *never* to ask what is going forward; and the consequence has well compensated all I had to go through from the reproaches of kind friends, who were very anxious that I should trouble them in that way. Our principle plainly forbids the practice; and nothing can therefore justify it. There is at first no temptation; for we had then rather miss the sayings of the wise men of Greece, than obtain them by such means; but the practice once begun, there is no telling where it will stop. Have we not seen — it sickens me to think of it — restless, inquisitive, deaf people, who will have every insignificant thing repeated to them, to their own incessant disappointment, and the suffering of every body about them, whom they make, by their appeals, almost as ridiculous as themselves. I never could tolerate the idea of any approach to the condition of one of these. I felt, besides, that it was impossible for me to judge of what might fairly be asked for, and what had better be let pass. I therefore obstinately adhered to my rule; and I believe that no one whom I have met in any society, (and I have seen a great deal,) has been enabled to carry away more that is valuable, or to enjoy it more thoroughly than myself. I was sure that I might trust to the kindness of my neighbours, if I was but careful not to vex and weary it; and my confidence has been fully justified. The duty extends to not looking as if you wanted to be amused. Your friends can have little satisfaction in your presence, if they believe that when you are not conversing you are no longer amused. "I wonder every day," said a young friend to me, when I was staying in a large well-filled country house, "what you do with yourself during our long dinners, when we none of us talk with you, because we have talked so much more comfortably on the lawn all the morning. I cannot think how you help going to sleep." "I watch how you help the soup," was my inconsiderate reply — I was not aware how inconsiderate, till I saw how she blushed every day after on taking up the ladle. I mentioned the soup only as a specimen of my occupations during dinner. There were also the sunset lights and shadows on the lawn to be watched, and the never-ceasing play of human countenances, — our grand resource when we have once gained ease enough to enjoy them at leisure. There were graceful and light-hearted girls, and there was an originality of action in the whole family, which amused me from morning till night. The very apparatus of the table, and the various dexterities of the servants, are matters worth observing when we have nothing else to do. I never yet found a dinner too long, whether or not my next neighbour might be disposed for a tête-à-tête —never, I mean, since the time when every social occupation was to me full of weariness and constraint.

Another rule which I should recommend is always to wait to be addressed : except in our own houses, where the exception must be made with our guests. Some, I know, adopt a contrary rule, for this reason, that if we ask a question to which we can anticipate the answer, the awkwardness of a failure at the outset is prevented. But my own feeling is against obliging any one to undertake the trouble of conversing with us. It is perfectly easy to show, at the moment of being addressed, that we are sociably disposed, and grateful for being made companions ; and I, at least, feel the pleasure to be greater for its having been offered me.

I think it best for us to give up also all undertakings and occupations in which we cannot mark and check our own failures ; — teaching any thing which requires ear, preaching, and lecturing, and music. I gave up music, in opposition to much entreaty, some reproach, and strong secret inclination ; because I knew that my friends would rather put up with a wrong bass in my playing, and false tune in my singing, than deprive me of a resource. Our principle clearly forbids this kind of indulgence ; therefore, however confident we may be of our musical ear, let us be quite sure that we shall never again be judges of our own music, or our own oratory, and avoid all wish of making others suffer needlessly by our privations. Listen to no persuasions, dear companions, if you are convinced that what I have said is right. No one *can* judge for you. Be thankful for the kind intentions of your

22*

friends; but propose to enjoy their private eloquence instead of offering your own in public; and please yourselves with their music, as long as you can, without attempting to rival it.   These are matters in which we have a right to be obstinate, if we are sure of the principle we go upon; for we are certainly much better able to judge what will be for the happiness of our friends, in their common circumstances, than they can be of ours, in our uncommon ones.

How much less pain there is in calmly estimating the enjoyments from which we must separate ourselves, of bravely saying, for once and for ever, " Let them go," than in feeling them waste and dwindle, till their very shadows escape from our grasp! With the best management, there is quite enough, for some of us, of this wasting and dwindling, when we find, at the close of each season, that we are finally parting with something; and at the beginning of each, that we have lost something since the last.   We miss first the song of the skylark, and then the distant nightingale, and then one bird after another, till the loud thrush itself seems to have vanished; and we go in the way of every twittering under the eaves, because we know that that will soon be silenced too.   But I need not enlarge upon this to you.   I only mean to point out the prudence of lessening this kind of pain to the utmost, by making a considerable effort at first; and the most calculating prudence becomes a virtue, when it is certain that as much must at best be gone through as will afflict our friends, and may possibly overpower ourselves, our temper and deportment, if not our principles and our affections.   I do not know how sufficiently to enforce these sacrifices being made with frankness and simplicity; and nothing so much needs enforcing.   If our friends were but aware how cruel an injury is the false delicacy which is so common, they would not encourage our false shame as they do.   If they have known anything of the bondage of ordinary false shame, they may imagine something of our suffering in circumstances of irremediable singularity. Instead of putting the singularity out of sight, they should lead us to acknowledge it in words, prepare for it in habits, and act upon it in social intercourse. If they will not assist us here, we must do it for ourselves. Our principle, again, requires this. Thus only can we save others from being uneasy in our presence, and sad when they think of us. That we can thus alone make ourselves sought and beloved is an inferior consideration, though an important one to us, to whom warmth and kindliness are as peculiarly animating as sunshine to the caged bird. This frankness, simplicity, and cheerfulness, can only grow out of a perfect acquiescence in our circumstances. Submission is not enough. Pride fails at the most critical moment. Nothing short of acquiescence will preserve the united consistency and cheerfulness of our acknowledgment of infirmity. Submission will bemoan it while making it. Pride will put on indifference while making it. But hearty acquiescence cannot fail to bring forth cheerfulness. The thrill of delight which arises during the ready agreement to profit by pain — (emphatically the joy with which no stranger intermeddleth) — must subside like all other emotions; but it does not depart without leaving the spirit lightened and cheered; and every visitation leaves it in a more genial state than the last.

And now, what may we struggle for? I dare say the words of the moralist lie as deep down in your hearts as in my own: "We must not repine, but we may lawfully struggle!" I go further, and say that we are bound to struggle. Our principle requires it. We must struggle for whatever may be had, without encroaching on the comfort of others. With this limitation, we must hear all we can, for as long as we can. Yet how few of us will use the helps we might have! How seldom is a deaf person to be seen with a trumpet! I should have been diverted, if I had not been too much vexed,

at the variety of excuses that I have heard on this head since
I have been much in society. The trumpet makes the sound
disagreeable; or is of no use; or is not wanted in a noise,
because we hear better in a noise; nor in quiet, because
we hear very fairly in quiet; or we think our friends
do not like it; or we ourselves do not care for it, if it
does not enable us to hear general conversation; or — a
hundred other reasons just as good. Now, dear friends,
believe me, these are but excuses. I have tried them
all in turn, and I know them to be so. The sound soon
becomes anything but disagreeable; and the relief to the
nerves, arising from the use of such a help, is indescribable.
None but the totally deaf can fail to find some kind of
trumpet that will be of use to them, if they choose to
look for it properly, and give it a fair trial. That it is not
wanted in a noise is usually true; but we are seldom in a
noise; and quiet is our greatest enemy, (next to darkness,
when the play of the countenance is lost to us.) To reject
a tête-à-tête in comfort because the same means will not
afford us the pleasure of general conversation, is not very
wise. Is it? As for the fancy, that our friends do not like
it, it is a mistake, and a serious mistake. I can speak confidently of this. By means of galvanism, (which I do not,
from my own experience, recommend,) I once nearly recovered my hearing for a few weeks. It was well worth while
being in a sort of nervous fever during those weeks, and
more deaf than ever afterwards, for the enlightenment which
I gained during the interval on various subjects, of which
the one that concerns us now, is, — the toil that our friends
undergo on our account. This is the last topic on which I
should speak to you, but for the prevalent unwillingness in
our fraternity to use such helps as may ease the lungs of all
around them as much as their own nerves. Of course, my
friends could not suddenly accommodate their speech to my

improved hearing; and I was absolutely shocked when I found what efforts they had been making for my sake. I vowed that I would never again bestow an unkind thought on their natural mistakes, or be restive under their inapplicable instructions; and, as for carrying a trumpet, I liked it no better than my brethren till then; but now, if it would in any degree ease my friends that I should wear a fool's cap and bells, I would do it. Any of you who may have had this kind of experience, are, I should think, using trumpets. I entreat those of you who have not been so made aware of your state, to take my word for what you are obliging your friends to undergo. You know that we can be no judges of the degree of effort necessary to make us hear. We might as well try to echo the skylark. I speak plainly; it may seem harshly; but I am sure you would thank me ere long if I could persuade you to encounter this one struggle to make the most of your remnant of one of God's prime blessings.

Another struggle must be to seize or make opportunities for preserving or rectifying our associations, as far as they are connected with the sense which is imperfect. Hunger and thirst after all sounds that you can obtain, without trouble to others, and without disturbing your own temper; and do it the more strenuously and cheerfully, the more reason you have to apprehend the increase of your infirmity. The natural desire to obtain as much pleasure as we can, while we can, would prompt us to this; but my appetite was much sharpened during the interval I spoke of; as yours would be, if you had such an interval. I was dismayed to find, not only what absurd notions I had formed on some small points, but how materially some very important processes of association had been modified by the failure of the sense of hearing. In consequence of the return and increase of the infirmity, I have now no distinct notion of what these intellectual faults are: but the certainty then impressed that they exist, has taught me more than one lesson. I carry about with me the consciousness of an intellectual perversion which I can never remedy in this world, and of which neither I nor any one else can ascertain the extent, nor even the nature. This does not afflict me, because it would be as unreasonable to wish it otherwise, as to pray for wings which should carry us up to the milky-way; but it has stimulated me to devise every possible means of checking and delaying the perversion. We ought all to do so; losing no opportunity of associating sounds with other objects of sense, and of catching every breath of sound that passes us. We should note street cries; we should entice children to talk to us; we should linger in the neighbourhood of barrel organs, and go out of our way to walk by a dashing stream. We cannot tell how much wisdom we may at last find ourselves to have gained, by running out among the trees, when the quick coming and going of the sunshine tells us that the winds are abroad. Some day will show us from how much folly the chirp of an infant's voice may have saved us. I go so far as to recommend, certainly not any place of worship for purposes of experiment, but the theatre and the House of Commons, even when "the sough of words without the sense" is all that can be had. The human voice is music, and carries sense, even then; and every tone is worth treasuring, when tones are likely to become scarce, or to cease. You will understand that it is only to those who can rule their own spirits that I recommend such an exercise as this last. If you cannot bear to enjoy less than the people about you, and in a different manner; or if you neglect what you came for, in mourning what you have lost, you are better at home. Nothing is worth the sacrifice of your repose of mind.

What else may we struggle for? For far more in the way of knowledge than I can now even intimate. I am not going to make out, as some would have me, that we lose nothing after all; that what we lose in one way we gain in another, and so on; pursuing a line of argument equally insulting to our own understandings, and to the wisdom and benignity of Him who framed that curious instrument, the ear, and strung the chords of its nerves, and keeps up the perpetual harmonies of the atmosphere for its gratification. The ear was not made that men should be happier without it. To attempt to persuade *you* so, would above all be folly. But, in some sense, there is a compensation to us, if we choose to accept it; and it is to improve this to the utmost that I would urge you and stimulate myself. We *have* some accomplishments which we may gratefully acknowledge, while the means by which we gain them must prevent our being proud of them. We are good physiognomists — good perceivers in every way, and have (if we are not idle) rather the advantage over others in the power of abstract reasoning. This union of two kinds of power, which in common cases are often cultivated at the expense of each other, puts a considerable amount of accurate knowledge within easier reach of us than of most other people. We must never forget what a vast quantity we must forego, but neither must we lose sight of whatever is peculiarly within our power. We have more time, too, than anybody else: more than the laziest lordling, who does nothing but let his ears be filled with nonsense from morning till night. The very busiest of our fraternity has, I should think, time every day for as much thought as is good for him, between the hours of rising and of rest.

These advantages make it incumbent upon us to struggle for such compensation as is placed before us. We must set ourselves to gather knowledge from whatever we see and touch, and to digest it into wisdom during the extra time which is our privilege. What the sage goes out into the

field at eventide to seek, we can have at table, or in the
thronged streets at noonday, — opportunity for meditation,
one of the chief means of wisdom. If to us the objects of
sight are more vivid in their beauty, and more distinct in
their suggestions than to others, — if to us there is granted
more leisure, and stronger inducement to study the movement of the mind within, from us may be expected a degree
of certain kinds of attainment, in which it is as much of a
sin as a misfortune for us to be deficient.

Finally, we, like all who are placed in uncommon circumstances, are so situated that our mental and moral constitution can scarcely fail of being either very weak or very
strong. If we are dull and slow of observation, and indolent in thought, there is little chance of our being much
wiser than infants ; whereas, if we are acute and quick of
observation, (and for us there is no medium,) and disposed
for thought, nothing is likely to prevent our going on to be
wiser continually. In like manner, there is an awful alternative as to our morals. If we cannot stand our trial, we
must become selfish in principle, sour in temper, and disagreeable in manners. If we are strong enough for our discipline, we cannot fail to come out of it with principles
strengthened, affections expanded, temper under control, and
manners graced by the permanent cheerfulness of a settled
mind, and a heart at ease. If you can make this last your
lot, you have little more to fear. If you have stood this
proof, you can probably stand any which comes in the shape
of affliction. If you have brought vigor out of this conflict,
you are not likely to be unnerved. If, in your enforced solitude, you have cultivated instead of losing your sympathies,
you can scarcely afterwards grow selfish. If, as your enjoyments were failing you, you have improved your serenity,
your cheerfulness will probably be beyond the reach of circumstance. The principal check which must be put upon

these happy anticipations, is the fear that while the privation cannot be lessened, the pain of it may disappear too soon and too entirely. I now suffer little or no pain from my privation, (except at moments when comparisons are forced upon me before I am ready for them;) and I cannot help dreading a self-deception, to avoid which I would gladly endure over again all I have suffered. I had infinitely rather bear the perpetual sense of privation than become unaware of any thing that is true, — of my intellectual deficiencies, of my disqualifications for society, of my errors in matters of fact, and of the burdens which I necessarily impose on those who surround me. My dependence for being reminded of these things is — not on those, who incur trouble and sacrifice for my sake, but on the few occasional mortifications which I still meet with, and which are always welcome for the sake of their office. We can never get beyond the necessity of keeping in full view the worst and the best that can be made of our lot. The worst is, either to sink under the trial, or to be made callous by it. The best is, to be as wise as is possible under a great disability, and as happy as is possible under a great privation. Believe me, with deep respect,

Your affectionate sister,

HARRIET MARTINEAU.

March 16, 1834.

ON COUNTRY BURIAL-GROUNDS.

THE feeling which first prompted men to bury their dead in the neighbourhood of their places of worship is natural and universal. If a stranger, an impartial person, unbiassed by our predilections in favor of long-established customs, were asked to point out the spot best fitted for so awful a deposit, he

23

would say, " Bury your dead in a place where strong, universal religious associations may protect their repose.   Make their
graves in some spot where they will often meet your eyes;
but be careful at the same time, by connecting the remembrance of the dead with your religious feelings, to preserve
its vividness and strength.   Bury your dead in or near your
places of worship."   A custom thus approving itself to every
man's feelings was adopted long ago, and became almost
universal : the consequence of which is, that some change
has become desirable, if not necessary.   The number of
dead in our cities has so outgrown that of the living, that
the very feelings which first appropriated our churchyards
to be the abode of the departed, are daily shocked and disgusted at the scenes which every passer by must unavoidably
witness.

If any philosophical reasoner should say that it cannot
matter to the dead what becomes of their remains; or to the
living, when the immediate relatives and friends are no more,
I reply, that when we behold the violations which are often
practised, we naturally look forward to the time when the
remains of those whom we love, and perhaps committed but
yesterday to the tomb, shall be cast out in the same manner.
It is not enough that we can now guard their repose, if the
suspicion comes across us that when our guardianship is
withdrawn, their ashes shall be held in no more respect than
the dust of the ground.   It is not enough that we can cast
our eyes on the hallowed spot as we enter the house of God,
and silently pay to it the tribute of our hearts, if we feel the
chilling conviction that in time that grave shall be levelled;
that the careless step shall tread upon it, and that the sanctity of the place shall be abolished.   Neither can it be right
that the respect which the heart naturally pays to the remains
of the dead, should be discouraged.   It cannot be right that
children should behold the subservience of this natural re-

spect to considerations of convenience and interest. If to the dead it matters not whether their bones crumble by natural decay, or are broken by the tool of the workman, to the gazer it matters much. If no friend be near to shudder at the violation, some delicate spirit may be wounded, and most probably some young mind will receive a hurtfnl impression, will have some sentiment of natural piety weakened, some emotion of religious awe chilled or destroyed. While this religious awe invests the memory of the dead, and is associated with their remains, it can be no light matter to treat this remembrance with carelessness.

While, in the midst of cities, temptations to violate, sooner or later, the repose of the dead exist, nature will be found a more faithful guardian of their rights than even the vicinity of the sanctuary. If its walls afford but a temporary protection, we shall be wise to seek that which is more durable; and if man may not be trusted with the sacred charge, we should remove it where it may at least be safe from the hand of the spoiler. By depositing our dead in some place removed from the habitations of man, we indeed deprive ourselves of the consolation of visiting their graves, when we go up to worship, and of beholding their tombs as we join in the service of the sanctuary. But the deprivation is more than compensated by the security and the repose of the country burying-place. No rash hand will be tempted to level the heap. Nature will pay her daily tribute to the hallowed spot. The sun will shine upon it every morning; the dews of heaven will visit it every evening, for ever. Where these influences of nature and religion can be united, as in a country churchyard, it is well. It is no small privilege to the survivors to have such a place to resort to, when they pay their tribute of affection. But the larger proportion of our population must forego one or other of the advantages of a country churchyard; and it seems to be high time to point

out to them the desireableness, if not the necessity, of relin-
quishing their predilections in favor of the old places of sepul-
ture, and of reconciling their minds to the new plan which
the increase of numbers will at length oblige us to adopt.

All have heard of the cemetery of Père la Chaise. Its
beauty, and the deep and tender interest which pervades the
place, are universally acknowledged. Why should not every
city in England have such a spot in its neighbourhood?
Not, perhaps, as beautiful; but as interesting, as hallowed?
That there are no valid objections to such a plan, we know;
for it has been adopted with entire success, in two or three
instances in England. They who have attended funerals
in the damp and cheerless churchyards of the city, feel the
contrast between such scenes, and the shade of trees, where
flowers spring, and the sun sheds his earliest and latest rays.
They who have known what it is to be deterred from visiting
the grave of a friend by the fear of observation, and who
find that in the midst of a city they cannot escape sights
and sounds uncongenial with their feelings, can best appreciate the retirement and repose of a country burial-ground,
where no eye marks the mourner, no step intrudes on his
solitude, and no harsh sounds break in on his meditation.

The burial-grounds of a city are exposed to profanations
of various kinds, from which those of the country are free.
Notwithstanding all that is said of the good moral effects of
interring the dead in the sight of the living, we are every
day shocked with the levity with which places so sacred are
regarded. If now and then an old man may go to
meditate among the tombs, and gather from them that "all
is vanity," how many busy and careless persons pass
by without remembering that they are on consecrated
ground! The man of business hurries on, and pursues his
calculations, without being reminded that he knows not the
measure of his days. The man of learning reflects not, as

the tomb-stones meet his eye, that beneath them no knowledge or device is found.   The gay and worldly tread the
soil so often that they think not of the corruption within it, —
a corruption which they must share.   The school-boy whis-
tles and plays his pranks as he leaps over the graves, and
loses his awe of death as its outward symbols cease to be
mementos to him.   The sounds of business, the laugh of
mirth, the voice of contention, even the oath and the curse,
echo discordantly among the tombs ; and if they reach the
ear of the mourner, send a shudder through his frame, and
a chill through his soul.   In the country these things cannot
be.   No call of business or pleasure leads the careless through
its paths.   None enter but those who have an interest in the
place itself — who go to think and to feel.   The still, small
voice which issues from the grave is there listened to.   No
careless step profanes the hallowed turf.   It is bright with
flowers ; the bee gathers sweets, and the butterfly lights
upon them.   All else is retirement and repose.

There is something highly gratifying to the mind in persons of all denominations being interred in the same spot.
In towns, Dissenters are compelled either to appropriate a
ground to the exclusive use of the members of their own
body, or to bury their dead near churches.*   The latter
alternative is disagreeable to them ; for however enlarged
their views may be, the spot which they would choose for
the final abode of their friends would certainly not be close
under the walls of a place of worship which they never entered, and among those *only* in whose rites of homage they
had never joined.   Those who have a place of burial of their
own, however sensible they may be, and ought to be, of their
privilege, may yet lament that the exclusiveness to which
they were compelled, by conscience, during life, should be

---

* Of the Establishment.

23*

continued after death. Though to the dead it matters not where, or among whom, they are laid, to their survivors, it is as instructive as it is pleasing, to behold those who were separated in life, in death taking their rest together, and all at length united in the same deep repose. It is sweet to look on their present involuntary union as an earnest of one more complete; to hope that as they have been brought from far and near, one by one, into this wide fold, to spend the long night in peace, they will, when the morning shall rise, with one heart and voice desire to part no more. If this union be attained, it can be only by burying the dead in ground unconnected with places of worship; if in ground apart from places of worship, there can be no question that the country is preferable to the crowded city.

The grand difficulty which has hitherto been found in the establishment of such cemeteries as we have described, is, that no one will begin. The dread of novelty, the fear of failing in the observance due to the dead, deters the survivors from depositing the remains of a friend in solitude; from depriving him of that companionship in death to which the heart clings with a superstitious affection. Such tenderness and such fear are natural, though they may be weak; and we cannot wonder at this reluctance, however strongly our reason may declare it to be unfounded. But may we not consider it an honor to our departed friend, that he is the first to dedicate a new spot to holy thoughts and pious feelings; the means by which a new charm is spread over a scene which is now first distinguished from other scenes of equal beauty; that at his call the angel of death first descends to take up his abode, and shed a peculiar calm within the sacred enclosure? The holy influences which guard the place enter with the first funeral train; they depart not with the mourners, but abide to watch awhile the solitary tomb, and then to welcome each new-comer to his long home. To their protection we may commend our treasure; and if we are tempted to linger near the new-made grave, and dread to depart, let us remember that there may be a better guardianship than that of our scruples and fears. If any object that our consolation is unfounded and superstitious, let him ask himself whether the reluctance we combat be not unfounded and superstitious also.

It is difficult to imagine any real objections to a plan which has already been tried, and met with entire success. Any rites of consecration which the scruples of some may require, any precautions against violation, which all are anxious to prevent, can be practised with as little difficulty in one place as in another.* Reason and feeling both point out the neighbourhood of towns as more fit to be made the depository of the dead than towns themselves. In crowded cities, the first object is the welfare of the population; and to this every unwholesome custom should be sacrificed; and as the numbers of the living increase, the dead should be removed where space can be allowed, without grudging, to their remains, and where their presence must be salutary to the mind, while it is not hurtful to the health.

As a matter of feeling, if the remains of the dead are to be treated with any observance at all, let us give them all

---

* It can scarcely be supposed that Dissenters are very anxious to have their new burial-grounds consecrated, when, for that purpose, they are obliged to deliver over their property to the Church of England without remuneration; especially as the church can then refuse interment to Dissenters in their own ground.

It is frequently objected to burial grounds intended for the use of all denominations, that the funeral service of the Church of England cannot be performed on unconsecrated ground. But if the objector will examine the Canon, he will find no such prohibition as is commonly reported to exist. The service may be performed in any place. The clergyman of the Establishment is only forbidden to use any other funeral service than that prescribed in the Book of Common Prayer of the Church of England.

that is in our power. Let us place them where they shall be exempt from profanation, and protected by the most hallowed influences which we can invoke. As we cannot always watch over their tombs, let us commit them to the keeping of nature. While we are engaged in the busy concerns of life, she will be dressing the graves with her fair flowers and springing verdure; she will be making melody with her many voices, and her clouds and sunshine will bring their daily tribute to the hallowed spot. And when the heat and burden of the day are past, hither may we repair to refresh the memory of the dead within us; and while we recall days that are gone by, and open our hearts to the sweet influences of the present time, here may we best anticipate the close of our day of life, and breathe a prayer that that hour may be calm and blessed like this. Here may we best reconcile our minds to the approach of the night of death, and realize and exalt our conceptions of the eternal morning which shall unclose every eye, and restore the long-suspended energies of every soul.

ON THE DUTY OF STUDYING POLITICAL ECONOMY.*

"In England and Scotland," says Dr. Cooper (p. 21), "no well-informed gentleman is permitted to be ignorant of the labors of Adam Smith, Malthus, and Ricardo, any more than of Shakspeare, Milton, or Pope." Alas! Dr. Cooper thinks too well of us, as he would find, if he would come over and walk about London for one day. If he went to the Exchange, he would hear hopes and fears about the

---

* Lectures on the Elements of Political Economy, by Thomas Cooper, M. D., President of S. Carolina College, and Professor of Chemistry and Political Economy. — London, Hunter, 1831.

exchange being in favor of, or against our country. If he went among the merchants' counting-houses, he would find petitions in favor of monopoly in course of signature. If he went to the West End, he would see tokens of an expenditure, liberal enough, but of a kind hurtful to the general interest. He would see beggars in the streets levying their toll on passengers, and advertisements of charities would meet his eye in every direction. He would find farmers praying for restrictions on the importation of grain, and shop-keepers mysteriously bringing out their smuggled goods, and beadles getting two paupers married, to rid their parish of the charge of the bride; and members of Parliament in the club-houses advocating petitions in favor of a fixed rate of wages. He would hear of riots in the manufacturing districts on account of the introduction of new machinery, and of rick-burning in the agricultural, where some capitalist was enclosing waste land. He could not sit in an inn an hour, or walk the length of a street, without perceiving that our gentlemen know nothing, generally speaking, of political economy. The few who do understand it are gentlemen, we admit. It is but too evident that the middling and lower classes are ignorant of it yet; but the few who are not, would form an almost indistinguishable portion of the nation, if their number were the measure of their importance. Their talents and philanthropy have brought notice and abuse upon them at home, and honor abroad; their talents and philanthropy alone, for they have no adventitious help. They are not in our ministry; they are not in our senate; they are not, with two or three exceptions, in our universities or public schools. The press alone is open to them; and that they have obtained for our nation such a reputation as the American Professor innocently assigns us, is a proof which it is exhilarating to receive of the greatness and stability of the power they have won, in opposition to the blind prejudices of the people, and the haughty irrationality of the aristocracy. Dr. Cooper refers to some of the principles of the administration of Lord Liverpool, Canning, and Huskisson, in proof of the advance of the science in this country. It is true that we owe a change for the better to these statesmen; but it would amuse any one who did not think the matter too serious for a laugh, to observe how obscure, and imperfect, and feeble, is the recognition of grand principles of policy among those who are looked upon as our most adventurous statesmen. They are all bit-by-bit reformers, when any departments of this science are in question. They all flounder among the details when the direct road to principles is open; and let the question relate to what it may, — to Indian affairs, or poor-laws for Ireland, or the corn-laws, or colonial monopolies, or any other politico-economical point, the time of the house, and the patience of clear-sighted men are invariably wasted by frivolous discussions on irrelevant subjects, or on difficulties which ought to have been laid to rest long ago. We cannot think that this would be the case in a debate on Macbeth, or Windsor Forest, though it possibly might on a question of the liberty of unlicensed printing. Many popular representatives prefer shooting and billiards to studying Ricardo, as much as Charles Fox preferred tending his geraniums to reading Adam Smith.

We hold, however, that the blame does not chiefly rest with these gentlemen themselves. We wish they represented their constituents as faithfully in all things as in their ignorance of political economy. If they did, the cry for reform would be very gentle, and would come from a different quarter. It is true that the representatives of the people ought to be able to point out to their constituents the origin and nature of whatever evils they know only in their effects. This is the only way of making representation as enlightened and effectual as it might be; and, as it seems to us, of keeping the conscience of the representative clear, and the harmony between him and his constituents unbroken. Suppose, for instance, trade in some manufacturing district is at a stand from a dispute about wages. Masters and men desire their representative to advocate a fixed rate of wages. If he does so, he commits an egregious blunder ; if he declines without having a good reason to give, he offends his constituents. He ought to be able to explain to them the absurdity of their request, to point out the real cause of their troubles, and to state what he can attempt for its removal. But this is more, it seems, than has hitherto been expected of the representatives of the people, who have tardily and imperfectly learned from the irresistible evidence of events, those truths at which the intelligent among their people had arrived long before by a shorter cut. Thus it has been, and thus it is ; and since it is so, the people must begin by informing themselves, if they wish for a better state of things. It is evident that they cannot even be sure of choosing their representatives better till they are clear as to what is requisite in their member, and can judge whether he possesses the requisites. The people, then, must become practically acquainted with the principles of political economy, before they can expect to have their interests properly taken care of by the government.

Nor is this less necessary, supposing the ruling portion of the commonwealth as well-informed respecting its duties as it ought to be. The execution of their measures depends upon the people, and enlightened coöperation is essential to their success. There would be little use in the removal of restrictions if voluntary monopolies still subsisted. If the abuses of the pauper system were abolished, and the wisest of all possible measures substituted, its operation would be impaired if the public persisted in giving alms and maintaining soup charities, and clothing charities, and other well-meant institutions which do little but harm. We do not mean that such a broad difference between government and people could long subsist while the government was in the right; but in proportion to the errors of the people would sound public measures fail of their effect; and in proportion to the cordial coöperation of the people would be their efficacy. Whether, then, the government be wise or foolish, ignorant or informed, it concerns the people to understand their own interests, — i. e., to learn political economy.

Viewing this science as we do, — as involving the laws of social duty and social happiness, — we hold it as a positive obligation on every member of society who studies and reflects at all, to inform himself of its leading principles. If he cares at all about the faithful discharge of his functions in the position he holds, he must feel himself obliged to learn what those functions are, and how they may be best discharged. He would not place himself at a lawyer's desk, or a merchant's counter, or mount a pulpit, or dispose of his services in any way without learning what was expected of him, or preparing himself to fulfil his contract. He would not pocket his salary, and accept any advantages that his position afforded him, while he trusted to haphazard, or to daily routine, to teach him what he must do, or how he must do it. No honest man would thus engage himself, even if he were born to his office, and were subject to no controlling power. Neither will an honest man accept the benefits of the social contract without learning how to fulfil his share of it. It is not enough for a member of society, any more than for a merchant's clerk, to be upright and industrious, and amiable, and generally intelligent. More is wanted in both. They must be skilful as well as laborious, and their skill must be appropriate to their office. The clerk must have studied the principles, and mastered the details of his trade, or he does not deserve his salary; and the member of society must have informed himself how he may best serve the community before he can fairly appropriate the benefits of living in a community. His general intelligence is not enough, if it does not guard him against particular errors in the discharge of his function; i. e., a merchant's good education will not nullify his support of a monopoly. His uprightness is not enough, if it does not preserve him from unconsciously encouraging fraud in others; i. e., a representative's honest zeal will not justify an ill-grounded party measure. His benevolence is not enough, if it operates to increase misery; i. e., a kind-hearted man's almsgiving will not make the growth of pauperism a good thing. Thus every honest man who writes himself a member of society must understand political economy. He who is philanthropic as well as honest lies under a double obligation, inasmuch as he knows it to be in his power to help to drive those above him, and to lead those below him to a similar recognition of the duty common to them all.

It is not till we see how deeply the laws of social duty and social happiness are involved in this science that we become aware how important it ought to be in the eyes of the philanthropist. We are not among those who mix up moral questions with political economy, as if they were not only connected but identical. We do not speak of demand and supply and heavenly-mindedness in the same breath, or bring exchangeable value into immediate connexion with filial piety; but we think that this study partakes much more of the nature of a moral than a mathematical science, and are quite certain that it modifies, or ought to modify, our moral philosophy more extensively than any other influence whatsoever. Political economy treats of the sources and acquisition of wealth, of its distribution and consumption, — including under the term Wealth whatever material objects conduce to the support, comfort, and enjoyment of man.

24

There is no question that a great proportion of national crime is generated by poverty: all the theft, and much of the licentiousness of which society has to complain is produced by want, or by the recklessness which attends a state of want. There is no question that the frauds and all the demoralizing methods of circumvention frequent in the commercial world are occasioned by institutions which make one man's gain another man's loss, and foster a spirit of jealousy and selfishness: — institutions equally bad as they regard morals and social economy. There is no question that idleness and imposition are encouraged by all methods which interfere with the free course of industry, or which, by affording a premium on over-population, cause the supply of labor to exceed the demand. There is no question that many and obstinate wars have been occasioned by the faulty framing of commercial treaties, and by commercial jealousies and national competitions, — all which are inconsistent with sound principles of political economy. We might extend our exemplification much further; but it is needless. It is as true of a nation as of a family that its individual members will be less exposed to temptation, and more enlightened to perceive, and more at liberty to discharge its duties in a state of ease than of poverty; and that its most favorable circumstances are those where there is harmony between the various members at home, and goodwill towards their neighbours abroad, — a harmony and goodwill secured by an union of interests and a reciprocity of good offices. Is it not the duty of all philanthropic persons to act upon this truth, — to ascertain the leading principles on which the national interests are based, and according to which they must be secured? If our philanthropists would but do this, — if they would but aim at rectifying principles, instead of ameliorating the consequences of such as are bad, how speedily would the worst of our social evils disappear! It grieves us to the heart to see how charity is misunderstood, — what labor and pains are spent, with the best intentions, for nothing, or worse than nothing, while the same exertions, rightly directed, would benefit thousands. Hundreds, every winter, give money, and time, and pains to supply the poor of our towns with bread and soup. The business is inadequately done, at the best; and the moral effect upon the poor of that sort of charity is so bad as probably to counterbalance the present advantage. If half the pains had been taken to procure a repeal of the corn-laws, directly, by urging the measure on government, and indirectly, by enlightening the public mind on the policy of such a proceeding, the poor of Great Britain might, by this time, have been well fed, without having lost their spirit of independence, and would moreover have the prospect of being well fed as long as they could work. In hard winters there have been committees in almost every town near the coast to furnish the poor with coals, at a similar expense of moral evil, trouble, and cash. A very few individuals who, last year, urged and carried the repeal of the tax on sea-borne coal, did more towards warming the population — without any counterbalancing evil — than all the gentlemen with open purses, and all the ladies in drab bonnets who benevolently busied themselves from year to year. Nor was fuel the only good procured. Bread and clothes and independence came in the same colliers, though nothing was charged for their freight. Manufactures which could not before be set up, on account of the expense of fuel, were established as soon as the obstacle was removed. A new market was opened to the industry of the people, and they earned their comforts instead of having to beg for them. In such cases as these, one individual, issuing a sound opinion through the press or in Parliament, may do more good than a score of charity committees with a score of members in each. Why do not more aspire after this truly effectual benevolence?

Another, and yet more important consideration to the good man is, that the application of moral principles varies with the social condition of man. Doubtless we shall find, when we reach a better state of knowledge, that these principles are immutable; but we cannot use them in an abstract form. We know of none which have admitted of precisely the same application from the beginning of the world to this time. Modes of action which are good in one age or position of circumstances, are bad in another, while the principle remains the same. If we attempt to frame moral systems, we must make them for present use only. We must provide for their being modified as the condition of society changes, or we shall do more harm than good. A moral system which is good for a child is unfit for a man. A moral system which is suitable to an infant colony, is perfectly inapplicable to an ancient empire. The regulations of a commercial must be different from those of an agricultural country. No man, therefore, can either teach or practise morals well, however sound in his general principles, unless he knows the circumstances in which his principles are to be applied. A clergyman may preach well on justice, and may have the most earnest desire to practise and encourage this virtue; but he more than undoes his own labor, if he persuades his people to countenance the interference of Government in the employment of private capital; i. e., to petition for penalties on any particular mode of investment. He may thus be injuring the interests of thousands, while he advocates the principles of justice. In like manner, if his week-day labors are directed to the encouragement of almsgiving, instead of better modes of expenditure, he does more for the increase of pauperism, wretchedness, and crime, than a whole year's preaching on benevolence can counteract. If he were a political economist, he would not preach the less fervently, but he would accompany his enforcement of these principles

with illustrations of their best application in the present state
of society.   He would be eloquent on the right of man to
employ what he possesses as he pleases; and would show
how, as every man knows his own interest best, and as the
interest of the public is that of congregated individuals, the
part of justice and benevolence is to interfere with none in
the direction of their own concerns.   He would show that
the principle of benevolence varies in its application, according to the position of events; and that almsgiving, however
appropriate an act of benevolence in so peculiar a polity as
that of the Jews, is not a virtuous deed at present, if it can
be proved to create more misery than it relieves; and such
proof he would afford.   These explanations, out of the
pulpit, would add force to his Sunday eloquence, instead of
nullifying it.

No words can describe the evil of proceeding on a false
principle, or of erring in the application of a right one, in
concerns so momentous as those of society; and there is,
therefore, no limiting the responsibilities of all its members
for the mode in which they employ their influence.   This
responsibility cannot be evaded, for every individual has
influence; the obligation to learn how to employ this influence cannot, therefore, be evaded.   To show what individuals may do of good or harm, we will adduce one case.

Mr. Sadler, a man who, by some means or other, has
acquired a degree of influence to which his qualifications do
not entitle him, and which cannot be long maintained, finds
that there was once a divine command to "increase, and
multiply, and replenish the earth."   This command was as
appropriate as possible when issued; viz., when a family
stepped out of the Ark into a depopulated world, where food
might be had, next season, for the gathering, and where the
deficiency was of human beings, and not of produce.   Mr.
Sadler chooses to apply this command to our country at the

24*

present time, where food is scarce in proportion to the population, and there is not employment enough to enable the
poor to surmount the restrictions which deprive them of
foreign grain. If Mr. Sadler can effect the removal of these
restrictions, or if he can transport the supposed subjects of
the command to lands which want replenishing, his principle
may hold good; but he is bound to do these things *before*
he advocates a now untenable principle. If his advice, as
it now stands, be followed, he may have the questionable
honor of having added to our population some thousands,
born in wretchedness, reared in vice, and expiring, the victims of want or crime. Compare with the deeds of Mr.
Sadler those of Arkwright. He is computed to have added
a million to the permanent population of Great Britain.
But how? By providing the employment which was to
support them. Arkwright, by furnishing the support of a
permanent million, calls them into a life which may be
honest, useful, and enjoyable. Sadler, by encouraging an
increase of some thousands, previously to providing the
means of support, calls them into a life which is not only
guilty and wretched to themselves, but injurious to others,
by consuming the resources which were already too small.
Such a case needs no comment. It shows us something of
onr responsibilities, and throws some light on the dispute
whether an increase of population is or is not a good, and
thus affords us a lesson as to the mode of using our influence.

Enough has been said, (though we seem but to have
bordered upon the subject,) to prove the *utility* of the study
of political economy. Much, very much, might also be said
of its *beauty*. Yes, its beauty; for notwithstanding all that
is said of its dryness and dulness, and its concentration in
matter of fact, we see great attractiveness and much elegance
in it. We might reason at some length upon the kindred

arguments, that there is ever beauty in utility, and that there is no beauty which is not involved in matter of fact. But for such we have no space. We will only ask if there is no beauty in those discoveries by which the resources of nature are laid open, or in those processes by which her workings are overruled, to the benefit of man? Is there no beauty in the simple and compound adaptation of means to ends, or in the creative processes of the human intellect, whose results are embodied by the ingenuity of the human hands? Is there no beauty in the principle of equalization which may be traced in workings more extensive, and with a finer alternation of uniformity and variety than in any region of research with which we are yet acquainted? Does it not gratify the taste, as well as the understanding, to discern how deficiency is supplied, how superabundance subsides, how influences reciprocate, by the natural workings of the principles of social polity? Is there no pleasure in marking the approach of Plenty to sow her blessings round the cottage of the laborer, and of Civilization to adorn the abode of the artisan? Is there not gratification for the finer faculties in tracing the advancement of a state from its infancy of wants and occupations to a period of prosperity, and thence through all its complications of interests, till the intricate organization works with all the regularity which distinguishes the processes of nature, while it is instinct with life, and (if left free from empiricism) would expand into a majestic growth of lasting grandeur? Is there no pleasure in finding in present events a key to the past: in unravelling the mysteries of policy and morals which perplexed the legislators and philosophers of former ages? Above all, is there no beauty in the dealings of Providence with man? Can it be a dry and irksome task, to explore the plan by which communities are wrought upon to achieve the great ends of human virtue and human enjoyment? Social institutions are the grand instruments in the hands of Providence for the government of man; and no labors can be more worthy of the disciple of Providence than that of deducing the will of God from the course of events — of ascertaining the Divine signature by which institutions are sanctioned or prohibited.

Whatever beauty there is in mathematical science, it is embodied here; for the relations of number and quantity, remaining immutable, exhibit a new series of results. Whatever beauty there is in mechanical science resides in this also; for no powers are so mighty, and nowhere are they so variously combined as in the mechanism of society. Whatever beauty there is in chemical science, is present here also; for there is a strong analogy between the mutual action of natural and moral elements. Whatever beauty there is in moral science appears preëminently here; for hence we draw our inductions, and construct our theories, and here or nowhere we must try the principles in which both result. Hither the finger of God directs us when we inquire for an oracle to expound to us the state, and prophecy the futurity of the race which He has destined to be lords of the earth, as a preparation for becoming citizens of a better state.

If there be any who think natural indications of the Divine will insufficient, and who look into the Bible for a sanction for their studies, as well as for other things, we beg to refer them, not only to the implied principles of political economy which abound from the first peopling of the earth up to the apostolic institutions, — but to as full and clear an exemplification as can be found in Adam Smith. Dr. Cooper points out that in the parable of the ten talents, — inexplicable to all who do not understand the principle on which it proceeds, — the great truth is illustrated, that capital hoarded and buried, instead of being applied productively, does not yield its result of good. It is true, this is only one application of the general law of increase which was adduced for a moral purpose by him who spoke the parable : but it is good political economy, and they who wish it may plead a gospel sanction for its pursuit.

Our author, who is not only the first professor of this science in his college, but the proposer of such a professorship, has done good service to the cause we have been advocating by the zeal with which he enforces the advantages of its pursuit. He vigorously and perseveringly exhorts his countrymen to study political economy, and urges our example upon them ; by which, as we have seen, he does us too much honor. The lectures before us are what they pretend to be, elementary, and we doubt not have done all the more good for keeping clear of the abstruser parts of the science. They comprehend as much as it is reasonable to expect the bulk of students to learn, — as much as would regenerate our country if fully understood by our statesmen, and pressed upon them by the people. Dr. Cooper's style is strong and lively, — a great advantage where this class of subjects is in question. He pins his faith to no man's sleeve, but takes and leaves opinions as his judgment directs, after an extensive survey of the works which have issued from various schools. He goes a great way with Adam Smith, of course ; a great way with Say, Ricardo, Malthus, and Mill ; combining their leading opinions into a system with which we have only trivial faults to find. Our great objection is to his deficiencies of arrangement. We cannot, indeed, discover any principle of arrangement ; and cannot but wonder that, much as he admires Mill, he should not have followed his, which appears to us the natural, and therefore palpably fit mode of evolving the principles of the science ; namely, by classing them under the heads, Production, Distribution, and Consumption, — interposing Exchange if it should be thought desirable to treat separately of this method of distribution.

We must gratify ourselves by giving one extract, in which is implied a valuable sanction of our preceding arguments.

"Much difficulty and deplorable mistake have arisen on the subject of political economy from the propensity that has prevailed of considering a nation as some existing intelligent being, distinct from the individuals who compose it, and possessing properties belonging to no individual who is a member of it. We seem to think that national morality is a different thing from individual morality, and dependent upon principles quite dissimilar : and that maxims of *political economy* have nothing in common with *private economy*. Hence the moral entity — the grammatical being called a NATION, has been clothed in attributes that have no real existence, except in the imagination of those who metamorphose a word into a thing, and convert a mere grammatical contrivance into an existing and intelligent being. It is of great importance that we should be aware of this mistake : that we should consider abstract terms as names, invented to avoid limitation, description, and periphrasis — grammatical contrivances and no more : just as we use the signs and letters of algebra to reason with, instead of the more complex numbers they represent.

" I suspect it will be very difficult for us to discover a rule of morality, obligatory on individuals, that would not apply to nations considered as individuals ; or any maxim of political economy that would not be equally undeniable as a rule of private and domestic economy ; and *vice versâ*. The more effectually we can discard mystery from this and every other subject, the more intelligible it will become ; and the less easy will it be for designing men of any description to prey upon the credulity of mankind. It is high time that the language and the dictates of common sense, founded upon propositions easy to be understood, and easy to be proved, should take place of the jargon by which our understandings have been so long cheated.

" Those maxims of human conduct that are best calculated
to promote a man's highest and most permanent happiness
on the whole of his existence, are the only maxims of conduct
obligatory on individuals.   There is no other rational basis of
moral obligation ; for what can be put in competition with
the greatest sum of happiness upon the whole of a man's existence?   There are no rules of morality — there is no such
thing as virtue or vice, but what originated from our connexion with other creatures whose happiness may, in some
degree, be affected by our conduct.   What rules of morality
can affect a man condemned to pass his days alone on an
uninhabited island, or in solitary confinement within the
walls of a prison ?   In like manner, those rules of conduct
which are best calculated to promote the mutual happiness
of nations, in their intercourse with each other as individuals,
constitute the only maxims of the law of nations obligatory
on all, because calculated for the permanent benefit of all.
So, in the domestic concerns of a nation, those rules and
maxims of conduct which, upon the whole, are best calculated to promote the permanent happiness of any nation, that
is, of the individuals who compose it in the capacity of members of a political economy, are the laws really obligatory
upon that nation ; and the force of the nation is properly
exerted to carry them into effect when enacted, against any
individual who may contravene them : always taking for
granted that those laws are enacted, not for the benefit of
rulers, but with a view to promote *the greatest good of the
greatest number* of citizens composing the community.   This,
then, is the true origin of moral obligation, whether applied
to national aggregates of individuals, or to any individual of
the number.   For what stronger or higher obligation can be
suggested than to pursue and practise systematically those
rules of conduct which can most effectually and permanently
secure our own happiness upon the whole ?   What higher or

different motive can we have? It will be found, on examination, that the particular rules and maxims, comprehended
in this general expression of them, are the same, whether
applied to the conduct of one individual or ten, — of ten, or
ten thousand, or ten millions." — pp. 28 - 30.

A SUMMER EVENING DIALOGUE BETWEEN AN ENG-
LISHMAN AND A POLE.

Pole. — You should not ask foreigners to praise your
country till you can show it them under such an aspect as
this. Its rural scenes should be entered upon at this very
hour of this very season. I have told you that you should
approach Heidelberg at sunset, and Venice when the full
moon has risen, and Genoa when the sun first peeps up from
the sea. Abroad, I would say, traverse the harvest fields of
England, when they wave in the golden light of an August
evening.

Englishman. — Is the beauty of our landscape peculiar?
I should have thought, without any allusion to your own
unhappy country, that you had seen many such prospects as
this in the flourishing agricultural regions through which
you have travelled.

Pole. — I have traversed many corn districts, during both
seed-time and harvest; and the song of the vine-dressers,
and the chant of the reapers, are alike familiar to me. But
there is a beauty in your rural districts which I discern in
no others. The haze on the horizon, which tells that a busy
city is there, enhances the charm of the balmy solitude;
and yonder lordly mansion among the woods, and the peasant's cottage in the lane, give a grace, by contrast, to each
other.

Englishman. — And their inhabitants, likewise, I suppose. Yonder whistling laborer, plodding homeward with his sickle in his hand, contrasts well with the mechanic loitering through the field, chewing straws. And that cottage mother, gleaning in the next field, with her tribe of little ones about her, forms as pleasant an object as Lord W. with his train of high-born sons and daughters — as graceful a riding party as ever was seen — emerging from the green lane upon the down.

Pole. — It is a tranquil and fair scene. The voices of the children, pulling dog-roses and bindweed, are as sweet to the ear as the cooing of the ringdove in the grove we have just left; and there is music in the village clock, which sets all these peasants converging towards their homes. If ever there was peace, it is surely here; and it is soothing, even to the lacerated heart of a Pole, to witness it.

Englishman. — Such are the outward shows of things in this world. Do you not know, my friend, that brows often ache under coronets, and that splendid smiles sometimes disguise the wounds of the heart? Even so this fair scene yields a false show of happiness.

Pole. — Nay; but here is fact. There is reality before our eyes, and within reach of our touch. Here is golden grain, bowing beneath its own weight, in this field; and, in the next, the wain is piled high with the fruits of the harvest. And these abodes and their occupiers — are they but visions?

Englishman. — None of these things are visions, any more than the field flowers which flourish on a tomb, or the fever-flush which brightens the eye of the sick; but it does not follow that there is not decay and pain beneath and within.

Pole. — You mean that there is mortal sorrow within the bounds of this horizon. True; where humanity is present, there is sorrow.

25

Englishman.—Ay; and not only unavoidable sorrow, but that of man's own choice. What I mean is, that there is hollowness under this apparent prosperity. Step a little this way, and I will show you the ugly walls of a workhouse, where you now see only a clump of elms. The mechanic loiters here, because he is afraid to face his half-fed family at home; yonder laborer doubts whether his wife's gleanings will serve this week instead of parish pay. Look at these ill-grown fences, these rickety gates! The farmer who is about to reap this crop has no heart to keep his fixtures in good repair; and his wife, seeing his despondency, dreads to hear of his being found drowned in one of his own ditches. As for Lord W. and his family, they are going abroad to live cheap, till the education of the sons is finished. It wrings their hearts to leave their beautiful seat; but the steward exhibits a list of rent-arrears four times as long as that of receipts. So much for all this apparent prosperity!

Pole.—But whence all this? You have no war, foreign or civil, to consume your resources; and Providence has blessed your land with three successive fruitful seasons. Whence is all this trouble?

Englishman.—The sufferers will tell you that it arises from that fruitfulness of the seasons, which you speak of as a blessing. Far from suspecting that, by our own mismanagement, we turn blessings into curses, they pray for the continuance of a policy which would make double crops, if we could get them, cause double dearth.

Pole.—You mean the extraordinary arrangement of taxing corn. In our country we cannot comprehend why you persist in raising corn at a vast expense, when from us you might have it cheap. We want fabrics made of your wool; and have so much corn to give in exchange, that we feed our cattle with wheat, and leave large tracts of fine land waste, because you will not buy, but rather choose to bury your resources in your own bad soils.

Englishman. — Whence little enough of it arises again.

Pole. — And of that little the greater part is taken by the landlord. Which is the most pernicious crime, — fraud, robbery, or waste?

Englishman. — There is little choice when the interests of a nation are in question. Of which do you accuse us, in respect of our corn regulations? For my part, I charge our system with both.

Pole. — It was of waste that I first thought, in reference to the raising of the landlord's rent. His rent rises with every new tillage of inferior land; but it is not only his portion, but that of the farmer, and that of the laborer, which becomes dear, because you will not have corn from abroad. Is not this waste?

Englishman. — Most destructive waste. The landlord's portion of the whole average corn produce of this kingdom is now about one-fourth. More corn being wanted, it is raised at a greater cost; the whole produce becomes dearer; so that all who eat pay higher for their three quarters of the produce, in order that the landlord's rent may be increased. This is robbery as well as waste.

Pole. — And robbery which avails little to any one, it seems, since Lord W. has to go abroad, as you say. His rents are, it appears, only nominally increased, since he cannot get them paid.

Englishman. — And he is oppressed with the burden of pauperism likewise. As soon as corn becomes too dear for laborers to buy, they must have it given them in charity. Lord W.'s steward stands on his right, the parish assessors on his left. " My Lord," says the steward, " your tenants can pay only half their rents; this good season has ruined them." " My Lord," say the assessors, " the workhouse is as full as ever. The abundance of the last harvest has not compensated the rise of price caused by the tillage of B.

common.   The laborers can buy little bread, and you must supply them with as much more as they want."   So a part of the diminished rent goes to paupers; Lord W. sells his stud, and goes abroad.

Pole. — Where he may chance to see our swine devouring the wheat, for want of which the children of this country are pining.   At least, he will implore the Government, in parting, to withdraw the restrictions which have proved so disastrous.

Englishman. — Not he.   He has always been told that these restrictions were formed for men of his class.   He hears of them under the term "protection," and he is afraid of not being protected, and therefore prays to be made poorer still.

Pole. — How much power there is in a name.   Not only is Lord W. seduced by the term "protection," but many tenants by the word "agriculture," as I have reason to know. I heard much of the " protection of agriculture," in answer to my pleas, that the wheat of my country might advantageously be brought hither; and when I inquired into the truth, I found that " agriculture" meant " landlords," though tenants are still disposed to think it also means " farmers."   These are strange uses of terms.

Englishman. — Very puzzling to a foreigner, no doubt ; though it can be scarcely less so to an experienced farmer, to find out how the protection he clings to never fails to bring on ruin, though there may be occasional intervals of prosperity.   It is somewhat the same sort of protection that is given to fowls which are cooped for the killing.   They have twice as much given them as they can pick up ; and so, each fowl of the poultry yard, hoping to have his turn, crows and claps his wings to the story of the protecting system, though it goes on to be fatal to the greedy ones.

Pole. — Indeed, it is too difficult to a foreigner to understand your terms, whether in your courts of justice, or in your Parliament. I lately asked what was meant by "death recorded," and was told "transportation." I asked what was meant by "transportation," and was told "imprisonment," in gaol or on board the hulks. I ask what is meant by "agriculture," and am told "landlords." Truly, yours is a difficult language. But what is the charm about dear landlords, that your nation should prefer them to cheap corn?

Englishman. — Nay; you must ask the landlords. They are the most sensible of their own charms, I believe. Meantime, you can tell us a good deal, I know, about cheap corn.

Pole. — Alas! yes; and in the same breath, of dear clothing. In our country you may see our cattle fed with grain; our peasantry shivering, half-clad, while they consume and waste twice as much corn as they need, if they had a supply of other things. You may see large tracts turned into pasturage, and others forsaken, after two or three years' tillage; and all this for want of a market; while in yonder great town, there are multitudes pining for bread, your warehouses being overstocked with cloth, for which *you* want a market. What folly is here! If cheapness be good, why should not you have cheap corn, and we cheap clothing, to the advantage of every party concerned?

Englishman. — Because not only our landlords fear a reduction of their rents, but our farmers dread being obliged to change their occupation. If we were freely supplied with corn from abroad, a large proportion of these fields would become sheep-walks, you see. We should want more wool to make your coats; and this very scene may present a verdant down, speckled with flocks, instead of stubble fields, rich in sheaves, or an expanse of uncut grain.

25 *

Pole. — And why not, if thus your peasantry may be well fed, and your agriculturists lifted out of ruin ? There might be fewer farmers, some becoming shepherds, and others manufacturers or merchants ; but is it not better to flourish as a manufacturer, than to drown one's self in one's own ditch, as a farmer?

Englishman. — It certainly seems to me that this country is destined, by nature and circumstance, to be a commercial rather than an agricultural country ; and it would in no wise trouble, but rather rejoice me to see her supplying every region of the world with her manufactures, and receiving, in return, from east and west, the produce of wider and more fertile fields than she can boast.

Pole. — Then would cease the lamentable cry, that your people are too many for your food. Then would there be work for all, and work would bring a sufficiency of bread. How is it that one class dares to stand in the way of such an arrangement? How is it that a few are permitted to intercept the good of all?

Englishman. — Because this one class has hitherto had a disproportionate share in the making of our laws. Not that this should rightly have prevented a rectification of our system; for it has been proved to them a thousand times, — and that the proof should have been so long rejected, is unaccountable, — that their own interest requires the throwing open of our ports for the importation of foreign grain. This has been proved to Lord W. and to his tenant, the cultivator of these fields, not only by reasoning, but by experience. Yet they will not have the Corn Laws touched; the one speaking for himself in the Upper House; the other through his representative in the Lower. The laborer, in the field or at the loom, who needs no further proof than his gnawing hunger, has no voice in the matter.

Pole. — His case, indeed, is clear. Even the first apparent increase of wages, from the rise of prices, profits not him, since that which his wages must purchase has also risen in price. Then when the farmer's profits are lowered by this increase of wages, it must follow that wages will again fall, while prices remain high. This is a clear case.

Englishman. — Then what is that of the farmer? He suffers both from his profits being lowered and from the dearness of the corn he eats. It is only while his lease is current that he has any compensation for this dearness. When the time for renewal comes, he hands over to his landlord all that arises from this increased price.

Pole. — It seems, then, that the landlord should be the gainer: by robbery, I grant; but still a gainer. What is it that obliges Lord W. to go abroad?

Englishman. — Not merely that he cannot at present get in his rents. It is the tremendous fluctuation in their affairs which ruins both landholder and farmer. This fluctuation is owing to our dependence on our own soils for food, and can be no otherwise guarded against than by having some better dependence. During the succession of bad seasons, which took place during the late war, the price of corn rose higher than the deficiency of supply warranted; for, corn not being an article which people think of doing without, they bid against one another in their fear of not getting it, till none but the rich could pay the market price for it; and thus the farmers profited enormously while the poor starved, for this was not a rise of prices of that permanent kind which raises wages. At this time the cultivator of these fields flourished, and flung his money about bravely; taking in new land, which he has since been obliged to give up, after a large outlay of capital upon it; sending his sons travelling, portioning his daughters, and so on; and, of course punctually paying his rents, and agreeing to a large increase at the expiration of his lease.

Pole. — Ah! I see. And when good seasons come, not only must his sons cease to travel, and his daughters to look for portions, and Lord W. to receive his rent in full; but the slightest excess over the average supply would lower prices as unduly as a slight deficiency had before raised them. There is little security of property in this case. Lord W. can never tell how much he is worth, any more than the speculator in the funds; however much may be said of the stability of landed property.

Englishman. — Hence also the apparent generosity of remitting a portion of his rents when it is impossible that he should be paid the whole. He knows that his rent is fixed too high ; but instead of lowering it, he takes the chance of a bad season or two occurring before the expiration of the lease, and parades his liberality in the newspapers, where it is told, year after year, how generously Lord W. has returned or remitted one-third or one fourth of the rents due. Meanwhile, that which he does receive comes out of his tenant's capital ; the farm buildings go out of repair, and the hedges, gates, and ditches, are presently seen in the condition of these about us.

Pole. — And all this fluctuation might be prevented by a free trade in corn ! Certainly there would not then be so much alarm at a small deficiency ; so much joy at a trifling excess. Where the whole world is looked to for a supply, there is pretty good security against a famine ; for the whole world may be considered to yield an average crop.

Englishman. — Besides this, the supply being constant, would be well regulated ; whereas, at present, a large quantity is sometimes hurried into the country, on a bare rumor of a scarcity, and its arrival is the signal for a fall of price equally ruinous to the foreign speculator and the home land-owner. We are thus liable to be overstocked, or to believe ourselves so ; which is much the same thing to the agricultural interest; and to be in a perilous panic when we are a very little understocked.

Pole.— Surely, then, it would be a benefit to the landowner to have the country regularly and sufficiently supplied with grain, that so he might know what he has to depend on; instead of being one year rich in substance, and the next only in arrears. As for his permanent interests, they must be safe; for land can never become a worthless possession.

Englishman.— And least of all in a thriving country. Whether the land be laid out in sheep-walks or corn-fields, it will always be in request while manufactures are extending, commerce flourishing, and the population increasing its productive consumption. If rents are nominally lowered, their payment will be secure, and the means of life and luxury will be much less costly. The same may be said, or nearly so, for the farmer. He may bring up few of his sons to be farmers, but there will be a better opening for them in other occupations. They may all live for less; and be no longer doomed to bury their capital in bad soils, till they have no capital left to bury. Instead, therefore, of dreading the fall of price which would follow a free importation of corn, farmers ought to see that it would bring its advantage in a fall of wages and of rent — a fall which will occasion a rise of profits to them, without injuring their landlords, or those who deserve much more consideration, their laborers. The worst that could befall them is less mischievous than the present system, under which the poorer class of families are breaking; the next preparing for bankruptcy by paying their rents out of their capital; and the richest perplexing themselves to account for the rapid diminution of their wealth, and to anticipate the issue of the present pauper system.

Pole.— Ah! that fatal pauper system! It seems that your farmers have more to pay to paupers than they can keep to live upon themselves.

Englishman.—Just so. The tenant of the ground we stand upon made terrible complaints, a few years ago, on having to pay £50 a-year to the parish. He now pays £190, while actually in the state of distress and despondency I described to you.

Pole.—Surely he deprecates the continuance of the system under which he suffers so cruelly.

Englishman.—He protests against any change, unless it be the imposition of a further duty on foreign grain. He calls out for more protection, not seeing, that the protection he really needs is, to be shielded from his own prejudices. An extraordinary infatuation; is it not?

Pole.—It makes me melancholy to find infatuation every where. Some unhappy persons in my ruined country called in the protection of the Russian despot; and bitterly have they suffered, and made others suffer by their blind appeal. But no despot, not even he of Russia, can tyrannize so fatally as bad laws. Let your landlords and farmers take this to heart.

Englishman.—I wish we could so persuade them. A despot's rule is short, and the consequences of his tyranny easily repaired in comparison with the influence and issues of bad laws. If a just ruler were to succeed to Nicholas, I should have hope of seeing your country even yet lift her worn brow to be again crowned with plenty, and smile once more in the face of him who would redeem her; but bad laws corrupt the very sources of prosperity. Their repeal brings evils almost as tremendous as their continuance. Ages will not repair the grievances inflicted by the system we have been condemning.

Pole.—True; for ages will not obliterate the moral stains which injustice and hardship leave. You should hasten, then, all the more eagerly, to rectify the errors of those who, for whatever reason, made these bad laws.

Englishman. — They will be rectified; they must soon be so, in the face of any opposition that can be brought. Then may we cease to feel shame in looking on such a scene as this, — in perceiving how much Providence has given to man, and how much man has done to stint his brethren of their share of these gifts; and, by grasping too much for himself, to ruin all.

Pole. — Would that your people would learn from us, — pilgrims from a ruined land, — how to prize what is in their own hands; how to be happy while the means remain. We would say, look to the equal distribution of your wealth while it exists. If, as a nation, you would be strong, knit your ranks together, as the interests of all classes are knitted together by the primary laws of your social state. If, as a nation, you would be free, let your higher ranks release themselves from the bondage of prejudice and groundless fear, and call up your indigent classes out of the slavery of hardship and discontent. If you would be happy as a nation, let the gifts of heaven be made as welcome to the heart as they are beautiful to the eye. Then shall these sloping sunbeams meet no scowling brows; for there will be few guilty, where none are poverty-stricken. Then shall fruitfulness cease to be a curse to any, and harvests like these shall be an actual possession to each and all. Then shall these stealing shadows, which now serve to hide too many tears, settle down on millions of dwellings tenanted by repose.

NORWICH, 1832.

PARABLES.

THE WANDERING CHILD.

In a solitary place among the groves, a child wandered whithersoever he would.

He believed himself alone, and wist not that one watched him from the thicket, and that the eye of his parent was on him continually; neither did he mark whose hand had opened a way for him thus far.

All things that he saw were new to him; therefore he feared nothing.

He cast himself down in the long grass, and as he lay, he sang till his voice of joy rang through the woods.

When he nestled among the flowers, a serpent arose from the midst of them; and when the child saw how its burnished coat glittered in the sun like the rainbow, he stretched forth his hand to take it to his bosom.

Then the voice of his parent cried from the thicket "Beware!"

And the child sprang up, and gazed above and around, to know whence the voice came; but when he saw not, he presently remembered it no more.

He watched how a butterfly burst from its shell, and flitted faster than he could pursue, and soon rose far above his reach.

When he gazed and could trace its flight no more, his father put forth his hand, and pointed where the butterfly ascended, even into the clouds.

But the child saw not the sign.

A fountain gushed forth amidst the shadows of the trees, and its waters flowed into a deep and quiet pool.

The child kneeled on the brink, and looking in, he saw his own bright face, and it smiled upon him.

As he stooped yet nearer to meet it, a voice once more said " Beware! "

The child started back ; but he saw that a gust ruffled the waters, and he said within himself, " It was but the voice of the breeze."

And when the broken sunbeams glanced on the moving waves, he laughed, and dipped his foot, that the waters might again be ruffled : and the coolness was pleasant to him.

The voice was now louder, but he regarded it not, as the winds bore it away.

At length he saw somewhat glittering in the depths of the pool ; and he plunged in to reach it.

As he sank, he cried aloud for help.

Ere the waters had closed over him, his father's hand was stretched out to save him.

And while he yet shivered with chillness and fear, his parent said unto him,

" Mine eye was upon thee, and thou didst not heed ; neither hast thou beheld my sign, nor hearkened to my voice. If thou hadst thought on me, I had not been hidden."

Then the child cast himself on his father's bosom and said, —

" Be nigh unto me still ; and mine eyes shall wait on thee, and mine ears shall be open unto thy voice for evermore."

FAITH AND HOPE.

ONE morning, as the sun arose, two spirits went forth upon the earth.

And they were sisters. But Faith was of mature age, while Hope was yet a child.

They were both beautiful. Some loved to gaze on the countenance of Faith, for her eye was serene, and her beauty changed not: but Hope was the delight of every heart.

And the child sported in the freshness of the morning; and as she hovered over the gardens and dewy lawns, her wings glittered in the sunbeams like the rainbow.

"Come, my sister," she cried, " and chase with me this butterfly from flower to flower."

But her sister was gazing at the lark as it arose from its low nest and warbled among the clouds.

And when it was noon, the child said again, " Come, my sister, and pluck with me the flowers of the garden ; for they are beautiful, and their fragrance is sweet."

But Faith replied, " Nay, my sister, let the flowers be thine; for thou art young, and delightest thyself in their beauty. I will meditate in the shade, till the heat of the day be past. Thou wilt find me beside the fountain in the forest. When thou art weary, come and repose on my bosom."

And she smiled and departed.

After a time, Hope sought her sister. The tear was in her eye, and her countenance was mournful.

Then Faith said, " My sister, wherefore dost thou weep, and why is thy countenance sad ? "

And the child answered, " Because a cloud is in the sky, and the sunshine is overcast. See, the rain begins to fall."

"It is but a shower," Faith replied; " and when it is over, the fields will be greener and the flowers brighter than before."

Now the place where they sat was sheltered from the rain, as it had been from the noon-day heats. And Faith comforted the child, and showed her how the waters flowed with a fuller and a clearer stream as the shower fell.

And presently the sun broke out again, and the woods resounded with song.

Then hope was glad and went forth to her sports once more. —

After a time, the sky was again darkened. And the young Spirit looked up, and, behold! there was no cloud in the whole circle of the heavens.

Therefore Hope marvelled, for it was not yet night.

And she fled to her sister, and cast herself down at her feet, and trembled exceedingly.

Then Faith raised the child, and led her forth from the shade of the trees, and pointed to the sun and said,

"A shadow is passing over the face thereof, but no ray of his glory is extinguished. He still walketh in brightness, and thou shalt again delight thyself in his beams. See! even yet, his face is not wholly hidden from us."

But the child dared not look up, for the gloom struck upon her heart.

And when all was bright again, she feared to wander from her sister, and her sports were less gay than before. —

When the eventide was come, Faith went forth from the forest shade, and sought the lawn, where she might watch the setting of the sun. Then said she to her young sister,

"Come and behold how far the glories of the sunset transcend the beauties of the morning. See how softly they melt away, and give place to the shadows of night!"

But hope was now weary. Her eye was heavy, and her voice languid. She folded her radiant wings, and dropped on her sister's bosom, and fell asleep.

But Faith watched through the night. She was never weary nor did her eyelids need repose.

She laid the child on a bed of flowers, and kissed her cheek. She also drew her mantle round the head of the sleeper, that she might sleep in peace.

Then Faith looked upwards, and beheld how the stars came forth. She traced them in their radiant courses, and listened to their harmonies, which mortal ear hath not heard.

And as she listened their music entranced her soul.

At length, a light appeared in the east, and the sun burst forth from the portals of the heaven.

Then the Spirit hastened to arouse the young sleeper.

"Awake, O my sister! awake!" she cried. "A new day hath dawned, and no cloud shall overshadow it. Awake! for the sun hath risen which shall set no more!"

HELI AND ANTAR.

Two brethren were wayfaring in the desert when the hot wind blew.

The angel of Death rode on the blast, and smote them to the earth.

"Why tremblest thou, my brother?" said the spirit of Heli, as he spread his radiant wings for flight.

"Alas! I fear," said Antar, "because I know not whither I go! Would I could tarry with the body wherein I have dwelt so long. But the sun grows dark, and I can no more feel the ground. I must depart, but not, like thee, rejoicing. Whence is thy joy?"

"Because I shall now see more clearly the light that I have loved, and hear more perfectly the music which my soul hath been intent to hear."

26*

"My brother, bring me whither thou hast been wont to go, that my peace may be as thine."

Then Heli brought his brother to the ruins of a mighty city, which were scattered over the plain. No living man abode there, but the echoes called one to another among the tombs, saying, "The sons of men, where are they?"

Antar drooped his head as he listened, but a light shone forth from the eyes of Heli.

Then they pierced the depths of the forest, where the tree of a thousand years was wont to flourish in its verdure; where the field-flower had blossomed, and bees had murmured around.

But now the tree was bare before the north wind. The bees were benumbed within the stem, and the flowers lay hid beneath the snow.

Again Antar mourned, but Heli smiled, as he pointed where summer gales came from afar.

Afterwards Heli hovered over the deep; and when he saw that his brother followed, he clave the waters, and sought the lowest caves of the sea. There no sunbeam had ever shone, nor had silence entered since the world began.

The roaring of the waves was more fearful to Antar than the thunders of the sky. But to Heli it was as the music of glad voices; and he sang with the chorus of the waters, saying,

"Come, and hearken to the voice of God, how his voice is mightier than the waves of the deep."

Then from darkness and thunder they ascended to light and silence.

In the uttermost part of the heaven was the eternal altar, whereon was kindled an unconsuming fire.

There spirits went to and fro to fill their golden urns, and shed radiance through the universe. Suns shone everlastingly around, and planets rolled swiftly beneath. But there was no sound.

Antar saw none of these things, for his wings were spread before his face. But Heli drew nigh to the altar, and mingled with the young spirits which thronged around; for he knew that they were brethren.

But while he ministered with them, he was not unmindful of Antar. After a while he again led the way, and brought his brother where he might repose.

It was nigh unto the regions of darkness, and a deep shadow spread over the firmament.

"I now know," said Antar, "that thy joy is because thou hast found thy home. But how knowest thou the way?"

"Because it hath been my wont to come often whither I have but now conducted thee."

"Nay, my brother, but who hath brought thee?"

"The spirit of a man, Antar, can wander afar, even while the earth is its abode. Thus was it with me.

"I saw the smile of God in the light of the calm sunset, and heard his voice in the music of the morning.

"Whither he called me I went forth, and where he pointed I sought out his glories.

"I found them when I mounted the sloping sunbeam, and trod the path of the moonlight over the deep.

"When the lark flew up from her dewy nest, I arose with her; and when night came on, I wandered to and fro among the stars.

"Then I knew that the earth was not my home. But neither have I yet brought thee to my true abode, because thou art already faint with wonder and fear. I can show thee greater things than these."

"Not yet," murmured Antar, trembling the more as his brother spake. "Leave me; and when I am as thou, I will follow thee to thy home."

THE SPIRITS OF THE NIGHT.

As the sun was withdrawing his light from one hemisphere, the guardian spirits of man followed his course, as they were wont, that they might visit every land in turn.

But two who had been busy among the abodes of men all the day, lingered, unwilling to leave those to whom they had ministered.

To the one had been committed the urn which held the waters of bitterness, and he was called WOE. His young sister was named PEACE; and in her hand was placed the lyre whose music was of heaven.

"There are some," said WOE, "who will not be ready to hearken to thee to-morrow, my sister, if I leave them already."

"There are also some, my brother, whom I have not yet soothed to deep repose. O! that we might tarry awhile!"

"We may not tarry, for there is need of us afar. Yet one thing may we do. Let us give of our power to another, that she may minister till we return."

So they called upon CONSCIENCE, and charged her to descend with the shadows of night, and to visit the abodes of men. The angel of WOE gave her of the waters of his urn, and said unto his sister "Give her thy lyre, for what other music needest thou than thine own songs? What other melody is so sweet?"

And when they had charged their messenger to await them at the eastern gate when the morning should open it unto them, they spread their wings and hastened down the west.

Their messenger gazed after them afar: and when she marked the dim majesty of the elder spirit, and the mild beauty of his sister, she bent her head and silently went her way.

"What hast thou beheld?" said the angels to their messenger, when the portals of light were unclosed. "Are the healing waters spent? Hath the lyre been tuneful?"

"The waters are not spent," she replied; "for mine own tears have made this urn to overflow. The lyre was tuned in Paradise; else my trembling hand had jarred its strings."

"Alas!" cried the younger spirit, "where then hast thou ministered?"

"When the evening star appeared, I descended among the shadows, where I heard a voice calling to me from afar. It came from a space where raging fires were kindled by the hands of priests. Night hovered above, but the flames forbade her approach, and I could not abide longer beneath her wings. He who appealed unto me stood chained amidst the fires which already preyed upon him. I swept the strings of the lyre, and smiles overspread his face. Even while the melody waxed sweeter, the dark-eyed spirit of the tombs came and bore him away asleep."

The young angel smiled as she said, "He hearkeneth now to nobler harmonies than ours! But was there none other amidst the flames to whom thou couldst minister?"

"Alas! there was one who lied through fear. He was led back to his cell, whither I followed him. I shed the waters into his soul, and the bitterness thereof tormented him more than any scorching flames which could have consumed his body. Yet must I visit him nightly till he dies."

"Droop not thy wings because of his anguish, my sister," said the elder spirit. "He shall yet be thine when he is made pure for thy presence."

"I have been," said the messenger, "beside the couch of the dying, in the palace, and beneath the lowly roof. I have shed into one departing soul the burning tears of the slave, and soothed the spirit of another with the voices of grateful hearts. I have made the chamber of one rich man echo with the cries of the oppressed, and have surrounded the pillow of another with the fatherless who called him parent. Kings have sought to hide themselves as I drew nigh, while the eye of the mourner hath lighted up at my approach. The slumbers of some have I hallowed with music, while they knew not I was at hand; and others have I startled with visions, who guessed not whence they came. I am filled with awe at mine own power."

"It shall increase," said the elder spirit, "while mine own waneth. The fountain of bitter waters wasteth continually. When it shall be dried up, I will break mine urn."

"And my lyre," said his sister; "shall it not be hushed by mightier music from on high?"

"Nay, my sister, not then, nor ever. No mightier music shall make men cease to love thine. They shall gather together to hear thee in their cities, and shall seek thee in wildernesses and by the sea-shore. The aged shall hear thee chant among the tombs, and the young shall dance unto thy lay. Unto the simple shall thy melodies breathe from amidst the flowers of the meadows; and the wise shall they entrance as they go to and fro among the stars."

Then the messenger sighed, saying,

"When shall these things be?"

"When thou art queen among men. Knowest thou not that such is thy destiny? Thou art now our messenger, but we shall at length be thy servants. Yea, when yonder sun shall wander away into the depths, and the earth shall melt like the morning cloud, it shall be thine to lead the myriads of thy people to the threshold whence the armies of heaven come forth. It shall be thine to open to them the portals which I may not pass."

THE HERMIT.

THERE was a lofty rock which had stood for ever. And a fountain sprang up beneath the rock, and the waters thereof were purer than any waters that were upon the earth.

A Hermit made his dwelling beside the fountain. He drank of the waters at their source, morning and evening; and he went lower down, and purified himself every day.

His dwelling was covered with vines: and the Hermit trained the branches thereof, and watered the roots, and rejoiced to behold the golden clusters, and watched with care those that were yet unripe.

Birds fed from his hand, and refreshed him with their song. Antelopes also were sheltered beneath his roof, and he loved to behold their sports.

It chanced, one day, that the Hermit was weary and slept. And when he awoke, lo! one stood beside him in his dwelling. And the Hermit wist not how he had found entrance therein.

And the stranger was of a gay countenance, and in his hand he held a cup. He drank thereof, and offered unto the Hermit.

The Hermit was afraid; but, after a while, he listened to the words of the stranger and drank.

The night passed away in mirth. The holy man knew not when the sun went down: neither did he repair to the fountain as he was wont.

Towards dawn, he sank down in a deep sleep; and when he awoke, lo! the stranger had departed.

When he went abroad, the sun rode high in the heavens; and as he looked around him, he saw that all was laid waste.

The vines were torn down from their supports and trailed along the ground. The birds had not been fed; therefore their song was hushed. The antelopes came not forth: they were stretched on the earth, fainting with thirst.

Then the Hermit went to drink of the fountain. But the stream was almost dried up, and the waters thereof were bitter.

He hastened to bathe his feverish brow. But when he bent over the pool, lo! his face was changed that he knew it not.

Casting himself down in fear and sorrow, he cried " an enemy hath laid waste my dwelling while I slept."

Presently, dark clouds arose, and thunders rolled afar off.

And the Hermit heard a voice calling on his name. He looked up, and beheld one whose eye was sullen, and his brow dark and lowering.

And he frowned upon the Hermit, saying, " He whom thou hast entertained is SIN. He hath despoiled thy habitation, and the waste can never be repaired."

Then the Hermit trembled, for the voice of the stranger chilled his soul.

" What then must I do?" he cried. And while he spake, the winds arose, and there was a great storm. And DESPAIR replied,

" Thou canst not remain here. Behold! the storm beats upon thy dwelling, and it shakes from its foundations. Follow after thy guest, for here is no abiding place."

" But he hath spoiled me already," cried the Hermit; " and if I follow him, he will destroy me utterly."

" Then," cried DESPAIR, " cast thyself down from a rock and die."

And the hermit fled to the edge of a precipice, and was about to cast himself down, when a hand restrained him. He turned, and beheld the form of a woman. She was clothed in dark raiment. Her countenance was severe, though calm. Her eye was mournful, and bore traces of tears that had passed away. Her voice was low, but sweet; and the Hermit, while he listened, felt the tumult subside in his soul.

"Return unto thy home," she said. "I am REPENTANCE; and I will aid thee to repair the desolation thereof."

"But," replied he, "the storm beats upon it, and will overthrow it, so that I can never more enter therein."

"Return with me," answered his protector. "Thou canst abide under the shadow of the rock till the storm be overpast."

So she took his hand, and the Hermit suffered himself to be led back.

"At length the black clouds parted, and a ray of light fell upon the fountain.

"Drink thereof, and refresh thyself," said his guide.

The Hermit feared to taste, because he knew that the waters were bitter: but he obeyed the voice of his guide.

As he stooped to drink, lo! the pure wave swelled to meet his lips. His tears flowed fast, and as they fell into the stream, the bitterness thereof passed away.

And he arose refreshed, and strengthened for his work.

And REPENTANCE guided him therein.

But when all was done, the habitation was not pleasant as before.

And when she was about to depart, the Hermit cried, "Remain with me, for my home is yet sad, and the beauty thereof hath vanished away. I also fear to be alone, lest SIN, my enemy, should return."

REPENTANCE answered, "Another now waiteth my help, and I must depart. But be thou watchful, lest thy enemy approach thee unawares. If thou behold him nigh, flee unto the shadow of the rock, and thou shalt be safe."

And when she had departed, the Hermit pondered her words continually.

After a time, Sin again drew nigh. He hoped to find the door standing wide, and the Hermit sleeping as before.

He marvelled when he saw how fair the dwelling and the garden appeared. And he said,

"Some one hath taught him to repair the ruin which I caused. I must beware how I approach."

And he looked, and behold! the Hermit was seated beneath the Everlasting Rock. Peace was in his countenance as he saw how all around was fair and promising. The last rays of day shone on his grey hairs.

And Sin dared not approach; but lingered till the darkness of night should come on.

When the sun disappeared, the Hermit repaired to the fountain, and knelt down to drink.

Then Sin hastened to unfurl his wings, and fled away.

A PARABLE.

In the depths of a cave young Life awoke as if from sleep.

And because she knew not whence she was, or whose hand had awakened her, she gazed intently towards the darkness behind her, and softly said, "Whence am I?"

When none answered, she lifted up her voice and cried aloud, Whence am I?"

The cry resounded through the depths of the cave, and was heard in lower depths, and lower, till it died away into silence.

Yet was there no reply.

Then the spirit turned towards the mouth of the cave. Roses hung around it, and the vine put forth its clusters among the roses.

One stood without, watching till young LIFE should come forth into the sunshine. When she saw the angel, she marvelled at the beauty of his countenance, and said,

"Comest thou from the depths even as I?"

And the angel answered, "Thou hast arisen out of darkness, but I dwell in the midst of light. Thou art but now awakened; but I have gone to and fro for ages of ages. I am from Him who awakened thee, and my name is LOVE. Fear nothing for I can guard thee whithersoever thou goest. Call on me, and I will be nigh."

Then seeing that the spirit looked on the flowers and fruits that hung around, he smiled, and laid aside the palm-rod that he bore, and gathered of the roses as many as she would: and the fruits which hung aloft he held within her reach.

When she went forward, at length, the whole earth was fair before her. She roved the meadows, and bounded over the hills, and trod the paths of the groves till she was wearied and athirst.

Then she looked around for the angel, but she beheld him not.

Remembering that he had promised to come when she had need, she called on his name; and he was there.

And he rebuked her, saying, "Are there not messengers sent unto thee from above and from beneath, and thou regardest them not? Wherefore art thou faint, when they are around thee who shall renew thy strength?"

Then LIFE gazed steadfastly, and saw that a multitude of spirits was near. They uprose from the flowers of the field, and thronged the thickets of the forest. They issued from the abyss, and came down from among the stars. They sang amid the clouds on the mountain-top, and their music floated on the still lake.

When the young spirit held out her arms, they came unto her, and ministered unto her more and more continually.

The angel LOVE also blessed her. When her path lay through the sultry desert, he made a shade for her with his wings. He opened a way for her in the tangled wilderness, and soothed her when the tempest burst around her head.

When she asked, " Shall there be always snares, and burning heats, and tempests?" he replied,

"Nay; but for a while. When thou art on yonder summit, a cloud shall bear thee where such things are not."

As she drew nigh the mountain, they that thronged around her went back one by one, so that when she reached the summit, behold! she was alone.

And she saw a thick black cloud rolling towards her, and fearing to be swept away, she clung to the earth, and cried fearfully to the angel; but he was no where seen.

Then the skirts of the cloud hid from her the gay, bright earth; and a heavy chill fell on her.

And as the damps compassed her round about, one looked forth brightly from the cloud and smiled.

It was the angel. He held forth his hand saying,

"Though thou hast ofttimes forgotten me, behold me here in thy utmost need."

Then was revealed bright glory within the cloud, and the spirit sprang into it eagerly.

And as they sailed away into the ether, the angel cleft the cloud with his rod, and showed unto his charge the path she had traversed. The glory in which she lay fell upon it, and made it wholly beautiful. The waters which had been dark now gleamed, and the tangled forests waved majestically in the golden light.

When she looked upwards, she saw how the radiance spread unto the depths of the heaven till her dazzled eye could see no further.

"Fearest thou?" said the angel, as she bowed her head; "I lead thee unto Him who awakened thee out of darkness."

"I would fain behold him," she replied; "and what should I fear when I am with thee?"

THE SOLITARY.

In the early morning, a Solitary went forth to worship on the sea-shore.

The sea was calm, and the beauty of the bright expanse delighted his eye, and the solemn murmur of the waves soothed his soul.

And he mused awhile, and was about to begin his prayer.

But children approached, and as they sported on the sands, their cheerful voices met his ear.

And he was vexed that the calm of his thoughts was disturbed. And he frowned on the little ones.

Soon some fishermen approached; and they cast their nets into a skiff which was on the beach, and committed it to the deep.

And the wife of one of them was there; and the Solitary heard her thank God that the sky was clear and the ocean calm.

But again he was vexed that he was not alone.

Soon he beheld a busy scene. The boatmen returned from their night voyage, and were met with a joyous greeting. Young and old also came forth to enjoy the freshness of the morning. Sea birds spread their long pinions and rose and fell on the surface of the waters.

Then the Solitary said, "I cannot worship here, where I love to behold the waves advancing to my feet: I will go higher, where all is still."

27*

He climbed a cliff which rose from the beach, and there he found an open down where the turf was soft and green. The blue sea spread a wider expanse before him. The small boats were cradled on the deep beneath, and fleets pursued their course along the horizon.

The Solitary composed his thoughts to prayer.

But soon music fell on his ear. To him it was harsh, for he wished for silence.

Then he turned, and beheld a shepherd leading forth his flock.

And the face of the shepherd was marked with thought, and a mild light beamed from his eye. The music of his pipe also was soft and sweet.

Yet the Solitary looked on him with anger, and arose hastily, and plunged into the depths of a wood which skirted the sunny down.

And he traversed its shades till he came to a quiet nook, where a spring burst forth from the thicket, and the closely-woven boughs shut out the sunshine.

" I can see no more the spreading main," said he to himself, " but here I can be at peace. No eye followeth me here, and no cup is dipped in this spring."

He drank thereof, and his soul was once more hushed to stillness.

But after a while the breeze brought a sweeter music than the rustling of the boughs or the plashing of the spring.

Infant voices were chanting near. The song of their praise was sweet, and the words thereof were holy.

The Solitary left his covert, and beheld a cottage which the thicket had hidden from him. It stood on a sloping grass-plat. It was open to the heavens. The sun shone on its humble roof, and the ivy which twined around tossed its branches in the breeze.

An aged woman sat on the bench beside the door, and around her were little children gathered.

She had read to them the words of life; but her feeble voice was not heard afar off.

She taught them to sing hymns: and their praises were holy as the Hermit's prayer. But his soul was not as a little child's, and he could not bend to listen.

And the aged woman rose up, and the children besought his blessing. But he hardened his heart, and yet again hastened away.

A rock towered high above the wood. The ascent thereof was steep, and the path rugged. But wrath glowed in the breast of the Solitary, and impelled his steps.

He paused not till he reached the summit, and planted his foot where the step of man had never before trod.

There again he beheld the sea spreading farther than eye could reach. The roar of its waves ascended not so high. The ships appeared to be motionless on its bosom; and the small boats were no longer seen.

Then the holy man exclaimed with joy, " Now at length I am alone ! "

But, as he spoke, a living cry arose. He turned, and behold ! the nest of an Eagle. And the flapping of wings was heard.

The young eagles arose at the approach of their parent; and she fed them from her beak.

Then the Hermit saw how she spread her wings, and bore her young thereon, and flew gently a short flight, and returned again, that they might not be weary.

And the Solitary looked down abashed and sighed.

And a still, small voice whispered within his breast,

" Behold ! in all the universe of God, praise aboundeth unto Him; and is thy worship so pure that none other may mingle therewith ?

" Lo ! the Eagle hath wings that bear her up to the gate of heaven. She can battle with the storms of the sky. She can also gaze on the noonday brightness of the sun; for her eye shrinketh not, nor is weary.

" Yet she heareth the cry of her little ones, and beareth with their weakness till they can soar with her on high.

" Therein is her wisdom greater, and her heart more expanded than thine."

POETRY.

THE LAST TREE OF THE FOREST.

TIME-HALLOWED Tree! still honored in decay!
The Ivy clings around thee and renews
The verdant beauties of thy earlier day.
The sunbeams gild thee with their richest hues:
The Naiad leads her streamlet to thy stem:
The Wood Nymphs seek thy solitary shade,
And deck the turf with many a fairy gem:
Yet doth thy strength decay, thy beauty fade.

Thus art thou cherished; yet thy fall is nigh:
For o'er thee years and centuries have passed.
Of all the forest brethren, towering high,
Sole thou art left, the strongest and the last.
Race after race this woodland scene hath sought,
And multitudes have thronged its verdant bowers;
And thou art left, sole record of each thought
Of joy, or woe, that marked the by-gone hours.

At eventide, the Hermit from his cave
Hath wandered here to meditate unseen;
The traveller came his burning brow to lave
At thy cool fount, and pace thine alleys green;
And Pagan priests have raised their altars here;
And Monks received the sinner's sorrowing vows;
The knightly plume, the Warrior's shield and spear,
Have gleamed afar, or waved beneath thy boughs.

What sounds have greeted thee! the Minstrel's verse,
The Huntsman's bugle, ringing through the glade,
The Pilgrim's orison, the Bandit's curse,
Childhood's light laugh, and Age's warning staid;
The wakeful bird that carolled all night long,
Rousing the echoes with her thrilling lay;
And the glad spirit's more melodious song,
That sought thy covert nook to praise and pray.

The stricken deer hath pierced the thicket's gloom,
And in some still recess the mourner wept:
The murdered wretch hath found a secret tomb,
And infants, tired with play, have peaceful slept.
The idle shepherd mused the hours away,
Watching the sunbeams as they danced afar;
The maiden here was wont at eve to stray,
And through the foliage mark each silver star.

Time-hallowed Tree! the thoughtful well might deem
A moral being was on thee conferred;
So conscious seem'st thou that thy records teem
With warnings which, though mute, are not unheard.
For thou canst tell how passions blazed and died;
Canst tell of friends and foes alike laid low;
How haughty youth was blasted in its pride,
How hoary heads, in turn, must bend — as thou.

And while thy verdure falls, thy branches greet
The passing gust, and bend them to its will,
How many thoughts and feelings, sad and sweet,
In their first freshness, cluster round thee still!
Such should not perish.   Yet they too must fall.
Thou hast outlived the brave, the wise, the gay:
And, in thy turn, like all that's great, and all
That's beautiful on earth, must pass away.

ODE TO RELIGIOUS LIBERTY.

O! SACRED LIBERTY!
Thou art of heavenly birth;
And angels tend thy steps, and follow thee.
"Good will to men" they sang,
At thy descent on earth;
And through the midnight sky their anthems rang.
Thou, like a conqueror, didst extend thy reign,
And vanquish sin and pain:
And holy hands thy banner reared,
Where'er the name of Christ was heard.
But persecution raised her rod,
And call'd thy followers to renounce thy sway.
They, loving thee, and faithful to their God,
An onward path still kept:
They trembled not, nor wept;
And, grateful, found in thee a still unfailing stay.

When from its lofty station hurled,
Thy glorious banner lay,
Thy wings were to the winds unfurled,
And thou didst flee away,
For foes encompassed thee on every side.
To Alpine vales retired,
Secure thou didst abide,
Where by thy smile inspired,
The mountain race the Tyrants' power defied.
There the high-souled Vaudois,
Obedient to thy law,
Thee cherished as a heaven-descended guest:
And each heroic breast
Was as a shield to guard thee from thy foes.
When from the vale thy watchword rose,

It echoed through the forest drear,
Sounding from heart to heart in accents clear.
When from the mountain-top thy beacon blazed,
That with its ruddy glow
Brightened the torrent's flow,
A glorious band their arms upraised.
All gentle virtues gathered there,
Fostered by thy sacred care,
And hallowed guests beside each cottage hearth.

Yet didst thou mourn, while wandering o'er the earth,
That, all unmindful of thy heavenly birth,
The nations from thy guidance fly;
And thou didst weep.
Echoing from steep to steep,
Thy followers heard the plaintive cry;
And every heart indignant beat, and glanced each kind-
ling eye.
While in the forests of thine Alpine land,
Or in its caves reclined,
Mourning the woes and perils of thy band,
Thou sat'st and pined,
From a far island of the sea
There rose an earnest cry to thee,
And Wickliffe called upon thy name.
Swift thou didst take thy flight,
And arm him with thy might.
He saw thee plant thy foot upon the strand,
And gather round thee an adventurous band,
Strengthened to bear the torture and the flame.
And from that hour 't was thine to tend
Thy saints and martyrs, and to lend
Power to the faint, and to the worn repose.
'T was thine to make them smile amidst their pain,

To wipe the dews of anguish from their brows,
  Till *Milton* rose,
Thy great High-Priest, the Prophet of thy universal
 reign.

He saw thy slaughtered saints uplift their eyes
To thee, and raise to thee their latest cries:
 And thou didst touch his lips with fire,
Red from the altar of that sacrifice:
 And in his hallowed hands didst place thy lyre.
  When in the still midnight,
  He sang thy bounteous might,
And called upon thee, knowing thou wert nigh:
 Thou could'st not then thy voice refrain,
 From echoing back his lofty strain,
And pouring on his ear thy heavenly harmony.
  Hark! on the quivering wire,
  The high-wrought tones expire,
While the rapt prophet listens to thy voice,
Swelling afar, or breathing near, to bid his soul rejoice.

But other realms now own thy sway.
The glimmering dawn has brightened into day.
   And where the chariot of the sun
   Reposes when the day is done,
A mighty land hath ta'en thee for her own.
There thou hast fixed thy steadfast throne,
   There driven afar
   Thy radiant car,
Before whose conquering wheels the tyrants bow them
 down.
  To thee the western nations turn,
  With love for thee their bosoms burn;
They court thy smile, and fear thy frown,
And gaze with awe on thy resplendent crown.

28

But there are lands still wrapt in shades of night ;
Lands where, in happier days,
Sages and heroes found an honored tomb.
No ray is there but the infernal light
Of Persecution's blaze,
And Learning's halls are darkened with deep gloom.
But soon before thy living ray
The mists shall roll away,
And towers and spires shall glitter in the blaze.
Th' imperial palace on the mountain's brow,
The peasant's cot in shaded vales below,
Shall feel thy gladdening influence ; — every field,
More verdant flourish, fountains purer spring ;
The earth her fruits, the flowers their fragrance, yield ;
While hov'ring o'er them with resplendent wing,
Thou, from thy golden urn, dost showers of blessing fling.

When in the dungeon of thy foes
The captive mourns his wrongs and woes,
Or, phrensied, thinks upon the flaming pile,
O, Liberty ! descend, and cheer him with thy smile.
Or where, imprisoned in the convent cell,
The maid regrets the world she loves too well,
Pines through the weary day,
And weeps the night away,
And dreads to hear the matin bell
Of every joy repeat the knell,
O ! whisper with the voice of hope the words that bring
. repose.
Tell her of days to come when hearts may love,
And smiles and tears be given to earthly things ;
When wandering forth to gaze on stars above,
Or pluck the flower that in the pasture springs,

The youthful soul may offer nobler praise,
Than in the cloister's gloom, where fear prevails and love
    decays.

There is an island, rising from the main,
    Where fields are green, and rivers flow,
    And lakes reflect the sunset glow,
    And mountains tower above the plain,
Whose people call on thee: O! must they call in vain?
    They dwell not in the gloom of night,
    Nor in the woes of slavery wail;
    Thou blessest them with partial light,
But dost from them thy full effulgence veil.
    Withdraw the envious cloud
    That doth thy features shroud,
Receive their homage when they bid thee hail.
    For fiery hearts are glowing there,
    And earnest tongues are heard in prayer,
    And hands are ready to prepare
    A temple for thy dwelling-place.
    Speak but the word — its walls shall rise,
    Its altars flame, its spreading dome
    Shall echo with thy harmonies.
      O! there unveil thy face,
And choose that verdant island for thy home.

Where'er thy vast dominion shall extend,
  O'er the wide earth, and to the utmost sea;
Where'er the tribes of men their streams shall blend,
  To swell the ocean of humanity,
      O! glorious Liberty!
  Still be the human heart thy holiest place.
    There let thy presence keep the ark divine,
      And guard the holy law.

Let all unhallowed things from thence withdraw,
  And come not near thy glories, as they shine;
Nor dare pollute the covenant of grace.
    O, glorious Liberty!
Shed o'er the soul the light that comes from thee,
And breathe around its still recess eternal sanctity

THE FORSAKEN NEST.

PARENTS and nestlings! are ye flown?
Here is your bed of moss and down
    Fallen from its lofty bough.
Here ye first saw the light,
Here tried your earliest flight.
    Where are ye now?

The Spring still decks your native tree,
Its branches wave as light and free
    As when they rocked your nest.
What has the world to give,
That here ye cannot live
    And still be blest?

The air is fresh with sun and showers,
And insects sport, and early flowers
    Here lavish all their bloom.
What new desires awake,
That ye must thus forsake
    Your early home?

And could ye leave the parent wing,
And rashly on the breeze upspring,

A gayer scene to find ;
And leave your lowly nest,
With all its peace and rest,
    So far behind ?

And what has been your various fate?
One may have found a home, a mate,
    And groves as sweet as this :
And one perchance may mourn
Days that shall ne'er return ;
    Young days of bliss.

One to the hawk has fallen a prey ;
One, captive, pours his thrilling lay
    When hope and joy are gone ;
One seeks a foreign shore,
And thence returns no more,
    But dies alone.

So human families must part ;
And many a worn and aching heart
    Pines for its early home ;
The cheerful board and hearth,
The looks and tones of mirth,
    The hopes in bloom.

And one may smile while others weep ;
But still one precious hope they keep
    Through all life's changing years, —
To pass through joy and pain,
And mingle once again
    Their smiles and tears.

28*

THE THREE AGES OF THE SOUL.

" To every thing there is a season, and a time to every purpose under
heaven." Eccles. iii. 1.

THERE is a time, — and childhood is the hour, —
To hear the surges break among the caves;
To hail with mirth and sport their awful roar,
And hear no deeper music in the waves.
There is a time to rove the lawn, the field, —
Chasing the hind, to thread the forest glade,
And cull no beauty but the flowers they yield,
Nor find more deep refreshment than their shade.

Then is the time to gaze upon the sky,
When the moon reigns, and sapphire hosts advance,
And feel no influence wafted from on high,
See nought mysterious in their radiant dance.
Then is the time to ask where *they* can be,
Whom death withdrew as side by side we trod;
And since no tongue can tell, no eye can see,
To turn and sport upon their burial sod.

There is a time, — and now the hour is come, —
When life breathes out from all these hues and forms;
When winds and streams sing of the spirit's home,
And ocean chants her welcome midst his storms.
Then nature wooes the ear, directs the eye,
Breathes out her essence o'er the sentient soul;
Fathoms the depths for her, and scales the sky,
And speeds her ardent flight from pole to pole.

Life now, — no mean creation of a day,
Held without thought and in the present bound, —

Looking before and after, holds its way,
Treading serene its bright, eternal round.
Now Death, familiar grown, aye hovers near,
To shadow forth the spirits fairest dreams;
To tend young hopes, to quell the low-born fear,
And chase, with light divine, earth's fitful gleams.

The time shall be, — O come the promised hour! —
When all these outward forms shall melt away,
Seas shall be dry, and stars shall shine no more,
Hushed every sound, and quenched each living ray.
Yet, treasured as the life, they cannot die. —
Part of herself, ethereal as the soul,
Hesperus shall still lead forth his hosts on high,
Still earth be gay, and ocean gleam and roll.

O! come the hour when the expanded mind, —
Here fed by Nature with immortal food, —
Within itself the universe shall find,
Survey its treasures and pronounce them good!
O! haste the hour when to the deathless fire
On the eternal altar, souls shall come,
Linked in one joy; — and while its flames aspire
Still throng around and feel its light their home!

CONSOLATIONS.

MOURNER! thou seekest Rest.
Rise from thy couch, and dry thy tears unblest,
And sigh no more for blessings now resigned.
Go to the fount of life which ever flows;
There thou mayest gain oblivion of thy woes,
There shall thy spirit own a sweet repose.
    Seek rest and thou shalt find.

Thou seekest Health; and how?
Let gloom and tears no more thy spirit bow;
Health springs aloft upon the viewless wind:
Up to the mountain top pursue her flight;
Over the fresh turf track her footsteps light,
In hawthorn bowers, 'mid fountains gushing bright,
   Seek her, and thou shalt find.

But Hope hath left thee too,
'Mid many griefs and comforts all too few.
Think not her angel-presence is confined
To earth; but seek the helps which God hath given
To aid thy feeble sight, and through the heaven
See where she soars, bright as the star of even.
   Then seek, and thou shalt find.

Dost thou seek Peace? and where?
'Mong thine own withered hopes? She is not there,
Nor in the depths of thine own darkened mind.
Lay thy heart open to the infants' mirth,
Send the bright hopes of others from their birth,
Look round for all that's beautiful on earth.
   Seek Peace, and thou shalt find.

Seek Peace and Hope and Rest:
And as the eagle flutters o'er her nest,*
And bears her young, all trembling, weak, and blind,
Up to heaven-gate on her triumphant wing;—
So shall the Lord thy God thy spirit bring
To whom eternal suns their radiance fling.
   Him seek and thou shalt find.

---

* Deut. xxxii. 11.

ADDRESS

TO THE AVOWED ARIANS OF THE SYNOD OF ULSTER.

Hail! faithful few, who love the light of truth
More than the praise of men! — Your choice is made;
And may that choice repay you! If ye lose
Much that the heart of man has learned to prize,
Stir not your noble spirits when ye think
What ye have gained? What honor from good men,
What peace within, what favor from your God!
Reason is on your side, and nature too: —
Nature, who bade the human soul be free,
Active and independent, gave it power
To seek the truth and energy to hold.

  The mind of man must keep its onward course,
And conquer prejudice and combat error,
Till truth prevail, clear, gentle, and serene.
Thus springs, within the bosom of a mount,
Work on their silent way, till, stronger grown,
They burst their barriers, and gush freely forth
To meet the eye of heaven: and if, convulsed,
The hills are rent, and falling rocks impede
The torrent's course, the proud wave higher swells,
And overflows them; till opposed no more,
It spreads afar its silent, blue expanse,
Where flowers behold their image, and the moon
Gazes upon herself. —
                          Then struggle on,
And hope for future peace: — but if in vain
Ye seek it among men; — if malice, scorn,
And tyranny should track your steps, and chafe
The immortal mind they never can subdue, —
O! still be thankful for your destiny.

Hold fast your glorious privilege, and impart
Where'er ye may, the liberty wherewith
The Gospel makes you free.   What though for this
Bigots alarm, and superstition scowl,
And friends desert, and calumny prepare
Her scorpion whip, — yet tremble not, nor shrink,
Nor deem the contest doubtful.   Ye have heard
The holy call which none may disobey,
Received the badge which none may disavow.
Say, — if the spirit of Truth, descending, place
His fiery symbol on your honored heads,
Can ye, with every energy awake,
Each power exulting, glowing every sense,
Under his influence, — can ye forget
The language he has taught?   Can ye despise
His holy revelations, or desert
The little band of friends who bear his mark ?
Can ye forswear the gifts of heaven, because
Earth's tyrants frown, earth's children mock, and griefs,
Perils, and snares, are thickly strown around ?
    O, no !   Ye cannot choose but speak the things
Your mental eye hath seen, your favored ear
Intently heard. — And if for this the storms
Of life should gather round you on your way,
Ye shall not shrink defenceless or afraid.
Conscience is nigh to shield, to soothe, to cheer.
Should poverty impend, and natural tears
Be shed, when the fond partner of your cares
Grieves for her children's lot and fears for you,
Conscience shall dry those tears, dispel that grief,
Sweeten the bread of virtuous poverty,
Beam consolation from your children's eyes,
And echo sounds of gladness from their tongues.
Around your heads, if Conscience still attend,

The lightnings of the world innocuous play,
And form a crown of splendor for your brows.
Conscience can bid the muttering storm be still;
And make from jarring discords of the earth
Celestial music; — strains which shall expire
Only in death; — strains which your waking souls
Shall recognise, when from the tomb ye rise,
And see heaven's portals open to the sound.

THE SURVIVOR.

PECULIAR blessings are upon thy head,
O thou survivor of an honored band!
Parents and brethren are among the dead,
And thou dost seem a stranger in the land.
Yet there is care in heaven for such as thou,
And many a sacred privilege is thine :
For in thy soul celestial warmth doth glow,
And in the gloom of night, a radiance round thee shine.

The words of wisdom and the charms of youth
Remembrance sanctifies and hope endears;
And hallowed in thy soul are words of truth,
And young aspirings heard in by-gone years.
And in the visions of the still midnight,
Spirits surround thy couch, and smile and speak.
The hoary head is there and tresses bright,
And childhood's sweet caress is thine till morning break.

The vernal flower through memory is dear;
The star of evening shines within thy soul;
The morning mists, the sunset calm and clear,
Can steal thy cares, thy busiest thoughts control.

A spiritual life, which never can decline,
Inspires and dignifies all forms for thee.
Nature for thee is dressed in hues divine,
And all things have for thee peculiar sanctity.

Each sound to thee a secret tale can tell —
When borne by breezes to thy listening ear,
The fitful music of the Sabbath bell
Speaks of the worship of a higher sphere.
All melodies are echoed as they flow,
Within thy soul, by power on thee conferred;
And from its chords the lightest airs that blow
Can wake celestial tones, by all but thee unheard.

This privilege is thine, — when human grief
Weighs down another's heart, — such heavy woe
As thou hast felt, there thou canst bring relief,
And sweeten drops of anguish as they flow.
And thou dost welcome, from amidst thy tears,
Those streams by which all holy thoughts are fed;
As its pure crest the water-lily rears,
And spreads its leaves to welcome showers from heaven
      shed.

A mournful gift is thine. — When fair the skies,
And calm the deep, — from thy prophetic soul
Afar thou seest the gathering clouds arise;
'T is thine to hear afar the thunders roll.
A better gift is thine. — When bursts the storm,
And fear and horror each weak bosom fill,
Amidst the waves 't is thine to see the form
That treads the billowy waste, and bids the winds be still.

And thou art welcome to the board and hearth:
For thou hast smiles for youth, and for the old

Thou hast the words of peace, though not of mirth ;
And in thine arms the little one dost fold.
But as a Pilgrim do they welcome thee :
To holier lands they know thy footsteps tend.
With awe they look upon thy sanctity,
Thy blessing seek, and with thee love in prayer to bend.

Pilgrim! thy path is hallowed by the prayer
Of every grateful heart which thou hast blest.
We follow thee in soul, thy struggles share,
And see thee gain the city of thy rest.
There spirits wait to take thee to thy home ;
Familiar faces mingling with the throng :
And when their strains exult that thou art come,
Loved voices meet thine ear in that rejoicing song.

THE FLOWER OF THE DESERT.

FLOWER of the desert! lone as thou art fair!
No fountain pours its coolness by thy side ;
Yet perfume floats around thee, and the glare
Withers not thee where none else can abide.
Thou grateful seem'st that life to thee is given,
Nourished by dews and beams and airs from heaven.

Bright in thy solitude, thy leaves unfold,
Breathing sweet welcome to the matin ray ;
Thy rainbow beauties, though no eye behold,
New radiance gather till the closing day.
When stars arise, how graceful bends thy head,
Patient to wait the dews that heaven may shed!

Meek in thy solitude, thou dost not deem
That winds and showers were sent for thee alone :
For wandering gales oft visit thee that teem
With foreign fragrance, richer than thine own,
And whisper tidings of a genial clime
Where groves and gardens flourish in their prime.

A soul there is, as pure as thou and rare ;
'Midst heartless crowds in solitude she dwells ;
Conscious that kindred spirits breathe afar,
And cheered by that prophetic hope which tells
That flowers shall spring where now no promise shows,
And e'en this desert " blossom like the rose."

THE MIGHT OF SONG.

[From the German of Schiller.]

A TORRENT from the clefted rock
Rushes with the thunder's sound ;
And mountain-ruins mark the shock,
And oaks from steep to chasm bound.
Astonished then with thrilling fear
The wanderer listens from afar ;
The gushing roar he stands to hear,
Yet knows not whence these tumults are :
    So the tide of music swells
    Out of undiscovered wells.

Linked with the awful sister-band
Who still the thread of being wind,
Who can the singer's tones withstand,
And who his magic thrall unbind ?

With power, like Hermes' wand, to move,
To make the spirit faint or glow,
He lifts its wondering flight above,
Or sinks to shadowy realms below:
  Sways it now from jest to thought,
  Poised on feeling's light support.

As if, amid the festal ring
Came, stalking with a giant-stride,
Dim as the ghosts that twilight bring,
An awful fate to quell its pride;
As earthly greatness crouches dumb
Before the stranger's piercing gaze,
As sinks the revel's babbling hum
And falls the mask from every face,—
  Truth with mighty victory there
  Melting falsehood's works to air:

So, casting off each burden vain,
Man, wakened by the voice of song,
His spirit's-rank learns to attain,
And treads in holy power along.
One with the heavenly rulers now,
Before him earthly spirits quail,
Before him dumb each power must bow,
And no fatality assail.
  Care must smooth the furrowed brow
  While the tides of music flow.

As, after hopeless, lingering years
Of banishment and deep unrest,
The child with hot repentant tears
Sinks down upon a mother's breast;—
So to the threshold of his days,
To peace long-lost and needed long,

From exile's strange and weary ways
The fugitive is led by song.
  Chilled by cold convention's grasp,
  His heart to warm in Nature's clasp.

REFORM SONG.

(*Air* — ' Scots, wha hae.')

Now 's the day, and now 's the hour!
Freedom is our nation's dower,
Put we forth a nation's power,
   Struggling to be free!
Raise your front the foe to daunt!
Bide no more the snare, the taunt! —
Peal to highest heaven the chaunt, —
   " Law and Liberty!"

Gather like the muttering storm!
Wake your thunders for REFORM!
Bear not, like the trodden worm,
   Scorn and mockery!
Waking from their guilty trance,
Shrink the foes as storms advance
Scathed beneath a nation's glance, —
   Where 's their bravery?

Waves on waves compose the main ; —
Mountains rise by grain on grain ; —
Men an empire's might sustain
   Knit in unity!

Who shall check the ocean tide? —
Who o'erthrow the mountain's pride? —
Who a nation's strength deride,
      Spurning slavery?

Hearts in mutual faith secure,
Hands from spoil and treachery pure,
Tongues that meaner oaths abjure, —
      These shall make us free!
Bend the knee, and bare the brow!
God, our guide, will hear us now!
Peal to highest heaven the vow, —
      " Law and Liberty!"

HYMN.

THE COMING OF CHRIST IN THE POWER OF HIS GOSPEL.

Lord Jesus, come! for here
  Our path through wilds is laid,
We watch, as for the dayspring near,
  Amid the breaking shade.

Lord Jesus, come! for still
  Vice shouts her maniac mirth;
And famished thousands crave their fill,
  While teems the fruitful earth.

Lord Jesus, come! for hosts
  Meet on the battle plain.
There patriots mourn; the tyrant boasts;
  And tears are shed like rain.

29*

Hark ! herald voices near
　　Proclaim thy happier day.
Come, Lord, and our hosannas hear !
　　We wait to strew thy way.

Come, as in days of old,
　　With words of grace and power !
Gather us all within thy fold,
　　And never leave us more.

CHRIST'S LEGACY OF PEACE.

I.

WHAT hope was thine, O Christ ! when grace
Its riches to thy soul made known !
Mid throngs that filled the holy place
Thy spirit rose to God alone.

II.

What peace was thine, when thou didst pour
Thy sorrows forth, and rest on God ;
Though midnight tempests lashed the shore,
And none the desert path-way trod !

III.

What joy, to bid the tomb unclose,
And the long-buried one arise !
Though ready thine own grave, and foes
Upreared the cross before thine eyes.

IV.

Jesus! we would not mourn for thee.
By love is life in bliss arrayed;
Prayer makes the spirit light and free;
And who like thee has loved and prayed?

V.

Thy griefs, thy cares, we cannot know;
Our own are all that we can bear:
But thou thy peace hast left below;
Thy hope, thy joy, hast bid us share.

DESIRE OF DIVINE WISDOM.

I.

WHEN Samuel heard in still midnight,
A voice amid God's presence bright,
He rose, and said, on bended knee,
"Speak, Lord! thy servant heareth thee."

II.

E'en such a voice I too may hear;
E'en such a light my soul may cheer;
For Wisdom's words by God were given,
And Reason is a ray from heaven.

III.

Then will I feed this sacred fire;
For wisdom's precepts still inquire;
Still pray, from pride and folly free,
"Speak! for thy servant heareth thee."

IV.

But not alone within his hall
Shall my hushed soul attend his call:
He whispers from the woods at noon,
And calls me forth beneath the moon.

V.

His voice shall drown the hum of men,
And echo from the deep again:
Where'er he is my prayer shall be,
" Speak! for thy servant heareth thee."

THE FRATERNITY OF MAN.

I.

ALL men are equal in their birth,
Heirs of the earth and skies;
All men are equal when that earth
Fades from their dying eyes.

II.

All wait alike on him whose power
Upholds the life he gave;
The sage within his star-lit tower,
The savage in his cave.

III.

God meets the throngs who pay their vows
In courts their hands have made,
And hears the worshipper who bows
Beneath the plantain shade.

IV.

'T is man alone who difference sees,
And speaks of high and low ;
And worships those and tramples these,
While the same path they go.

V.

O ! let man hasten to restore
To all their rights of love :
In power and wealth exult no more ;
In wisdom lowly move.

VI.

Ye great ! renounce your earth-born pride,
Ye low ! your shame and fear :
Live, as ye worship, side by side ;
Your common claims revere.

STANZAS.

BENEATH this starry arch,
   Nought resteth or is still ;
But all things hold their march
   As if by one great will.
      Moves one, move all ;
      Hark to the foot-fall !
         On, on, for ever.

Yon sheaves were once but seed ;
Will ripens into deed ;
As cave-drops swell the streams,
Day thoughts feed nightly dreams ;

And sorrow tracketh wrong,
As echo follows song,
          On, on, for ever.

By night, like stars on high,
    The hours reveal their train;
They whisper and go by;
    I never watch in vain.
        Moves one, move all;
        Hark to the foot-fall!
          On, on, for ever.

They pass the cradle head,
And there a promise shed;
They pass the moist, new grave,
And bid rank verdure wave;
        They bear through every clime,
        The harvests of all time,
          On, on, for ever.

SONNET.

THE echoes of thy voice are heard afar,
O Happiness! through all the listening world;
While hovering o'er us, thy bright wings unfurled,
Thou tellest us what heavenly raptures are.
We hear them in the little skylark's song;
In infant laughter; and they come and go
In youthful breasts, and visit oft and long
The pious heart. — But still thine accents flow
As of one warbling in an unknown tongue.
The music is expressive, and we know

That we *could* comprehend the theme sublime,
Now wrapt in mystery. — O come the time
When all the understanding, all the soul,
Shall join the seraph lays which through heaven's regions roll!

1827.

THE BREATH OF LIFE.

Joy is the spirit's element,
   And joy is every where;
Not in a local heaven pent,
   But free as vital air.
For ever hath she fed the soul:
For aye her melodies shall roll.

The morning stars together sang,
   In answer to her call;
When earth to life and beauty sprang,
   She graced and quickened all:
Unveiled shall be her perfect day,
Whene'er the heavens shall pass away.

Where Alpine torrents plunge and hiss,
   And urge their wild career,
There, breathless, o'er the dim abyss,
   The shepherd bends to hear
How, sporting in the viewless showers,
Joy her deep song of homage pours.

Now smiling in a Lapland home,
   Or couched in turfy vales;
Now awful, throned in the simoom,
   Or winged with ocean gales;

Now entering halls where princes dwell;
Now, borne by dreams, the prison cell:

Deep is her power to sway the will,
   Chaunting in nature's lays;
With deeper power her accents thrill
   In apostolic praise:
But deepest when — awhile aloof —
She speeds to hallow heaven's reproof.

Joy is the spirit's element,
   And joy is every where.
Away, then, with the weak complaint,
   Away with dread and care!
Around her is a radiant throng;
Help thou their everlasting song.

THE SPIRIT'S HISTORY.

Through the low gate of life how heedless bounds
   The infant spirit on her echoing way!
Nor knows that every careless step resounds
   Through the far regions of futurity.
Now, idly scared, seeking some friendly arms;
   Now, thankless, bursting from the mild restraint;
She seizes as her own creation's charms,
   In joy presumptuous, wayward in complaint.
     When sinks her hope in death,
      With impious wail she weepeth;
     Nor trusts the voice that saith,
      " It is not dead, but sleepeth."

How awful when, along the way of truth,
　　With stealthy tread, the listening spirit comes;
Doubt in her eye, thought on her brow of youth,
　　And undried tears dewing her cheek's soft blooms.
Following afar the funeral train, that bear
　　Her life's-stay to the burial,—taught by woe,
She seeks some brooding presence in the air,
　　And asks if there be help above, below.
　　　　She starts the voice to hear,
　　　　　　That can her peace restore;
　　　　Nor knows who stays the bier,
　　　　　　And bids her weep no more.

How calm before the spirit's tranquil gaze,
　　Strengthened by grief and joy, creation lies!
No lurking fears in its untrodden ways,
　　No wrecks upon its shores, mists in its skies!
So bright the sunshine, mild the shadows there,
　　They woo the spirit to a deep repose;
And if long-vanquished spectres still appear,
　　'T is in a dream; they vanish at its close.
　　　　Then breaking from the throng,
　　　　　　Weeping, she goes in faith
　　　　To him whose word is strong
　　　　　　To burst the bands of death.

How holy, when the chequered day is o'er,
　　Heaven's splendors by the spirit else unseen!
Its orbs, in thrilling silence evermore
　　Winning their way amid the deep serene!
How whispers echo, starting from the vault!
　　How piercing are those myriad steadfast eyes!
She dimly sees where winged armies halt,
　　To hail the eternal morn that soon must rise,

30

She haunts the hallowed tomb,
    As breaks that holy day;
And angels, mid the gloom,
    Chase all her cares away.

SURVIVORSHIP.

THOU mayst not mourn thy loneliness of soul.
What though the spirit, whose benign control
Was thy mind's strength and blessing, now be fled;
What though no voice, no token from the dead
Stills thy wild questionings, or helps thy prayers;
What though the thrilling thought no bosom shares,
Which uttered dies away; and gushing tears,
Whose source is hid, are still referred to fears,
And transient griefs thy soul has risen above;
What though the intensest fires of human love
Are back repressed, till heart and brain they burn;
Thy loneliness of soul thou mayst not mourn.

Each hope unshared that on thy soul recoils,
Its force concentred, prompts to nobler toils.
The intellectual glance, not lingering now
To meet response, discerns and pierces through,
Makes inquisition into things unknown,
And wins the world of being for thine own.
Nor shall thy love, though from its kindred rent,
Pine like a captive in his dungeon pent,
Waiting release, and destined still to wait:
Wide as the soul its growing powers dilate.
Embracing all, — yet sacred still to one;
Living for all, — yet dwelling still alone; —

Made strong thro' weakness, free thro' harsh control,
Thou mayst not mourn thy loneliness of soul.

Go to the grove where beechen shadows lie ;
There hushed in thought, shrouded from human eye,
List while the winds, that traverse land and sea,
Whisper the tidings that they bring for thee : —
Tell thee where sister spirits mourn the dead ;
How kindred hearts with thine have thrilled, have bled ;
How some, e'en now, are glowing with a flame
Kindled like thine, for purposes the same,
To cheer the watch, to daunt a common foe ;
Like signal fires on many a mountain's brow.

Rise from thy couch, to hail the midnight star,
And question what that eye beholds afar,
That thou mayst love and pray for.   Now its beam
Falls on the brow, and mingles with the dream
Of some young sleeper smiling in his rest,
Or wearied pilgrim waiting to be blest.
Now the fixed gaze it meets of watchful sage,
Or with the lamp illumes the student's page ;
Now, like the eye of God, it glances through
The guilty soul, and damps the hardened brow ;
Or cheers the vigils, calms the sighing breath
Of love that hovers round the couch of death.

Thus winds and stars bring kindred to thy side.
If still for nobler sympathy thy pride,
'Midst heaven-fraught souls, aspire to claim a place,
Turn to the written records of thy race.
Where'er, in calm endurance, man has borne,
For holy cause, the frowns of kings, the scorn
Of multitudes ; — where'er the scourge, the fire,
From souls that on their inward strength retire,

Nor abject prayers, nor wrath, nor groans have wrung ;
Where'er the nerves of woman have been strung
Such strength to foster, and such pangs behold,
Such lot to share, lest heavenly love grow cold ;
There mayst thou, if such links like souls may bind,
Communion hold with each immortal mind ;
From saint to hero, chief to martyr, turn,
And in thy solitude forget to mourn.

There is a Presence — awful, yet most sweet,
Where all that's holy, holy things may greet.
There throng, unite, and dwell in commune free,
They that have been, that are, that yet shall be.
The eye may not behold, nor ear drink in,
The light, the music, breathing from within ;
The grave may interpose, long ages roll,
And land and sea may sever soul from soul,
Yet in eternal union still they dwell ;
The same love cheers, the same emotions swell.

Each impulse that the Will divine hath given,
Thrills from earth's lowest deep to highest heaven ;
Each influence that the Love divine hath shed,
Gives beauty to all life — life to the dead ;
Beams from the sanctum of a common home,
And lights the path where thronging pilgrims come.
Conscious of that pervading Presence mild,
Blest with the freedom of a favored child,
Look round, while earthly shadows from thee roll,
And dream no more of loneliness of soul.

END OF VOL. I.

Lightning Source UK Ltd.
Milton Keynes UK
UKOW06f1935301013

220119UK00010B/202/P